BrightRED PUBLISHING

BGE LEVEL 3

GEOGRAPHY
COURSE BOOK

Rhona Maclean

First published in 2020 by:
Bright Red Publishing Ltd
Mitchelston Drive Business Centre
Kirkcaldy
KY1 3NB

A CIP record for this book is available from the British Library.

ISBN 978-1-84948-319-3

With thanks to:
PDQ Digital Media Solutions Ltd, Bungay (layout), Sian Jarman (copy-edit).
Cover design and series book design by Caleb Rutherford – e i d e t i c.

Every effort has been made to seek all copyright-holders. If any have been overlooked, then Bright Red Publishing will be delighted to make the necessary arrangements.

Acknowledgements
Permission has been sought from all relevant copyright holders and Bright Red Publishing are grateful for the use of the following:

visdia/Shutterstock.com (pp 8–9); Image(s) licensed by Ingram Image (pp 10 & 13); Mopic/Shutterstock.com (p 11); RIBI Image Library (CC BY 2.0)[1] (p 12); James St. John (CC BY 2.0)[1] (p 14); Colin Smith (CC BY-SA 2.0)[2] (p 14); robin2/Shutterstock.com (p 15); Massimo Pietrobon (CC BY 3.0)[4] (p 15); Sanjay Acharya (CC BY-SA 4.0)[5] (p 16); BlueRingMedia/Shutterstock.com (p 18); Norbert Nagel (CC BY-SA 3.0)[3] (p 22); Walter Siegmund (CC BY-SA 3.0)[3] (p 24); Top1963/Tryfon Topalidis (CC BY-SA 3.0)[3] (p 26); Mentnafunangann (CC BY-SA 4.0)[5] (p 27); BenAveling (CC BY-SA 4.0)[5] (p 29); Heidi Soosalu (CC BY-SA 3.0)[3] (p 30); Brocken Inaglory (CC BY-SA 3.0)[3] (p 30); Marco Verch Professional Photographer and Speaker (CC BY 2.0)[1] (p 30); Mapswire.com (CC BY 4.0)[6] (p 30); gnuckx (CC BY-SA 2.0)[2] (p 31); Ingo Kuebler (CC BY 3.0)[4] (p 32); William Crochot (CC BY-SA 4.0)[5] (p 32); Yamaguchi (CC BY-SA 3.0)[3] (p 33); Michael R Perry (CC BY 2.0)[1] (p 36); Vardion (CC BY-SA 3.0)[3] (p 38); UN Photo/Logan Abassi United Nations Development Programme (CC BY 2.0)[1] (p 38); United Nations Development Programme (CC BY 2.0)[1] (p 39); Haha169 (CC BY-SA 3.0)[3] (p 41); Cory Doctorow (CC BY-SA 2.0)[2] (p 42); CIR Online (CC BY 2.0)[1] (p 42); modisketch/Shutterstock.com (p 43); Andy Maguire (CC BY 2.0)[1] (p 43); Ophelia Jane Julia (CC BY-SA 2.0)[2] (p 45); Ævar Arnfjörð Bjarmason (CC BY-SA 3.0)[3] (p 46); Symac (CC BY-SA 3.0)[3] (p 47); travellight/Shutterstock.com (p 47); Illustration © 2008 Public Library of Science (CC BY 2.5)[7] (p 51); Narongsak Nagadhana/Shutterstock.com (p 51); Frederik/Wikimedia/NASA (p 52); McKay Savage (CC BY 2.0)[1] (p 52); outdoorsman/Shutterstock.com (p 53); Wojsyl (CC BY-SA 3.0)[3] (p 53); Ulamm (CC BY-SA 3.0)[3] (p 54); Dirk Beyer (CC BY-SA 2.5)[8] (p 55); Michael C. Rygel (CC BY-SA 3.0)[3] (p 56); Colin Smith (CC BY-SA 2.0)[2] (p 59); David Crocker (CC BY-SA 2.0)[2] (p 59); Marcel Wiesweg/Zacharie Grossen (CC BY-SA 3.0)[3] (p 59); Alan O'Dowd (CC BY-SA 2.0)[2] (p 59); Thilo Parg (CC BY-SA 3.0)[3] (p 62); Gareth James (CC BY-SA 2.0)[2] (p 63); Alan O'Dowd (CC BY-SA 2.0)[2] (p 64); Bill Boaden (CC BY-SA 2.0)[2] (p 64); Gareth James (CC BY-SA 2.0)[2] (p 65); Petr Šmerkl, Wikipedia (CC BY-SA 3.0)[3] (p 65); Mick Knapton (CC BY-SA 3.0)[3] (p 65); EzhilanG (CC BY-SA 4.0)[5] (p 67); Munro1986 (CC BY-SA 4.0)[5] (p 67); Callum Black (CC BY-SA 2.0)[2] (p 67); Images Money (CC BY-SA 2.0)[2] (p 68); Ian Balcombe (CC BY-SA 2.0)[2] (p 68); Smelov/Shutterstock.com (p 68); Barney Moss (CC BY 2.0)[1] (p 69); Peeperman (CC BY-SA 3.0)[3] (p 70); sobolevnrm (CC BY-SA 2.0)[2] (p 70); Andrew Tryon (CC BY-SA 2.0)[2] (p 70); Luc Viatour / https://Lucnix.be (CC BY-SA 3.0)[3] (p 70); Peter Mulligan (CC BY 2.0)[1] (p 70); Anne Burgess (CC BY-SA 2.0)[2] (p 71); Jim Barton (CC BY-SA 2.0)[2] (p 71); I See Modern Britain (CC BY 2.0)[1] (p 71); dzaky murad/Shutterstock.com (p 72); Richard Sutcliffe (CC BY-SA 2.0)[2] (p 72); Paul Arps (CC BY 2.0)[1] (p 72); Des Colhoun (CC BY-SA 2.0)[2] (p 73); Map reproduced by permission of National Parks UK (p 74); baaker2009 (CC BY 2.0)[1] (p 74); Alan Findlay (CC BY-SA 2.0)[2] (p 74); Michael_Saint/Shutterstock.com (p 75); JF Hobbs (CC BY 3.0)[4] (pp 76–77); CIAT (CC BY-SA 2.0)[2] (p 80); Ville Koistinen/Bertrand Grondin (CC BY-SA 3.0)[3] (p 81); worldclassphoto/Shutterstock.com (p 85); Dinesh Valke (CC BY-SA 2.0)[2] (p 85); Dinesh Valke (CC BY-SA 2.0)[2] (p 86); SaveJungle/Shutterstock.com (p 88); Marcelina Zygula/Shutterstock.com (p 88); Douglas Fernandes (CC BY 2.0)[1] (p 90); Agência Brasil (CC BY 3.0BR)[9] (p 90); Gleilson Miranda/Governo do Acre (CC BY 2.0)[1] (p 90); Lano Lan/Shutterstock.com (p 90); Dr Morley Read/Shutterstock.com (p 91); Ji-Elle (CC BY-SA 3.0)[3] (p 91); GrrlScientist (CC BY 2.0)[1] (p 91); JialiangGao www.peace-on-earth.org (CC BY-SA 4.0)[5] (p 92); Thai National Parks www.thainationalparks.com (CC BY-SA 2.0)[2] (p 92); Jason Rothmeyer (CC BY 2.0)[1] (p 92); Rameshng (CC BY-SA 3.0)[3] (p 92); Hans Denis Schneider/Shutterstock.com (p 92); Theeradech Sanin/Shutterstock.com (p 94); Pedarilhosbr/Shutterstock.com (p 94); kakteen/Shutterstock.com (p 95); 2 images by Dr Morley Read/Shutterstock.com (p 97); crustmania (CC BY 2.0)[1] (p 98); greensefa (CC BY-SA 2.0)[2] (p 98); Agência de Notícias do Acre: Gleilson Miranda/Governo do Acre (CC BY 2.0)[1] (p 99); NASA LBA-ECO Project (p 100); Ibama (CC BY 2.0)[1] (p 101); Irina Fischer/Shutterstock.com (p 103); Brocken Inaglory (CC BY-SA 3.0)[3] (p 105); Wescottm (CC BY 4.0)[6] (p 105); Strebe (CC BY-SA 3.0)[3] (p 106); Syed Wali Peeran (CC BY-SA 4.0)[5] (p 108); John D Sirlin/Shutterstock.com (p 108); Bureau of Land Management (CC BY 2.0)[1] (p 108); Ian D. Medeiros (CC BY 4.0)[6] (p 110); Summerdrought (CC BY-SA 4.0)[5] (p 111); Michael Grindstaff (CC BY-SA 3.0)[3] (p 111); El Guanche (CC BY 2.0)[1] (p 112); James St. John (CC BY 2.0)[1] (p 112); Moyan Brenn (CC BY 2.0)[1] (p 112); Tomas Castelazo (CC BY-SA 2.5)[8] (p 113); USFWS Pacific Southwest Region (CC BY 2.0)[1] (p 114); Rawpixel Ltd (CC BY 2.0)[1] (p 114); Bidgee (CC BY 3.0)[4] (p 114); John O'Neill (CC BY-SA 3.0)[3] (p 115); Gabriel White (CC BY-SA 2.0)[2] (p 117); South African Tourism (CC BY 2.0)[1] (p 117); Mark Dingemanse (CC BY 2.5)[7] (p 118); Akly (CC BY-SA 4.0)[5] (p 118); Сашка Денисов (CC BY 3.0)[4] (p 120); Viator.com (CC BY-SA 2.0)[2] (p 120); EpicStockMedia/Shutterstock.com (p 120); Bahnfrend (CC BY-SA 4.0)[5] (p 120 & 121); Ltz Raptor, edited by Base64 (CC BY-SA 3.0)[3] (p 120); Land Rover MENA (CC BY 2.0)[1] (p 121); Charles Sharp (CC BY 2.0)[1] (p 122); Viator.com (CC BY-SA 2.0)[2] (p 122); Charles Gadbois (CC BY 3.0)[4] (p 122); Geograph (CC BY-SA 3.0)[3] (p 129); Ansgar Walk (CC BY-SA 3.0)[3] (p 129); Artenex/Shutterstock.com (p 129); Jgrahn (CC BY-SA 3.0)[3] (p 131); Andrea Pokrzywinski (CC BY 2.0)[1] (p 131); Andreas Weith (CC BY-SA 4.0)[5] (p 132); evgenii mitroshin/Shutterstock.com (p 134); Andreas Trepte (CC BY-SA 2.5)[8] (p 135); kees torn (CC BY-SA 2.0)[2] (p 138); Gretarsson (CC BY-SA 2.0)[2] (p 139); Bureau of Land Management Alaska (CC BY 2.0)[1] (p 139); Angela (CC BY 2.0)[1] (p 140); 2 images by ARLIS Reference (CC BY-SA 2.0)[2] (p 140); Marine Photobank (CC BY 2.0)[1] (p 140); U.S. Fish and Wildlife Service Headquarters (CC BY 2.0)[1] (p 141); Wazefaire (CC BY-SA 3.0)[3] (p 141); Walter.bender (CC BY-SA 3.0)[3] (p 143); Frank K. (CC BY 2.0)[1] (p 144); ADialla (CC BY 2.0)[1] (p 144); Woodwalker (CC BY-SA 3.0)[3] (p 145); NASA Goddard's Scientific Visualization Studio/Cindy Starr (p 147); Phantom Open Emoji maintainers and contributors (CC BY 3.0)[4] (p 149); Sam Fentress (CC BY-SA 2.0)[2] (p 153); AridOcean/Shutterstock.com (p 154); Jim Barton (CC BY-SA 2.0)[2] (p 155); Defence Images (CC BY-SA 2.0)[2] (p 155); Anne Burgess (CC BY-SA 2.0)[2] (p 156); David Baird (CC BY-SA 2.0)[2] (p 157); James T M Towill (CC BY-SA 2.0)[2] (p 157); Humannet/Shutterstock.com (p 157); Robin Sones (CC BY-SA 2.0)[2] (p 159); Humphrey Bolton (CC BY-SA 2.0)[2] (p 159); Stefan Kühn (CC BY-SA 3.0)[3] (p 160); Tim Green (CC BY 2.0)[1] (p 160); Henrik (CC BY-SA 3.0)[3] (p 160); wk1003mike/Shutterstock.com (p 160); Maigheach-gheal (CC BY-SA 2.0)[2] (p 160); Richard Allaway (CC BY 2.0)[1] (p 161); Langspeed (CC BY-SA 3.0)[3] (p 162); Notafly (CC BY-SA 3.0)[3] (p 163); Frasmacon (CC BY-SA 3.0)[3] (p 163); Tom Harpel (CC BY 2.0)[1] (p 163); Sfortis (CC BY-SA 3.0)[3] (p 164); Famartin (CC BY-SA 4.0)[5] (p 164); Typhoonchaser (CC BY-SA 3.0)[3] (p 164); Simon A. Eugster (CC BY-SA 3.0)[3] (p 165); Ian Capper (CC BY-SA 2.0)[2] (p 166); Alfred Gay (CC BY-SA 3.0)[3] (p 167); Joe Mabel (CC BY-SA 3.0)[3] (p 167); Leoboudv (CC BY-SA 3.0)[3] (p 167); L. Shyamal (CC BY-SA 3.0)[3] (p 168); Tiia Monto (CC BY-SA 3.0)[3] (p 168); Charles Harker/Shutterstock.com (p 171); Wilfredor (CC BY-SA 4.0)[5] (p 173); chensiyuan (CC BY-SA 4.0)[5] (p 173); Dariusz Jarzabek/Shutterstock.com (p 176); Sara Berdon/Shutterstock.com (p 176); Images Money (CC BY 2.0)[1] (p 178); Image from: https://simd.scot/2016/#/simd2016/BTTTFTT/9/-4.0000/55.9000/ (OGL v3.0)[12] (p 179); The UN flag © United Nations[13] (p 180); Diagram 2 – 'The five Ps model of sustainable development' taken from https://un.org.au/files/2015/09/Infographic_five_elements.png, by Division for Sustainable Development Goals, © 2015 United Nations[13] (p 180); UN Sustainable Development Goals logo, infographic and icons by Division for Sustainable Development Goals © 2015 United Nations[13] (p 180 & 182–5); La Priz (CC BY-ND 2.0)[10] (p 181); Serge (CC BY 2.0)[1] (p 181); NOAA Marine Debris Program (CC BY 2.0)[1] (p 181); Image © Why Green Economy? (p 182); Nilfanion (CC BY-SA 3.0)[3] (p 186); John Lindie (CC BY 2.0)[1] (p 187); BIG ALBERT (CC BY 2.0)[1] (p 187); pio3/Shutterstock.com (p 188); SEDACMaps (CC BY 2.0)[1] (p 189); Shao (CC BY-SA 3.0)[3] (p 189); Biswarup Ganguly (CC BY 3.0)[4] (p 189); pictures Jettcom (CC BY 3.0)[4] (p 189); Roberto De la Parra (CC BY 2.0)[1] (p 189); Quinn Dombrowski (CC BY-SA 2.0)[2] (p 192); CIAT (CC BY-SA 2.0)[2] (p 193); Widad Sirkhotte (CC BY-SA 2.0)[2] (p 193); Gajus/Shutterstock.com (p 194); Paulrudd (CC BY-SA 3.0)[3] (p 199); Balaram Mahalder (CC BY-SA 3.0)[3] (p 199); Balaram Mahalder (CC BY-SA 3.0)[3] (p 199); SEJustice (CC BY-SA 3.0)[3] (p 200); Vespertunes (CC BY-SA 4.0)[5] (p 200); Planemad (CC BY-SA 3.0)[3] (p 203); Anja Disseldorp (CC BY 2.0)[1] (p 203); Development Planning Unit University College London (CC BY 2.0)[1] (p 203); Derek Harper (CC BY-SA 2.0)[2] (p 207); Oregon State University (CC BY-SA 2.0)[2] (p 207); Pauline E (CC BY-SA 2.0)[2] (p 207); Philip McErlean (CC BY-ND 2.0)[10] (p 208); Freddie Phillips (CC BY 2.0)[1] (p 208); Stefan Krause (CC BY-SA 3.0)[3] (p 208); Phillip Capper (CC BY 2.0)[1] (p 208); Peter Trimming (CC BY-SA 2.0)[2] (p 209); Anne Burgess (CC BY-SA 2.0)[2] (p 209); Images from https://www2.gov.scot/Resource/0052/00521305.pdf & https://www2.gov.scot/Topics/Statistics/Browse/Agriculture-Fisheries/AgriculturalMaps/Farmtype (OGL v3.0)[12] (p 212); Image from: https://blog.metoffice.gov.uk/2014/10/20/what-is-the-wettest-city-in-the-uk/. (OGL v3.0)[12] (p 212); AridOcean/Shutterstock.com (p 212); Philip Halling (CC BY-SA 2.0)[2] (p 213); Johannes Jansson/norden.org (CC BY 2.5 Denmark)[11] (p 213); Soil-Science.info (CC BY 2.0)[1] (p 213); Aqua Mechanical (CC BY 2.0)[1] (p 214); Peter Trimming (CC BY-SA 2.0)[2] (p 214); Andrew Curtis (CC BY-SA 2.0)[2] (p 214); SasinTipchai/Shutterstock.com (p 215); U.S. Department of Agriculture (CC BY 2.0)[1] (p 215); eGuide Travel (CC BY 2.0)[1] (p 215); neil smith (CC BY-SA 2.0)[2] (p 217); RSPB Hope Farm field plan is reproduced with permission of RSPB (p 217); Sk Hasan Ali/Shutterstock.com (p 218); ILO Asia-Pacific (CC BY-ND 2.0)[10] (p 220); Planemad (CC BY-SA 3.0)[3] (p 222); Jasvipul Chawla (CC BY-SA 2.0)[2] (p 222); urbz (CC BY 2.0)[1] (p 222); YGLvoices (CC BY 2.0)[1] (p 223); Ting Chen (CC BY-SA 2.0)[2] (p 223); urbz (CC BY 2.0)[1] (p 223); Nathan Hughes Hamilton (CC BY 2.0)[1] (p 223); urbz (CC BY 2.0)[1] (p 224); Logan King (CC BY-ND 2.0)[10] (p 226); M M (CC BY-SA 2.0)[2] (p 227); Jon Hurd (CC BY 2.0)[1] (p 227); M M (CC BY-SA 2.0)[2] (p 228); urbzoo (CC BY 2.0)[1] (p 228); Greg Younger (CC BY-SA 2.0)[2] (p 228); Shadowgate (CC BY 2.0)[1] (p 231); Ellen Thompson (CC BY 2.0)[1] (p 231); Steve Cadman (CC BY-SA 2.0)[2] (p 231); David P Howard (CC BY-SA 2.0)[2] (p 231); Eric Gaba, NordNordWest (CC BY-SA 3.0)[3] (p 233); Allan Harris (CC BY-ND 2.0)[10] (p 233); Saffron Blaze, via http://www.mackenzie.co (CC BY-SA 3.0)[3] (p 233); Duirinish Light/Shutterstock.com (p 233); Engel Ching/Shutterstock.com (p 234); Kim Traynor (CC BY-SA 3.0)[3] (p 234); Richard Webb (CC BY-SA 2.0)[2] (p 234); Lydia (CC BY 2.0)[1] (p 236); Colin Smith (CC BY-SA 2.0)[2] (p 236); AsiaTravel/Shutterstock.com (p 236); Andrew Gray (CC BY-SA 2.0)[2] (p 237); S.m.u.d.g.e/Shutterstock.com (p 237); Neil Mitchell/Shutterstock.com (p 237); 1000 Words/Shutterstock.com (p238); Jorge Maricato/Shutterstock.com (p238); Peter Trimming (CC BY 2.0)[1] (p 239); Airwolfhound (CC BY-SA 2.0)[2] (p 239); leungchopan/Shutterstock.com (p 239); Julien Harneis (CC BY-SA 2.0)[2] (p 240); DFID – UK Department for International Development (CC BY 2.0)[1] (p 240); Trocaire (CC BY 2.0)[1] (p 241); Rod Waddington (CC BY-SA 2.0)[2] (p243); hris1johnson (CC BY 2.0)[1] (p 243); Dvermeirre (CC BY-SA 4.0)[5] (p 244); 2 images by SuSanA Secretariat (CC BY 2.0)[1] (p 244); Tibor Végh (CC BY 3.0)[4] (p 246); Valentin Ottone (CC BY 2.0)[1] (p 246); Surrey County Council News (CC BY-ND 2.0)[10] (p 247); Theo Crazzolara (CC BY 2.0)[1] (p 249); Julius Volz (CC BY-SA 2.0)[2] (p 249); Morgan (CC BY 2.0)[1] (p 249); Thirteen Of Clubs (CC BY-SA 2.0)[2] (p 249); AL.Eyad (CC BY 2.0)[1] (p 249); steve estvanik/Shutterstock.com (pp 252–3); Eden, Janine and Jim (CC BY 2.0)[1] (p 255); AridOcean/Shutterstock.com (p 255); Pyty/Shutterstock.com (p 255); NOAA Great Lakes Environmental Research Laboratory (CC BY-SA 2.0)[2] (p 256); Randi Hausken (CC BY-SA 2.0)[2] (p 256); Dennis Jarvis (CC BY-SA 2.0)[2] (p 261); Robbie Shade (CC BY 2.0)[1] (p 263); Ordnance Survey Maps © Crown Copyright. All rights reserved. Licence number 100049324 (pp 63, 64, 65, 66, 265 & 267).

Printed and bound in the UK.

CONTENTS

INTRODUCING BRIGHTRED BGE GEOGRAPHY

INTRODUCTION

Welcome to the BrightRed BGE Geography textbook. This book should guide you through all the Outcomes and Benchmarks for Geography for the Scottish Curriculum in a fun-filled, colourful way.

Teachers should never have to worry about covering or assessing Benchmarks ever again, and students should be able to glide effortlessly from Level 3 and progress to some areas of Level 4 while learning about topics that are not only enjoyable, but also should concern all of us about the modern world we live in. The selected topics target learning pathways that build on prior knowledge and help progression into National and Higher Geography. In addition, the activities offered will ensure challenge and rigour for all students, from accessing and understanding key words to evaluating digital data.

Topics covered build on information acquired as students work through the book. Unit 6, 'Mapping Skills', covers the basics to assist any students who may never have experienced working with latitude, longitude or OS grid references, as well as some basic activities included in the BGE Benchmarks.

Skills for life and work

This has been included to highlight the large variety of skills Geography introduces to us. Students can review these, identify their key strengths and match them to the examples of careers and further study to which each Geographical unit in the book can lead in the Homework Helpers.

Command words

Three command words are focused on throughout the activities in this book. The understanding and use of these command words should ensure better progress for students into assessment at National 4, 5 and Higher levels.

Classroom challenges

These are all formulated to cover the BGE Level 3 and some Level 4 Benchmarks and Outcomes. They have been designed to ensure pace, challenge and enjoyment for all abilities.

Homework Helpers

Activities that are suitable for extending learning beyond the classroom have been highlighted. We also have a wonderful bundle of links to videos and extension work available online at www.brightredpublishing.co.uk

Teaching Notes

Printable templates and useful teaching resources have been collated in our Teaching Notes bundle and are available to download for free from the Bright Red website.

SKILLS FOR LIFE AND WORK

Sometimes 'Skills for life and work' are referred to as part of 'Developing the young workforce'. It is important that students experience and develop these skills as part of their learning. Recognition of key strengths within these skills can help students enter positive destinations after school.

The activities in this book cover the following key skills.

- Creating
- Writing
- Digital skills
- Numeracy
- Summarising
- Problem-solving
- Listening
- Explaining
- Processing
- Note-taking
- Thinking
- Describing
- Reporting
- Independent learning
- Following instructions
- Evaluating
- Analysing
- Researching
- Organising
- Working with others
- Presenting
- Leadership
- Citizenship
- Teamwork

WHAT ARE COMMAND WORDS?

Command words used in questions and tasks tell us how we should answer them. Sometimes they get the nickname of 'bossy words' as a result.

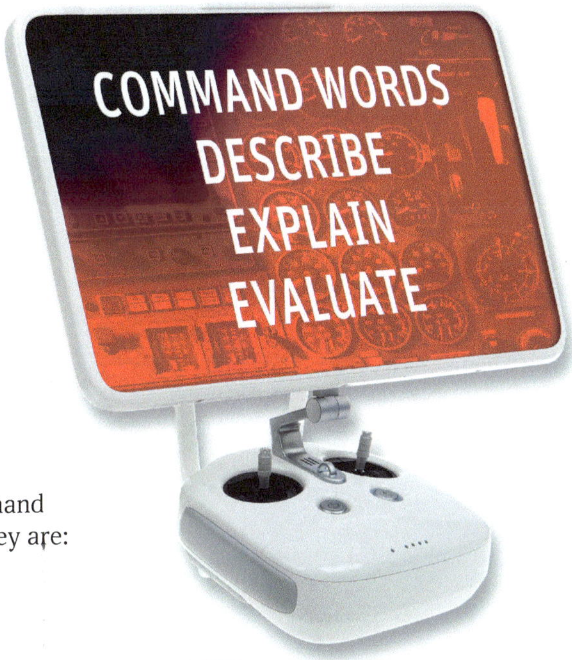

In this book, three main command words appear in questions. They are:

DESCRIBE – This means to give details about the main characteristics of something. It is a bit like painting a picture of something but using words instead of paint. What does it look like? What are the main features?

EXPLAIN – This is when you either give the meaning of something, or give the reasons for something happening or existing. Often this means thinking about the words 'how' or 'why'. It could also be suggesting what the impact of something could be. What caused it and what are the effects?

EVALUATE – This is a bit trickier than describing or explaining. It often means looking at the advantages and disadvantages of something. However, it also means you have to come up with a 'conclusion' or 'judgement' based on the evidence you have. It is a bit like being a judge or detective.

EARTH FORCES

If you think this planet we live on is a safe, solid lump of rock – it's time to think again!

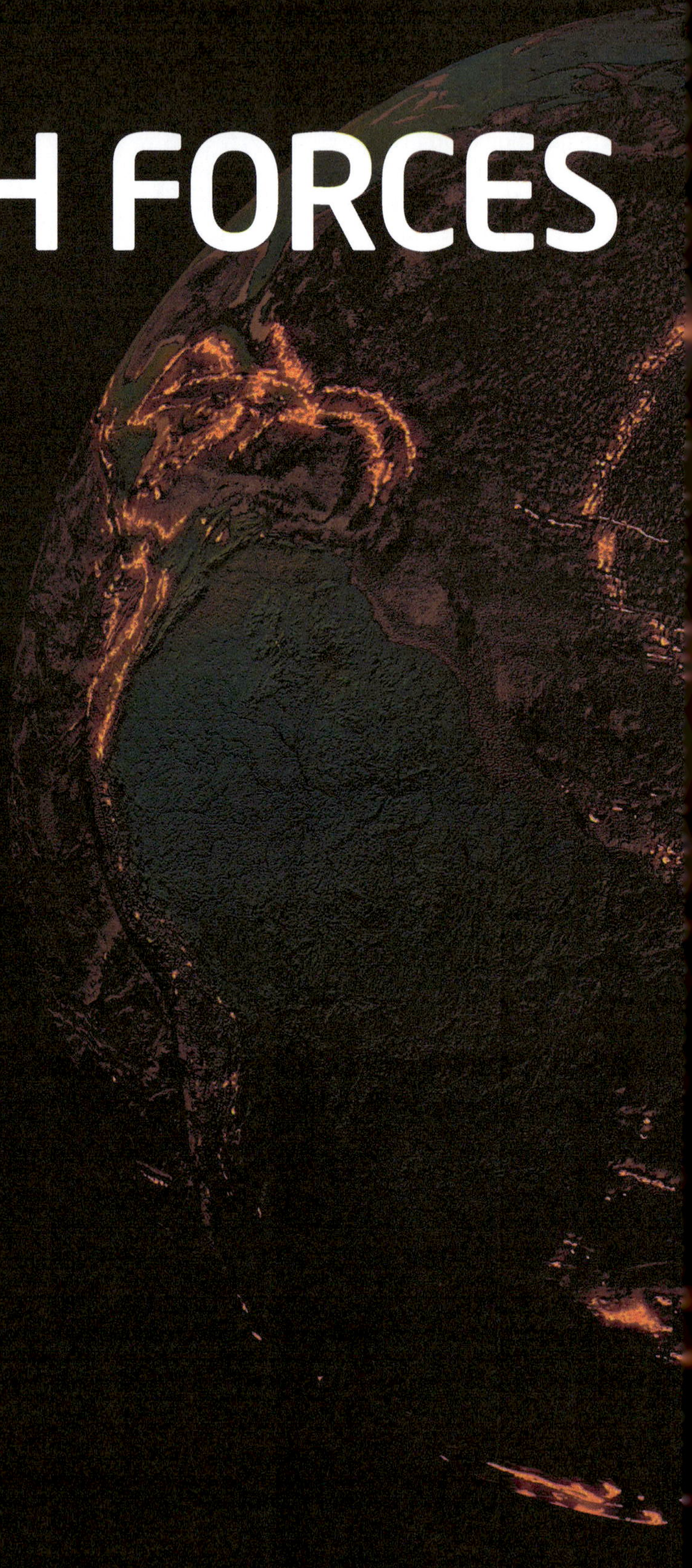

EARTH FORCES

Having investigated processes which form and shape landscapes. I can explain their impact on selected landscapes in Scotland, Europe and beyond. SOC 3-07a

Benchmarks

- Identifies the processes which form landscapes across the world.
- Provides a simple explanation of at least three processes involved in the development of any chosen landscape, for example, coasts, volcanic, rivers or glaciated.
- Reviews at least two simple graphical sources to interpret information and form a conclusion, for example, a map and a graph.

What's coming up?

- What are the zones of the Earth?
- Finding out about the Earth's crust.
- What is Pangea and what are the causes of continental drift?
- What causes plates to move and cause continental drift?
- Getting to know all things volcanic.
- Why do we have earth-shattering earthquakes?
- What causes terrifying tsunamis?

WHAT ARE THE ZONES OF THE EARTH?

We tend to think of our planet as being a lump of solid rock. However, if we were to take a bite out of the Earth and have a look inside, we would see that it is made up of different parts.

If we were to imagine that we were going on a journey to the centre of the Earth, we would actually pass through four separate zones. The outer zone is the thinnest and is known as the **crust**. It is made of solid material. Below the crust is the thickest zone, known as the **mantle**, which is molten (liquid rock called **magma**). In the centre of the Earth is the core, which has two parts. The **outer core** is also believed to be molten, and the **inner core** is thought to be solid and probably made of dense, heavy iron.

DON'T FORGET

The distance from the surface to the centre of the Earth is 6378 kilometres!

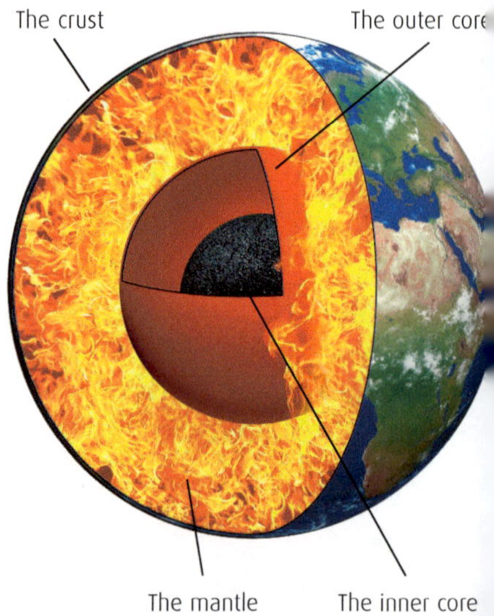

Diagram 1 – The zones of the Earth

Molten, newly born Earth starting to cool

How the crust formed

The Earth was created under so much heat and pressure that it formed as a molten (liquid) planet. As it orbited (moved in a curved path) around the sun, it gradually began to cool and settle. It was during this time that the outer zone of the Earth – the crust – formed around the planet, rather like skin forming on a bowl of custard or porridge as it starts to cool. Although the crust may feel thick and solid under our feet, when compared to the overall size of the Earth it is as thin as the skin on an apple and as fragile as the shell on an egg.

Notice how thin the shell on this egg is!

The Earth's plates

What makes things difficult for humans is the fact that the crust is also broken up into large pieces known as **plates**. The boundaries of these are the Earth's danger lines where **volcanoes**, **earthquakes** and **tsunamis** regularly occur. In addition, these plates are constantly on the move, jostling and bashing into each other, or ripping apart to open up chasms leading to the mantle below. It is this movement that has ultimately caused great loss of human life on our planet over the centuries.

There are some great film clips on our Homework Helpers to help you imagine what planet Earth was like when it first formed.

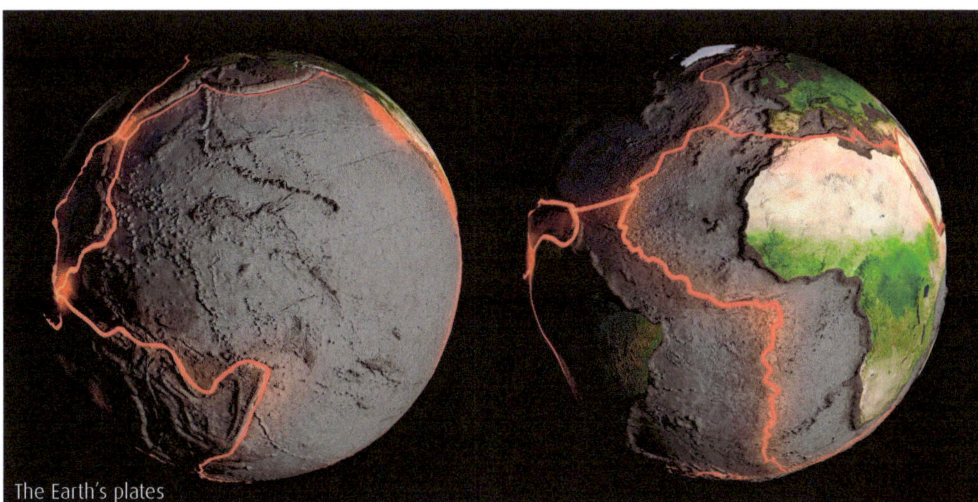

The Earth's plates

Image of earthquake damage on a plate boundary in Haiti in 2010

Classroom challenge

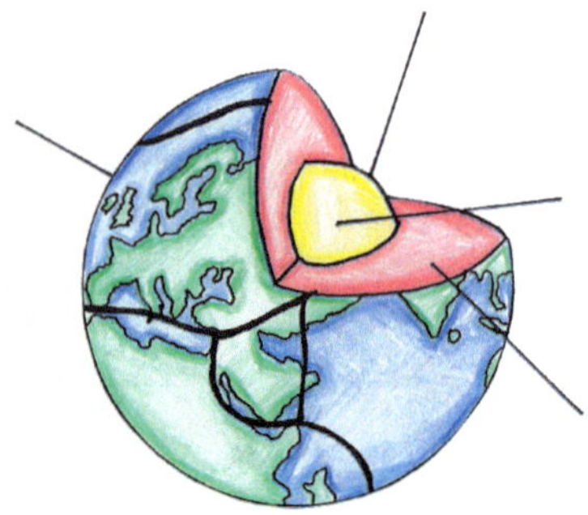

1. Make your own diagram of the zones of the Earth in your workbook. You can do this by tracing or sketching the diagram opposite, or on a printed template. Colour it in carefully and add the following labels: Crust, Mantle, Outer Core and Inner Core. Use Diagram 1 on page 10 to help you.
2. Which two zones of the Earth are made of solid material?
3. Which two zones of the Earth are molten?
4. Use the words in the box below to copy and complete the following sentences:

EARTHQUAKE PLATES VOLCANO
PLATE BOUNDARIES MANTLE CRUST

The thin skin around the Earth that formed when it cooled is called the ________.

A dangerous mountain that can kill people when it erupts is a ________________.

A shaking of the land that makes buildings collapse is an ________________.

The layer of molten rock below the crust is the ______________.

The large sections of the Earth's crust are called ___________.

The edges of plates where many people have been killed over the centuries are called ____________ ____________________.

5. **Explain** how the Earth's crust formed.
6. How many other words can you make out of the phrase – ZONES OF THE EARTH? For example: TEN, HEAT, ...

TEACHING NOTES

A printable template of this image is available to download online at www.brightredpublishing.co.uk

FINDING OUT ABOUT THE EARTH'S CRUST

So far, we have discovered that our planet is not a solid lump of rock, but is made up of four distinct zones. These zones get hotter and hotter as you travel towards the centre of the planet, with the mantle being on average around 3000°C. However, the inner core reaches a whopping 5500°C! Humans would vaporise before they could get anywhere near temperatures such as these!

Inside our planet

What we now need to find out is what causes the plates to move, and therefore start to understand the causes of volcanoes, earthquakes and tsunamis. To do this, we need to know more about the Earth's crust.

Scientists believe that the Earth is around 4550 million years old. You can perhaps appreciate how old this is when you consider that modern humans made their first appearance on Earth only 200 000 years ago. So, in fact, humans have been around for a mere 0.004% of the planet's history. This fact makes it difficult for us to understand and imagine what Earth was like in the millions of years before we existed.

Check out the 'What if Earth only existed for 24 hours?' link in the Homework Helpers.

What Earth would have looked like 4550 million years ago

When the Earth was in its early, molten stage, we have already learned that the crust formed on the surface of the planet as it started to cool down. The crust itself, though, can be split into two types – the continental crust and the oceanic crust. As their names suggest, the **continental crust** formed where the great continents are, while the **oceanic crust** is found under the oceans.

Classroom challenge

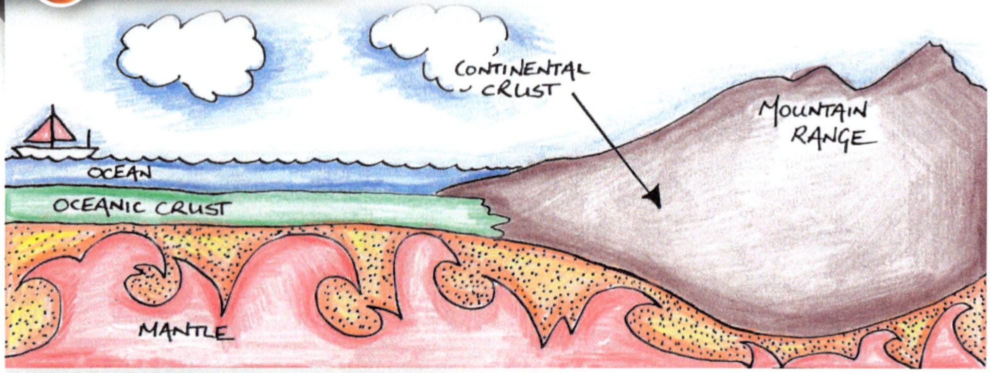

1. Find out more about the Earth's crust by sketching, tracing or using a template of the diagram above. **Annotate** it by adding the following labels beside the correct arrows.

Continental crust: up to 70 km thick under mountains. Formed from lighter materials and over 3500 million years old. Rock type - Granite

Oceanic crust: 6 km thick. Formed from heavier materials and less than 200 million years old. Rock type - Basalt

TEACHING NOTES

You can find a printable template of this resource in our Teaching Notes at www.brightredpublishing.co.uk

2. Now, colour in your diagram following these instructions:
   OCEAN = BLUE
   OCEANIC CRUST = GREEN
   CONTINENTAL CRUST = BROWN
   MANTLE = RED

3. Copy and complete the following paragraph in your workbook, choosing the correct words. You will need to look carefully at the diagram you just completed for help.

Basalt columns at Fingal's Cave, Staffa, Scotland

Granite rock

The continental crust is formed from **heavier/lighter** materials while the oceanic crust is made of **heavier/lighter** materials. The oceanic crust is **6 km/70 km** thick, which is much thinner than the continental crust, which is **6 km/70 km** thick. The oldest is the **continental/oceanic** crust at **200 million/3500 million** years old. The main rock type making up the continental crust is **granite/basalt**, but the main rock type making up the oceanic crust is **granite/basalt**.

Explore the Earth's crust and other zones further by using the Homework Helpers activities.

WHAT IS PANGEA AND WHAT ARE THE CAUSES OF CONTINENTAL DRIFT?

The Earth's crust is a very complicated zone, as it is rather like a giant jigsaw puzzle. As we have already learned, it is broken up into pieces called **plates**.

We have also learned that these plates do not sit still. They are constantly on the move.

The study of plates and their movements is known as **plate tectonics** and comes from the Greek word for building. This theory helps to explain how, about 250 million years ago, the continents of the world were all joined together to form one huge land mass called **Pangea**. So, believe it or not, the land masses we see on a map of the world today were once joined together. It seems that the plates that our continents lie on have drifted apart to take up their present positions (and they are still moving). This is known as **continental drift**. This idea or theory was first thought of by a German scientist called Alfred Wegener in 1912.

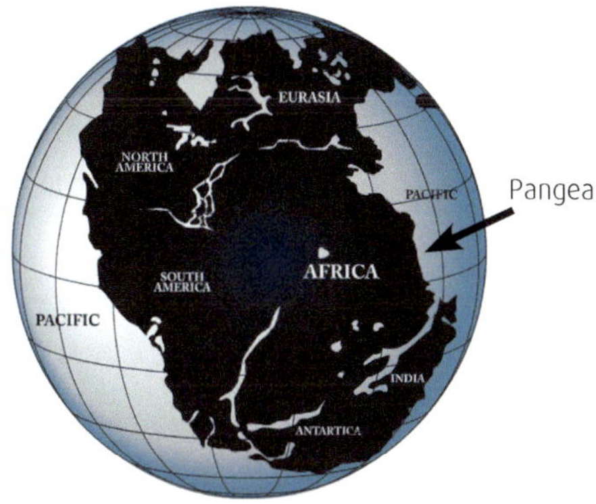

How the Earth would have looked 250 million years ago

DON'T FORGET

Continental drift is happening at around the same speed as your nails grow.

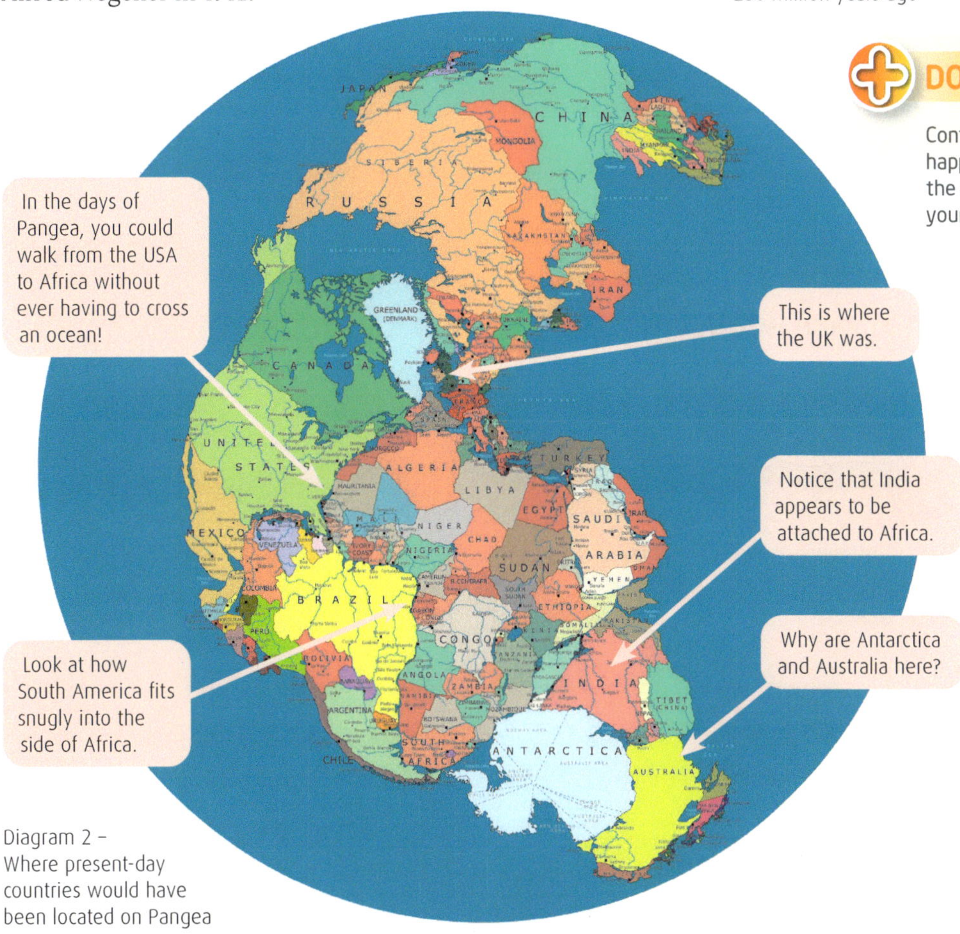

Diagram 2 – Where present-day countries would have been located on Pangea

Evidence for Pangea

This does all seem very far-fetched, though! How do we know that the continents once fitted together? Well, scientists seem to have the answer to this.

Diagram 2 on page 15 shows that the shapes of the continents of today fit neatly together like a jigsaw puzzle. Even more convincing, though, is the fact that when they are fitted together, the places where the same types of **fossils** have been found also slot neatly together.

DON'T FORGET

Fossils are the remains of prehistoric plants and animals preserved in rock.

Fossil embedded in rock

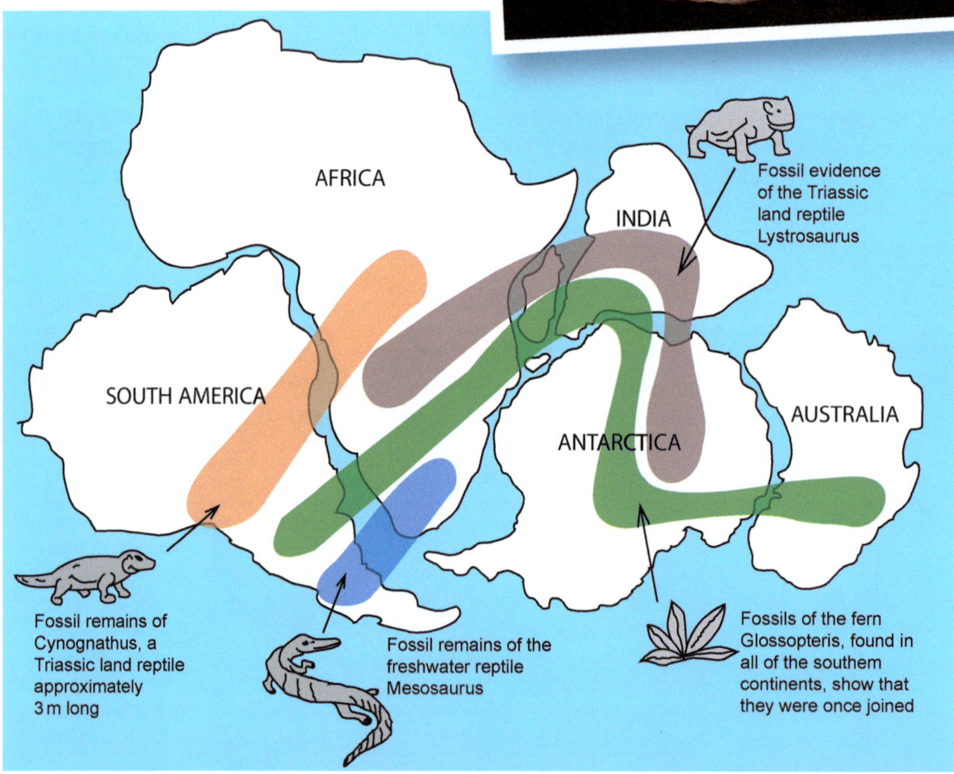

Diagram 3 – Evidence for Pangea

Classroom challenge

1. **Describe** what Pangea is.
2. How long ago did Pangea exist?
3. The word **tectonics** comes from Greek. What does it mean?
4. Imagine you are Alfred Wegener. Study Diagrams 2 and 3 on pages 15 and 16. Write down two pieces of evidence that he might have used to convince his friends that the continents were once joined together.

Alfred Wegener

Go Digital!

Print the template for this activity by heading to www.brightredpublishing.co.uk and downloading the Teaching Notes bundle.

5. Collect template maps of South America and Africa from your teacher. Cut them out and fit them together like a jigsaw. Glue them in this position into your workbook. Using the diagram below, add the evidence that they were once joined together onto your maps. Colour them in neatly.

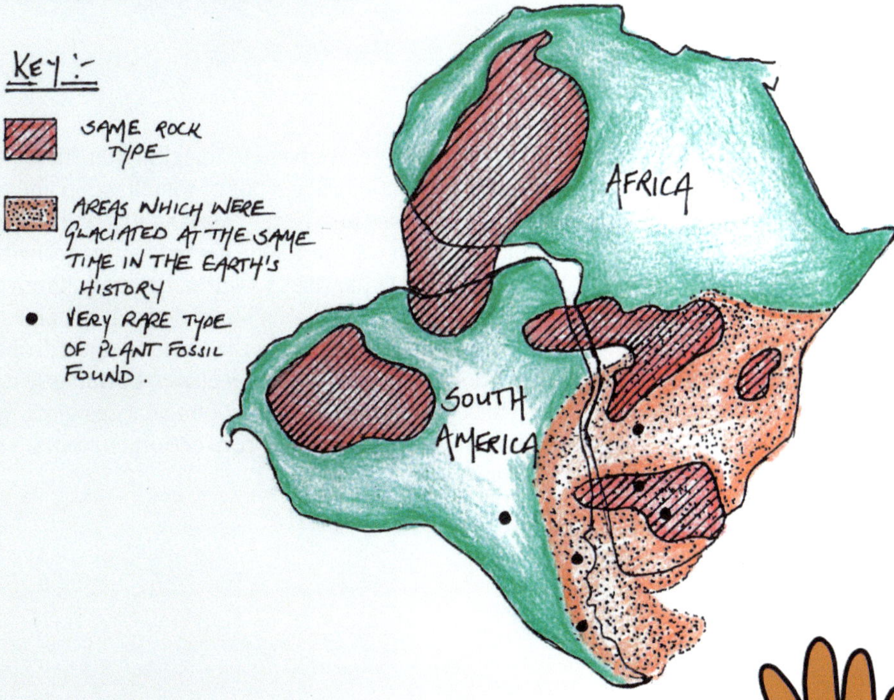

6. You have been asked to stand up and tell your class five things you have learned about plate tectonics and the zones of the Earth. What five things would you list?

WHAT CAUSES PLATES TO MOVE AND CAUSE CONTINENTAL DRIFT?

Convection currents

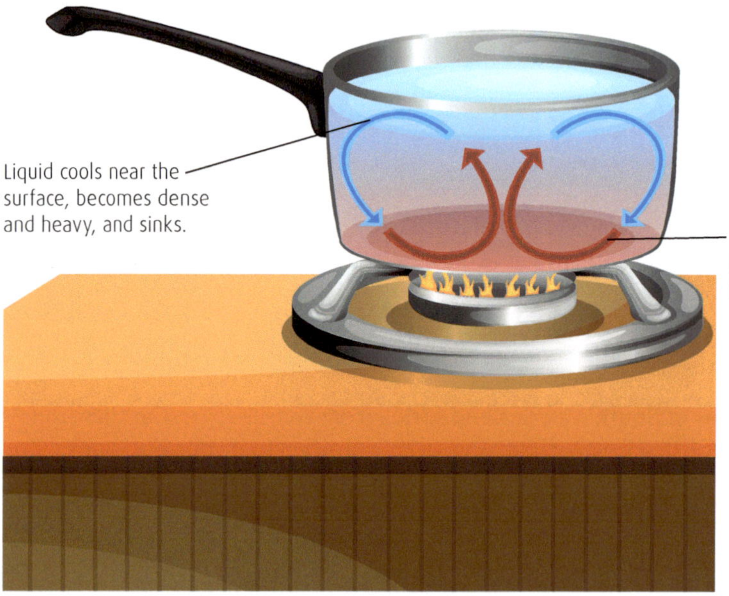

Diagram 4 – How liquid moves in a pot when you heat it up

To explain how plates move, we need to be scientific. We have to imagine that the core of the Earth is like a flame on a cooker, and the mantle is like a pot of tomato soup above it. When any liquid is heated up, it becomes less dense and rises. This happens within the Earth's mantle. Magma (the molten rock found in the mantle) is heated by the core and rises upwards towards the crust. As this liquid magma rises towards the crust, it moves away from the heat of the core and starts to cool. If we cool a liquid down, it becomes dense and heavy, and starts to sink. In the mantle, this means the liquid magma drops back down towards the core. Once back down near the core, it heats up, becomes less dense and rises upwards once again. This cycle of heating and cooling causes giant circular movements of the liquid magma in the mantle called **convection currents**. These currents are what cause the plates to move.

DON'T FORGET

Some parts of the Earth's crust are drifting faster than other parts. India, for example, is charging into the continent of Asia at a speed of 17 cm per year!

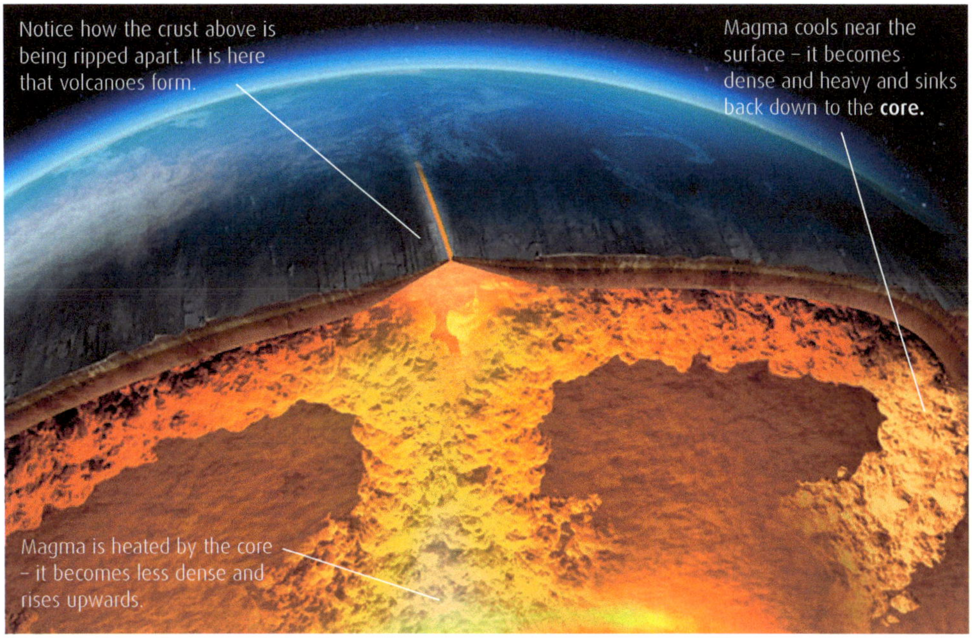

Diagram 5 – Convection currents in the Earth's mantle

The movement of the plates

As a result of convection currents, the Earth's plates move in three main ways. These are shown in Diagram 6 below.

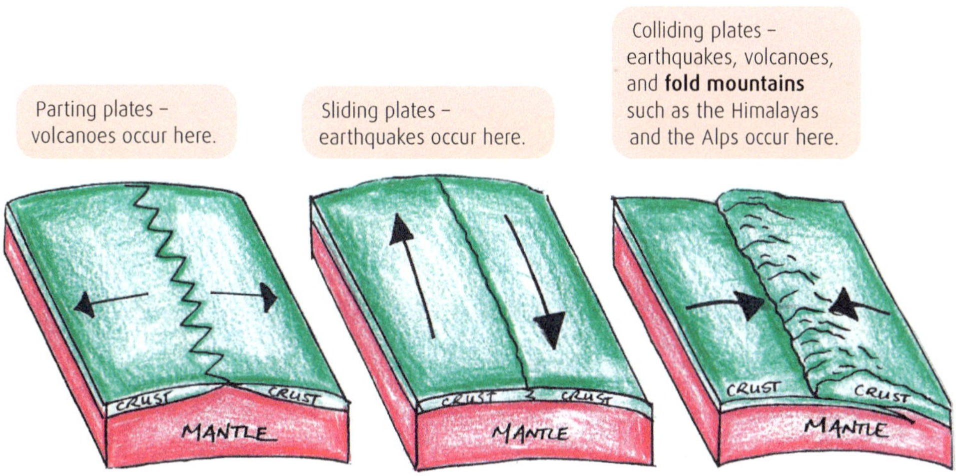

Diagram 6 – The different ways in which plates move

The plates of the Earth all have names, and the directions they are moving in are shown in Diagram 7 on page 20.

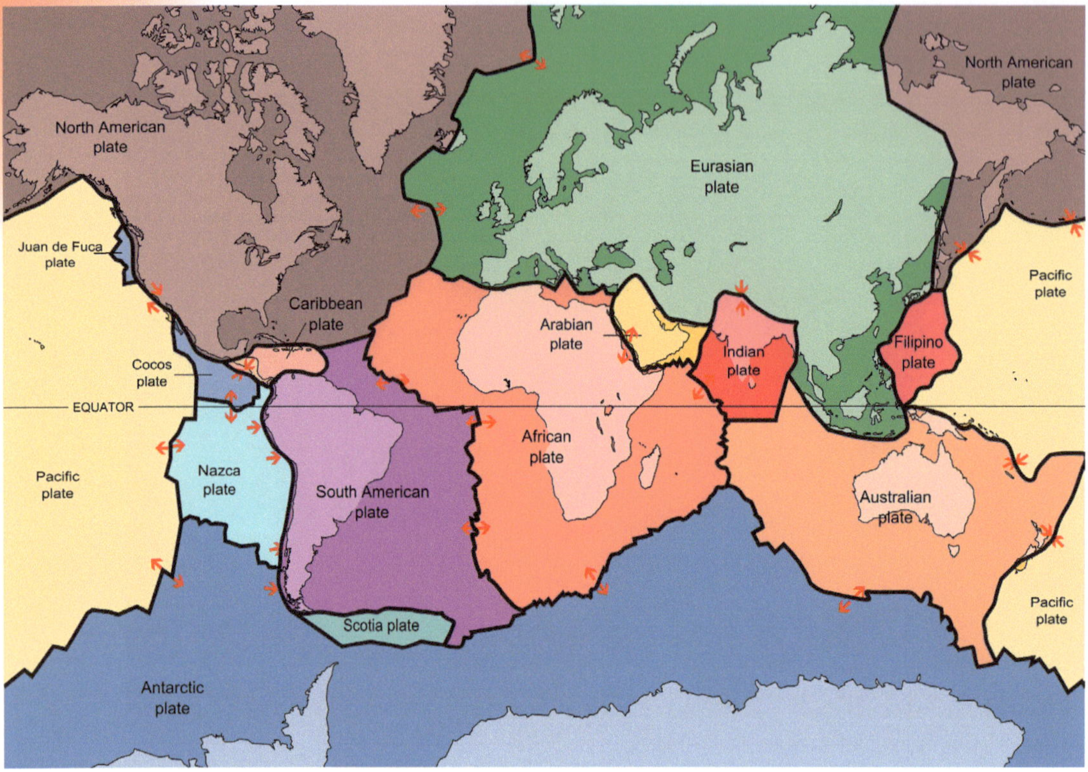

Diagram 7 – The Earth's plates and their names

Direction of movement

Moving away from each other

Moving towards each other

One of the most famous plates in the world is the Pacific plate. This is because the edges of it are called the **'Ring of Fire'** since so many earthquakes and active volcanoes are found there.

Active volcanoes, plate tectonics and the 'Ring of Fire' around the Pacific plate

Classroom challenge

1. Key word conundrum!
   Unscramble the words and phrases below and write them in your workbook.

   AREASUNI TEALP NONTICVECO RUNTRESC
   GAMMA DOLF TAMUNOSIN GRIN FO RIFE

2. Look at the words you have just unscrambled. Which words give the name of the circular movements that occur in the Earth's mantle?
3. Imagine that you had to **explain** what causes these circular movements to your parents/carers. Write down what you would say to them. You may want to draw some diagrams to help with your explanation.
4. Study Diagram 7 on page 20 of the Earth's plates. Can you find the UK on it? Once again, look at the words you unscrambled in Question 1. What is the name of the plate that the UK sits on?
5. **Explain** why you think there are no volcanoes or major earthquakes in the UK. **Hint** – look at where the UK sits on the plate.
6. Use Diagram 7 on page 20 to decide if the following statements are true or false. Write the sentences out and add the word 'true' or 'false' at the end.

   The African plate is moving away from the South American plate.

   The Eurasian plate is moving towards the North American plate.

   The Antarctic plate is moving away from the Australian plate.

   The Pacific plate is moving towards the Nazca plate.

7. Match up the following 'heads and tails' in the table below. Write the correct sentences out in your workbook.

A plate is a	like a giant jigsaw.
Plates fit together	is called plate tectonics.
Plates move towards or	huge piece of the Earth's crust.
The study of plate movement	away from each other very slowly.

8. If plates move on average only 5 centimetres a year, how long would it take the Eurasian plate to move 1 kilometre away from the North American plate?
9. Trace or sketch Diagram 6 on page 19 and then **annotate** your drawing with how the plates move, and carefully colour them in.

Go Digital!

10. Your teacher will give you a template of the Earth's plates. Cut them out, mix them up and then try to fit them back together again. Once you have done this, stick them into your jotter.

TEACHING NOTES

Templates for this activity can be found in our Teaching Notes bundle to help your students with this activity.

For more details and scientific terms on plate movement, as well as some entertaining activities, check out our Homework Helpers bundle at www.brightredpublishing.co.uk

Download our Teaching Notes bundle at www.brightredpublishing.co.uk to print out the template for this activity.

GETTING TO KNOW ALL THINGS VOLCANIC

Types of eruption

A **volcano** is generally understood to be a cone-shaped mountain from which lava pours. However, volcanoes can actually come in different shapes and sizes and do not always eject lava when they erupt. In general, there are two types of eruption, as shown in Table 1 below.

What we imagine a typical volcano to look like

Type of eruption	What comes out of the volcano?
Effusive	Lava, steam, gas, volcanic bombs – Mount Etna
Pyroclastic	Explosion of ash, gas and pumice – Mount Vesuvius eruption that destroyed Pompeii

Table 1 – Different types of volcanic eruption

Lava eruption

Explosive pyroclastic ash eruption at Mount Saint Helens, Washington State, USA

Pumice stones from a volcano

Pumice can be used to rub away hard skin on your feet!

We can describe how active a volcano is by using the three terms shown in the table below.

Extinct	The volcano will never erupt again.
Dormant	The volcano is sleeping and will erupt in the future.
Active	The volcano has had at least one eruption in the last 10 000 years.

Volcanoes usually occur as a result of the two different ways in which the plates move: parting plates and colliding plates.

Parting plates

If plates move away from each other, a crack in the Earth's crust opens up, and magma (the name given to lava when it is under the ground) will burst upwards onto the surface, forming volcanoes. Diagram 8 below shows parting plates under the Atlantic Ocean where the North American plate is ripping away from the Eurasian plate. This area is known as the **Mid-Atlantic Ridge** and is, quite literally, where the bed of the ocean is splitting open. Unfortunately for the island of Iceland, it sits right on the Mid-Atlantic Ridge and this explains why it has so many volcanoes and eruptions.

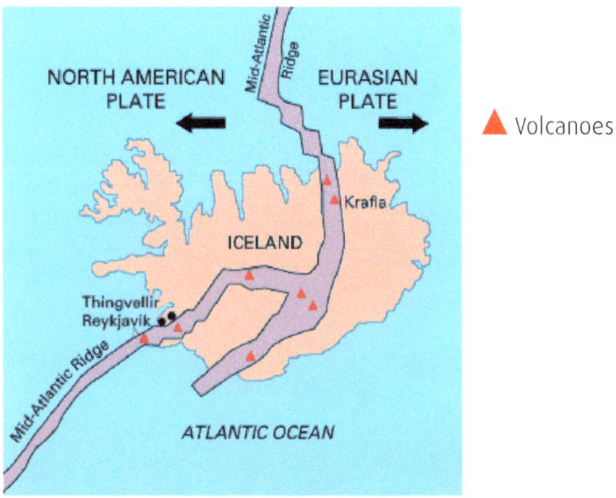

Iceland and the Mid-Atlantic Ridge

The Mid-Atlantic Ridge in Iceland attracts many tourists

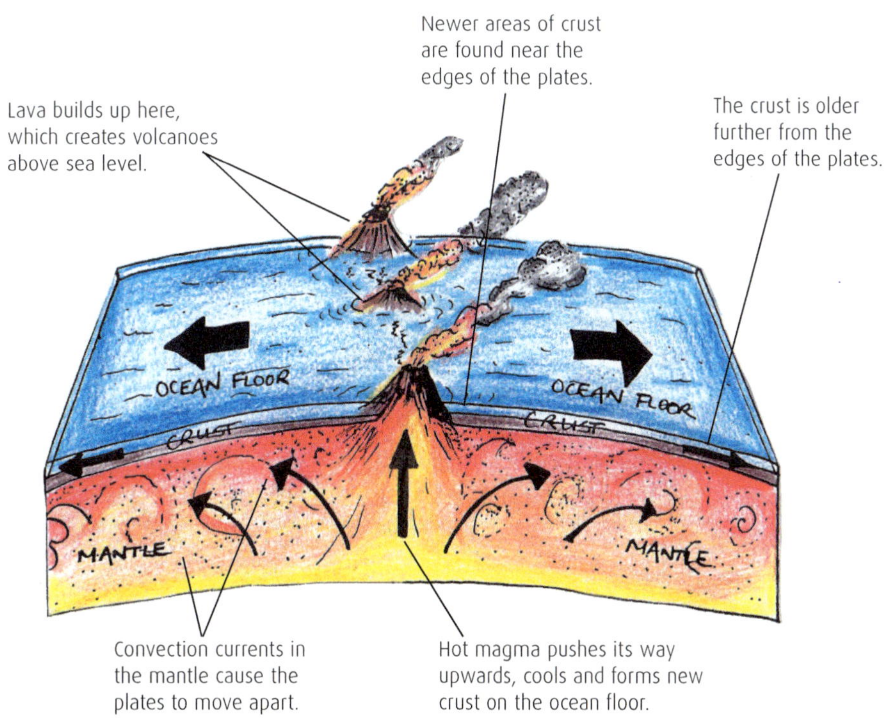

Diagram 8 – Action along the Mid-Atlantic Ridge

Colliding plates

Volcanoes may also form where plates collide, such as where the Pacific plate meets the North American plate. This happens because the heavier oceanic crust is forced downwards under the continental crust; it then melts in the heat of the mantle, creating extra magma and pressure. This pressure causes magma to move upwards, forming volcanoes.

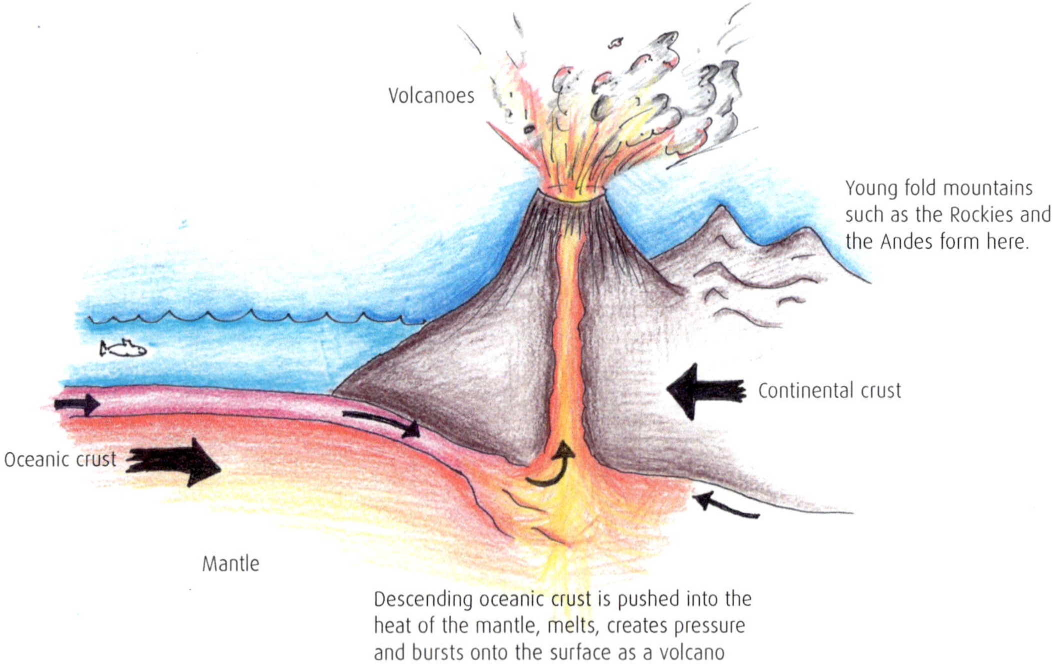

Diagram 9 – Why colliding plates form volcanoes

Mount Rainier, Washington State, USA – a volcano formed due to colliding plates

Classroom challenge

1. Above is an image of Arthur's Seat in Edinburgh. Is it an **active**, **dormant** or **extinct** volcano?
2. Study Table 1 on page 22. What are the names of the two different ways volcanoes erupt, and what type of material comes out of them?
3. (a) What name is given to the area where the North American plate is splitting from the Eurasian plate? (**Hint** – it is under the Atlantic Ocean.)
   (b) Look at Diagram 8 on page 23. **Explain** in your own words why we get volcanoes here.
4. Study Diagram 9 on page 24. To **explain** why we get volcanoes where plates collide, you can either:
   - Draw or trace your own annotated (labelled) diagram, or
   - Make up some true or false statements for your classmates to try.
5. Read the section on colliding plates. Give an example of where plates are colliding by naming the plates, and give the name of a volcano that has formed as a result.
6. Stump your teacher! Make up a question to ask your teacher on what you have learned about volcanoes so far. Make it quite difficult!

Arthur's Seat in Edinburgh, UK

Go Digital!

7. Visit the link to the British Geological Survey website on the Homework Helpers to make your very own model of Arthur's Seat.

Check out our Homework Helpers for more activities, film clips and quizzes on volcanoes.

Composite volcanoes

One of the main types of volcano is a **composite volcano**. They have three main features:

- They are usually cone-shaped.
- They are usually formed from layers of ash and lava.
- At the top, there is a bowl-shaped area known as the **crater**.

If we were to cut open a volcano and have a look inside (a **cross-section**), then we would see the features shown in Diagram 10 on page 27. This diagram also shows us that it is not just lava that bursts out of a volcano when it erupts. There are other deadly materials involved too!

Mount Mayon in the Philippines has the characteristics of a composite volcano

Look at how the lava from this eruption is eating up this road!

Lava flow in Hawaii, USA

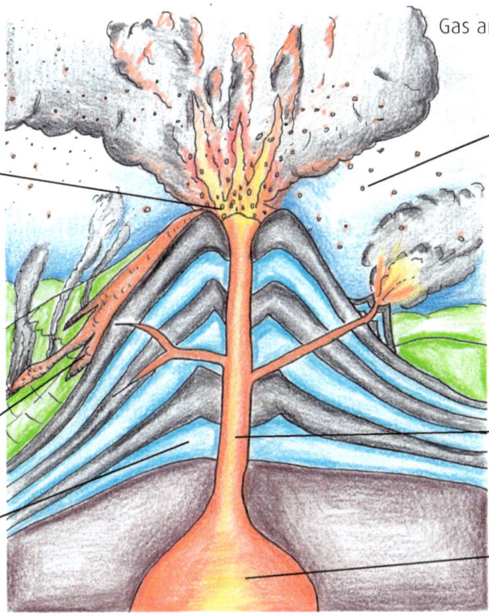

Diagram 10 – Features (a cross-section) of a composite volcano

Four ways in which a volcano can kill you

Cooked to a crisp by red-hot poisonous gases	Super-heated gases such as carbon dioxide, sulphur dioxide, hydrogen sulphide and carbon monoxide can mix with ash and travel down the sides of a volcano at speeds of 450 miles per hour. This is known as a **pyroclastic flow** – and the most famous eruption of this type was at Pompeii in AD79 when Mount Vesuvius erupted. It boiled the brains of victims, vaporised their flesh and blackened their skeletons. This is the most deadly type of eruption, and you cannot outrun it!
Drown in red-hot mudflows	Sometimes volcanoes are so high they have snow, ice and glaciers at the top. If a pyroclastic eruption melts these, they mix with the ash to form hot mudflows called **lahars**. They can travel very fast and can bulldoze entire towns, as they carry big boulders with them.
Flattened by hot volcanic bombs	These are lumps of red-hot lava that measure more than 65 mm and can be thrown huge distances. They can be very big – over 5 metres in size – and have the potential to kill groups of people.
Suffocated by deadly ash clouds	Ash can fall like snow from a volcanic eruption and settle on the roofs of houses. The weight of this can cause buildings to collapse, killing people inside them. Even more worrying is that ash can be ejected in large quantities into our atmosphere, block incoming sunlight and cause the Earth to cool. Scientists think that a huge eruption of this type caused the extinction of 96% of the Earth's species during the Permian era.

Table 2 – Four ways in which a volcano can kill you

Charred skeletons at Herculaneum

Classroom challenge

There is a template for this in our Teaching Notes bundle.

1. Make a tracing, or sketch your own annotated (labelled) diagram of a composite volcano for your workbook. Use Diagram 10 on page 27 to help you.
2. Copy and complete this paragraph by adding the missing words. Choose words from the box underneath.

> Before an eruption, magma builds up in the ____________ c________. Magma will rise up the m_____________ _________ as an eruption begins. When a volcano erupts, ______ will be ejected from the c_____________. Rising magma inside a volcano causes many small ________________ to be felt. Volcanoes also eject ____________ gases, volcanic __________ and a_______.

MAIN VENT	LAVA	EARTHQUAKES	ASH	BOMBS
MAGMA CHAMBER	POISONOUS	CRATER		

3. Make a copy of the diagram below. Use Table 2 on page 27 to add descriptions of your own to **explain** why each type of eruption can be deadly.

Check out our Homework Helpers activities for more on deadly volcanoes.

Four ways a volcano can be deadly

- **Poisonous gases** –
- **Mudflows** –
- **Volcanic bombs** –
- **Ash clouds** –

Go Digital!

4. Do your own research. Go online and try to find out the ten most deadly volcanoes in the world today. List them and say why they are considered deadly.

DON'T FORGET

Did you know that scientists use the Volcanic Explosivity Index (VEI) to grade how violent a volcano is? It goes from 0 to 8, with 8 being classed as 'mega-colossal'. Check out the Homework Helpers for more on this.

Question 4 can be set as a homework task.

Why live close to a volcano?

If there are so many ways that a volcano can kill you, why do more than 800 million people worldwide live within 60 miles (100 km) of an active volcano? Indeed, if we know that between 1500 and 2017 more than 278000 people were killed during an eruption or by the effects following one, why do people continue to rebuild their homes and their lives next to active volcanoes?

The diagram below explains why.

TEACHING NOTES

You can find a link to a lesson on the 'Montserrat eruption role play' in our Teaching Notes bundle.

Diagram 11 – Mount Etna in Sicily is very populated!

Classroom challenge

1. How many people in the world live within 60 miles of an active volcano?
2. Read through the whole 'Getting to know all things volcanic' section again and study Table 2 and Diagram 11 on pages 27 and 29.
   Evaluate whether people should live next to volcanoes.

To **evaluate** something is a very important skill in geography. It means you must think about all the good things that volcanoes offer, but also all the problems that can be experienced living close to them. You should then state whether people should live next to volcanoes or not, and give your reasons why. Try to give at least two reasons why people should live near volcanoes and two reasons why they should not.

Reasons why people should live by a volcano.	Reasons why people should not live by a volcano.
Conclusion. State whether you think people should live beside volcanoes and your two reasons why.	

Evaluation table

How can people predict, plan and prepare for a volcanic eruption?

If 800 million people worldwide live within 60 miles of an active volcano, they must be confident that they will be safe if an eruption were to happen. How can people predict, plan and prepare themselves?

Predict

The images below show some measures that are used to attempt to **predict** when an eruption will occur and to try to reduce loss of life.

Diagram 12 – How can people predict an eruption?

What can people do to fight an eruption?

People living close to Mount Etna in the area of Zafferana in Sicily (see Diagram 13 below) are very familiar with how to deal with eruptions since it is Europe's most active volcano! Diagram 14 on page 31 sums up some of the techniques that have been used.

Diagram 13 – Location of Mount Etna and Zafferana, Italy

DON'T FORGET

USGS stands for the United States Geological Survey. It is a US government bureau that provides scientific advice on many things, including how to deal with natural hazards such as volcanoes and earthquakes.

Mount Etna erupts at least once a year.

Ash can be shovelled off roofs to stop them collapsing under the weight.

Explosives can be used to create holes in the mountain for lava to flow into.

Helicopters can drop huge concrete blocks onto the lava flow to try to block or divert it.

High-pressure water hoses can be aimed at the lava to cool it and stop it flowing.

Emergency services (police, fire service, nurses and doctors) are trained in what to do during an eruption.

Bulldozers can be used to make rock and soil dams to block and divert the lava flow.

Diagram 14 – Living in the shadow of Mount Etna, Sicily

DON'T FORGET

Did you know that 25% of Sicily's population lives on the slopes of Mount Etna?

Classroom challenge

1. Study Diagram 12 on page 30.
   (a) Below are names of instruments that are used to help us predict if a volcano is about to erupt. You will need to use the Code Buster to swap each number for the correct letter to find out their names, but the letters have also been jumbled up! Try to unscramble them, and write the instrument names in your workbook.

A	B	C	D	E	F	G	H	I	J	K	L	M
1	2	3	4	5	6	7	8	9	10	11	12	13
N	O	P	Q	R	S	T	U	V	W	X	Y	Z
14	15	16	17	18	19	20	21	22	23	24	25	26

19 18 12 1 19 5   18 9 20 5 12 13 20 20 5   13 18 5 13 5 19 20 9 19 15 5
19 3 3 15 5 16

(b) What is the name of the US organisation that can be called in to help predict if a volcano is about to erupt, and can advise people when to leave?
(c) **Explain** why you would bury a seismometer on a volcano.
(d) What happens to the pH of lake water if a volcano is about to erupt?
(e) What is the name of a gas that is released before an eruption?

2. Zafferana is a beautiful town in Sicily, which is very popular with visitors.

Zafferana

Mount Etna erupting close to Zafferana

However, it is also close to Mount Etna, and the people who live there often have to fight the volcano to save their town.

Study Diagram 14 on page 31. Make up a poster called 'Fighting Mount Etna', which tells people about the ways they can battle with a volcano to save their town.

Download the Homework Helpers and check out the film clips on Zafferana and Mount Etna.

A volcanologist sampling lava. Would you like to do this job?

3. A volcanologist is a person who studies volcanoes and often tries to predict when they will erupt. Having studied lots of detail on volcanoes – would you like to be a volcanologist? Give two reasons for your answer.
4. Write out the letters of the alphabet in your workbook. Try to think of a word to do with volcanoes for every letter. For example, A = Ash.

WHY DO WE HAVE EARTH-SHATTERING EARTHQUAKES?

What is an earthquake?

In simple terms, earthquakes are a rumbling, shaking or rolling of the Earth's crust. They usually occur when two plates slip past one another suddenly, or crash into each other at plate boundaries. However, they can also be experienced when plates are being forced in opposite directions, or even when magma rises inside volcanoes!

TEACHING NOTES

Look at the great 'Activities' on earthquakes in our Teaching Notes to enhance learning.

There are over 150 000 earthquakes every year, but most are so gentle they can only be detected by highly sensitive instruments called **seismometers**.

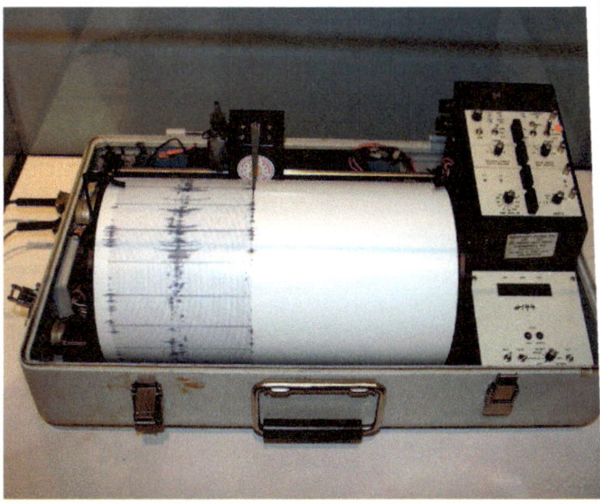

A seismometer

Building damage, Haiti, 2010

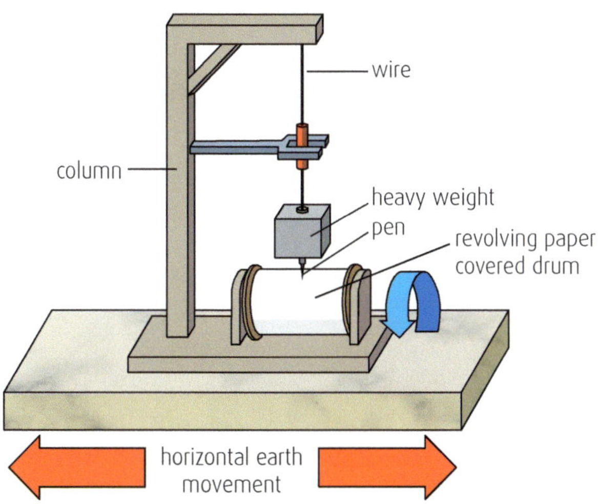

Make a simple seismometer

When an earthquake occurs, it sends out **shock waves**. These are usually detected by seismometers, and measured on a special scale called the **Richter scale**. Many believe that this scale goes from 0 to 10, with 10 being the worst. However, in theory, there is no upper limit to the scale. In terms of human survival, though, a magnitude 12 earthquake would be the equivalent of a planet the size of Mars crashing into the Earth! The Richter scale is a logarithmic scale, which simply means that a magnitude 6 earthquake would actually be ten times more powerful than a magnitude 5.

Magnitude	Description	How often	Feels like how many kilograms of TNT	Impact
1	Small	Every minute	0.6 to 20 kg	Humans cannot feel these.
2	Small	Every hour	600 kg	Very sensitive people or animals may feel these.
3	Small	Every day	20 000 kg	Felt by people sitting down – feels like the rumble of heavy traffic going by.
4	Small	Every week	60 000 kg	Ceiling lights may swing – can wake people from their sleep.
5	Moderate	Every 10 years	20 000 000 kg	Furniture moves, ornaments fall, plaster begins to crack.
6	Moderate	Every 30 years	60 000 000 kg	Chimneys fall, walls crack, difficult to stand up, severe structural damage to houses.
7	Major	Every 50 years	20 billion kg	Severe structural damage to houses, many houses collapse, underground pipes crack, gas leaks cause fires, cracks open up in the ground.
8	Great	Every 100 years	60 billion kg	Most buildings, bridges etc. destroyed, total destruction, ground actually rises and falls.
9	Great	Every 300 years	20 trillion kg	Rare and unbelievable damage would result (Japan 2011).
10	Super	No recordings of this	Unimaginable!	The Earth can be moved on its axis. The equivalent of a large asteroid hitting the Earth.

Table 3 – The Richter scale of earthquake energy

Classroom challenge

1. **Describe** what an earthquake is.
2. How many earthquakes are there every year?
3. What is the name of the instrument we use to measure earthquakes?
4. What is the name of the scale we use to measure earthquakes?
5. Study Table 3 above. Draw ten boxes in your workbook. In each box, sketch out a scene for a movie to represent the impact of each stage on the Richter scale from 1 to 10.

TEACHING NOTES

Don't forget to visit www.brightredpublishing.co.uk for more interactive ways of learning about earthquakes.

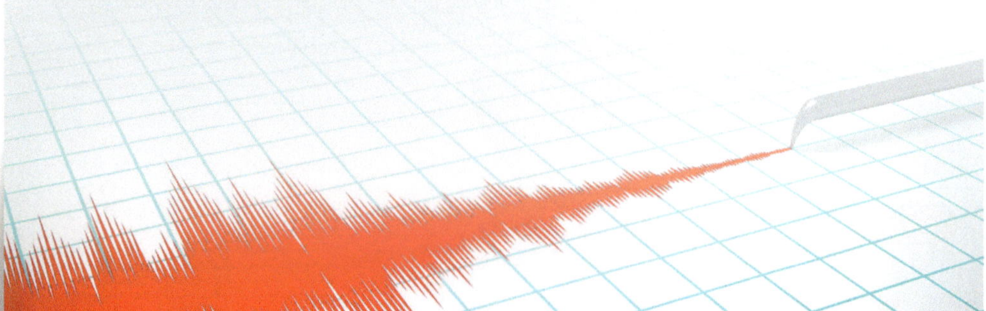

Features of an earthquake

We have already learned that when an earthquake occurs it gives out **shock waves** (sometimes called **seismic waves**). These are rather like flinging a stone into a pond. The point on the surface of the crust where the actual centre of the earthquake is felt is called the **epicentre**. This is where most earthquake damage will occur. The shock waves move in ripple-like motions from this point, just like the ripples on a pond when a stone hits the water. People who have experienced earthquakes have even witnessed the ground rolling up and down like waves on the sea! The point where the rocks have moved under the ground is called the **focus**. For some time after an earthquake, there may be more ground movement as the plates settle. These are called **aftershocks**.

Ground movements called shock waves after an earthquake are like ripples in a pond

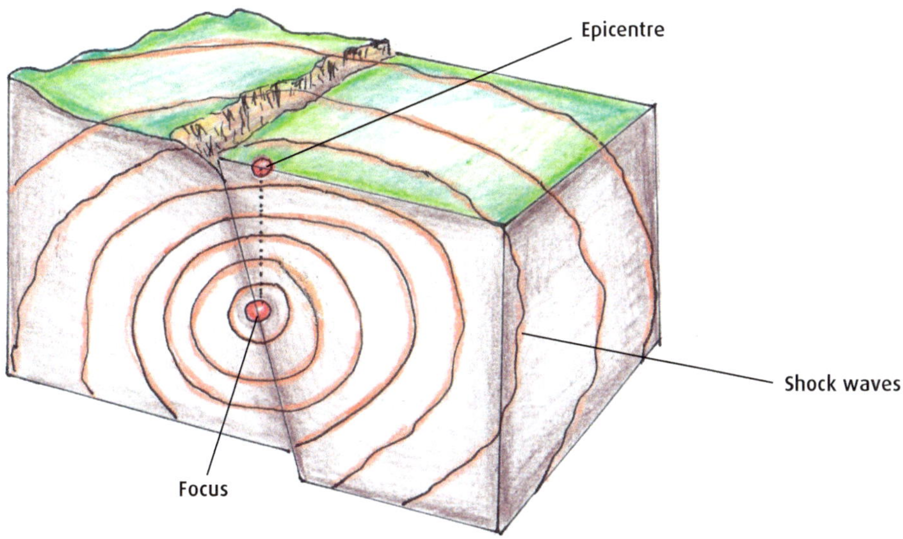

Diagram 15 – The structure of an earthquake

Sliding plates – the San Andreas Fault

Most of the movements that cause earthquakes occur along large cracks called **faults**. One of the most famous faults in the world is the **San Andreas Fault**, where the Pacific plate is trying to slide past the North American plate. Usually the movement is so slow that it is hardly noticed. In fact, there is at least one **earth tremor** along the San Andreas Fault every day. However, problems arise when the plates get stuck. This allows pressure to build up, and eventually the plates free themselves with a huge jerk that shakes the ground massively. Unfortunately, some areas of the San Andreas Fault have been stuck for quite a while now, and the residents who live on or close to these are expecting a huge earthquake to happen at any time. The last significant quake happened in San Francisco in 1906. Another medium quake hit the city in 1989, called the Loma Prieta earthquake. The people of California refer to this situation as 'waiting for the big one'.

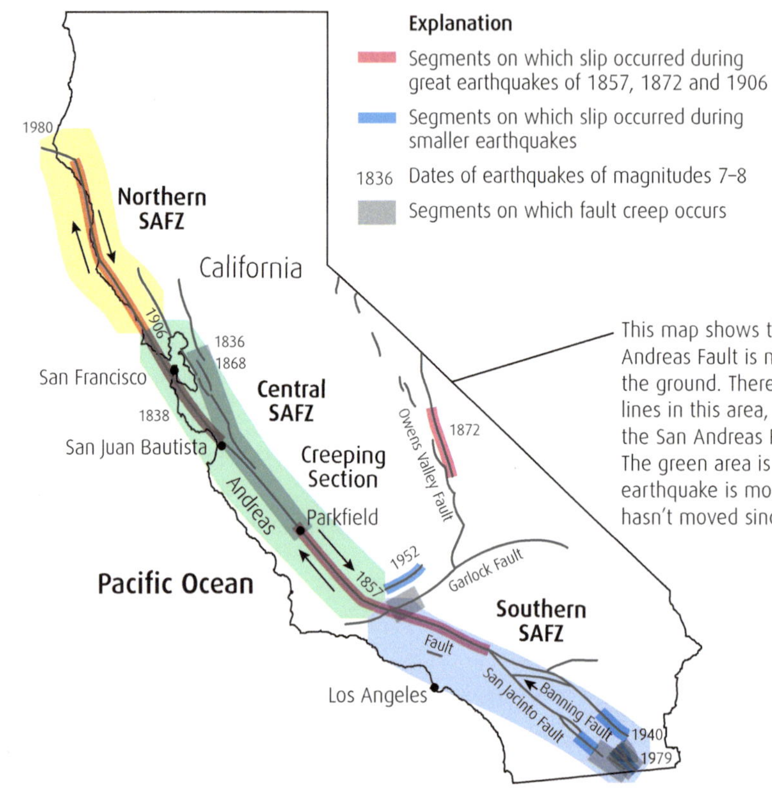

This map shows that the San Andreas Fault is not a simple line in the ground. There are lots of fault lines in this area, and so it is called the San Andreas Fault Zone (SAFZ). The green area is where the next big earthquake is most likely, because it hasn't moved since the 1800s!

The San Andrea Fault system in California, USA

The San Andreas Fault

What makes this situation even worse is the fact that two of the biggest cities in the USA – San Francisco and Los Angeles – are located on, or very close to, this fault. In fact, over 15 million people live in the area affected.

Classroom challenge

1. Copy and complete the sentences below by filling in the missing words. The first letter has been put in for you. Diagram 15 on page 35 will help you with this.

   The point where an earthquake has occurred underground is called the f__________.

   The centre of an earthquake above ground, where the damage is worst, is called the e____________.

   The two names given to the waves that spread out from the centre of an earthquake are s__________ or s______________ waves.

   One of the most famous fault lines in the world is called the S_____ A________ F______.

   The two plates that are sliding past each other along this fault are the N______ A__________ plate and the P_________ plate.

2. Either draw or trace your own version of the San Andreas Fault diagram below for your workbook. Carefully label it and colour it in.

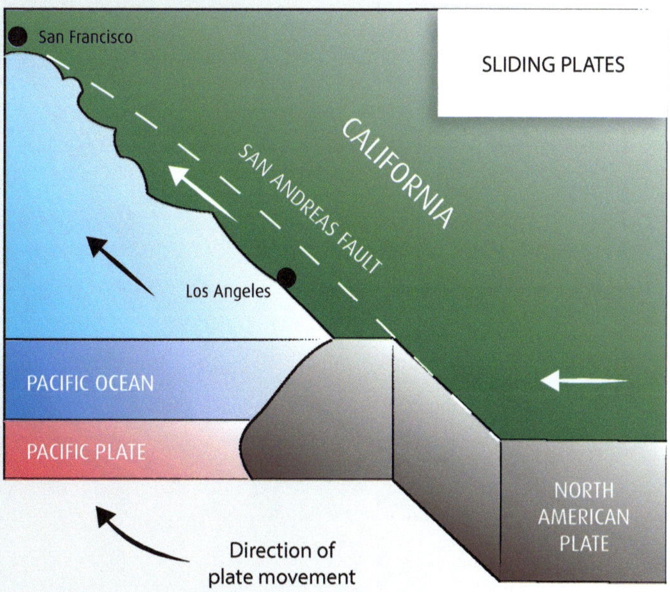

3. **Describe** what shock waves are said to be like.
4. **Explain** what has happened to the sliding plates along the San Andreas Fault that means a really big earthquake is now more likely.

Find out more about the Loma Prieta quake of 1989 in our Homework Helpers!

Earthquake in Haiti, 2010

What happened?

On 12 January 2010, an earthquake, measuring 7 on the Richter scale, hit the country of Haiti. Haiti is part of a large island called Hispaniola, which it shares with the Dominican Republic. It is here that the Caribbean plate is sliding past the North American plate.

Haiti, unfortunately, is one of the poorest countries in the world and struggled to cope with such a huge disaster. Its capital, Port au Prince, was only 25 km from the epicentre.

Location of Haiti

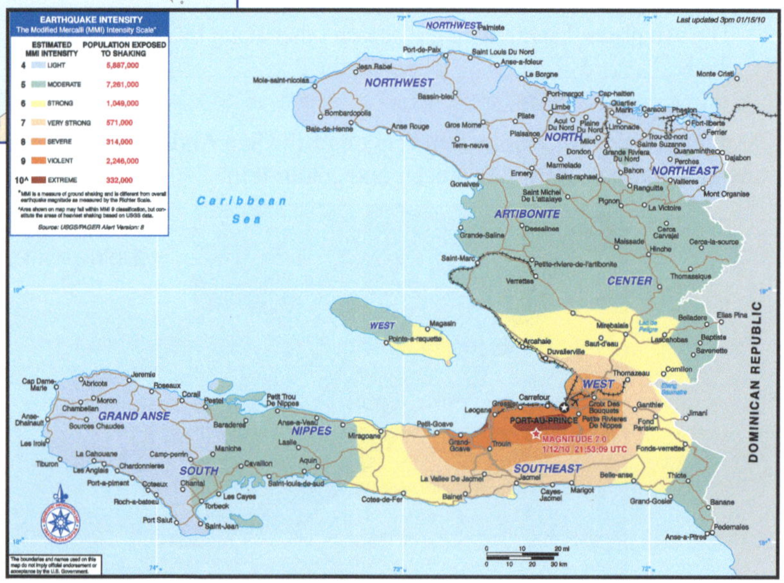

Map of earthquake intensity for 2010 earthquake in Haiti

Many of the houses in Haiti were made from loose bits of wood, breeze blocks and corrugated iron, and they lacked foundations. They collapsed easily.

Diagram 16 – Destruction in Haiti, 2010

The Haiti Times

Earthquake Disaster Newsfeed

- Buildings collapse as shock waves move across the ground.
- People are trapped in the rubble.
- 250 000 residences and 30 000 commercial buildings collapse or are severely damaged.
- Electricity cables break and spark – fire breaks out. These are difficult to deal with because water mains have been burst.
- There are sewage spills and no access to drinking water.
- People loot shops in search of food and for mattresses to sleep on outside.

Digging out survivors

- Aftershocks cause more deaths as unstable buildings collapse on survivors and rescuers.
- There are so many bodies that they have to be put into mass graves to stop the spread of disease. This means relatives may never find their loved ones.
- No electricity, as cables and pylons have collapsed.
- People face homelessness and disease.
- It takes three days before any aid starts to arrive. Aid and rescuers struggle to get in as roads, railways and bridges have collapsed in the quake.
- The economy is ruined.
- Three million people are affected by the quake. The Haitian Government reports that 230 000 people have been identified as dead, 300 000 are injured and an estimated 1 000 000 are homeless.
- Diseases such as cholera break out due to filthy conditions and broken pipes for water and sewage.
- People are unemployed and have no money because their place of work has been destroyed.

Earthquake damage

Classroom challenge

1. Make your own map of the countries of the Caribbean.
Use an atlas or the online atlas from the Homework Helpers to help you add the following labels to your map.

USA, Mexico, Caribbean Sea, Pacific Ocean, Haiti, Dominican Republic, Cuba, Jamaica, Venezuela, Colombia

Neatly colour in your map and stick it into your workbook.

TEACHING NOTES

There is a blank map of the countries of the Caribbean in our Teaching Notes to help with this.

2. **Primary effects** are things that happen because of the earthquake itself. **Secondary effects** are things that happen in the hours, days and weeks after the quake.
Read the *Haiti Times Newsfeed*. Decide which events are **primary** or **secondary effects**, and list them in the table below.

Primary effects	Secondary effects

3. Use this table and Diagram 16 on page 38 to give at least three reasons why so many people were killed or injured as a result of the Haiti earthquake.

TEACHING NOTES

There are some film clips in the Teaching Notes to help with this.

What can you do to survive an earthquake?

The earthquake tragedy in Haiti was so bad because it is one of the poorest countries in the world and can't afford to put earthquake precautions in place. However, people who live in earthquake zones in wealthy countries, such as the population of California living near the San Andreas Fault, are well informed and trained in what to do in an earthquake. This is called the '3 Ps Policy' – Predict, Plan and Prepare!

Predict

Diagram 17 – The San Andreas Fault, and signs an earthquake may be about to occur

Protect

The biggest killer in an earthquake is building collapse. Therefore, to try to save lives, attempts should be made to make buildings earthquake-proof, such as the Transamerica Pyramid in San Francisco. It has the features shown in Diagram 18 here.

Diagram 18 – The Transamerica Pyramid – is this the ultimate 'earthquake-proof' building?

In addition, there are strict building regulations in place, and regular safety checks are made. Older buildings and bridges have been strengthened and reinforced. Any structures that are likely to suffer damage in an earthquake have signs on them to warn people that they risk their lives by entering.

Enter at your own risk!

DON'T FORGET

Did you know that the Transamerica Pyramid cost $32 000 000 to build?

Find out more about the amazing Transamerica Pyramid at www.brightredpublishing.co.uk

Prepare

The city of San Francisco has a Department of Emergency Management that has a very detailed website issuing instructions to citizens on how to prepare for an earthquake.

Download our Homework Helpers to learn more about how San Francisco manages earthquake preparation.

If possible, get outside to an open space away from where buildings will collapse – but only after the shaking stops.

Get under a table – this offers some protection from a collapsing ceiling. 'Drop, Cover, Hold On'.

People participate in the 'Great ShakeOut' earthquake drill.

Schools and public buildings have regular earthquake drills.

People should turn off the gas (to stop explosions), fill the bath with water (to fight fires if water mains burst), and store food, bottles of water, batteries, radio and first-aid kits.

Families should make plans for what to do in an earthquake and where to meet afterwards.

Emergency services (fire, police, ambulance) are trained in what to do. Areas are designated as command centres, and temporary hospitals are zoned away from the danger areas.

Diagram 19 – The soft ground of the Marina District in San Francisco wobbled like a jelly in the 1989 quake. How can people prepare for this?

In the past, the advice given to people for what to do in an earthquake was to stand in a doorframe. It was believed that this was the strongest part of a wall and it was the least likely part to collapse. However, experts now advise against this and, having studied reports from survivors of earthquakes, believe that the best advice is 'Drop, Cover and Hold On'.

Drop, Cover and Hold On!

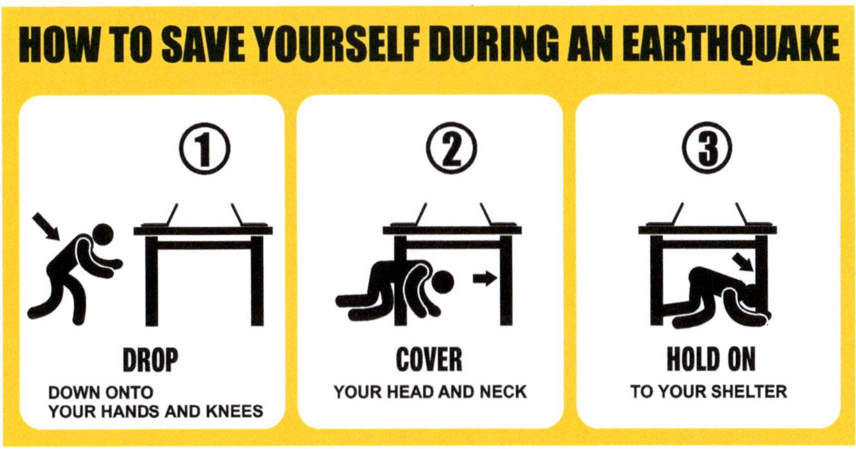

Diagram 20 – Earthquake advice

Within the home, there are also some basic things people can do to make their living environment safer in an earthquake. These can be as simple as not having heavy objects on shelves, which could fall on people in a quake. Also, anchor or tie heavy furniture such as fridges and cupboards to the walls or floor to stop them toppling over.

Finally, countries at risk of earthquakes worldwide now participate in the **'Great ShakeOut'**. This occurs at a certain time and date every year and involves everyone in these areas practising what to do in an earthquake.

Check out the link to the 'Great ShakeOut' in our Homework Helpers.

Classroom challenge

1. Study Diagram 17 on page 41.
   (a) **Describe** natural signs that warn us that an earthquake is about to happen.
   (b) Name two pieces of equipment that can help us to detect if plates are starting to move.
2. Study Diagram 18 on page 41. **Explain** why the Transamerica Pyramid can be described as the ultimate earthquake-proof building. What features does it have?
3. Imagine you and your family live close to the San Andreas Fault. Study Diagrams 19 and 20 on pages 42 and 43.

Now make up a detailed checklist of what you and your family should do in an earthquake.

There are some film clips and interesting links in our Homework Helpers to investigate this further.

4. Every family should have an earthquake survival kit if they live in a quake zone. This picture shows the items that you can buy for this.

Working in pairs, complete the table below. You must identify the items from the kit, say what you would need them for, and suggest items that are missing from this picture that you would also need for you and your family (there are a few crucial things missing!).

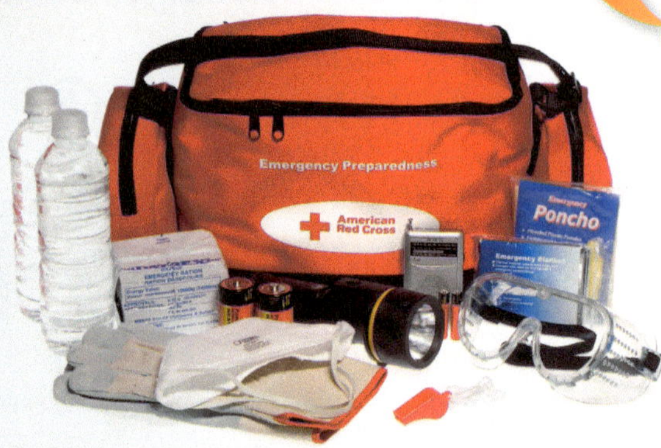

Earthquake survival kit

When complete, convince your class what they should have in an earthquake survival kit and the reasons why. You could make up a slide presentation, poster or leaflet.

TEACHING NOTES

Why not use the SF72 link in our Teaching Notes to help you here?

Item	What is it needed for?
Extra item	**What is it needed for?**

WHAT CAUSES TERRIFYING TSUNAMIS?

What is a tsunami?

A tsunami is a large ocean wave, usually triggered by an underwater earthquake. The name comes from the Japanese language and means 'harbour wave'.

Tsunami damage, Japan, 2011

Tsunamis are often caused by tectonic plates crashing together under the ocean. This can result in pressure forcing one plate to jump up above the other one. This, literally, lifts the ocean water above that plate – and that is what makes the ocean pull away from the land around it. Perhaps the best way to visualise this is to imagine a tea towel lying flat on a table. The tea towel represents the ocean water. If you pinch the middle of it and then lift it a little, you notice the edges will pull inwards. This is exactly what happens to ocean water in a tsunami.

So, the first sign that a tsunami is about to occur is water disappearing rapidly from a beach. If you see this happening, run inland or get up high fast!

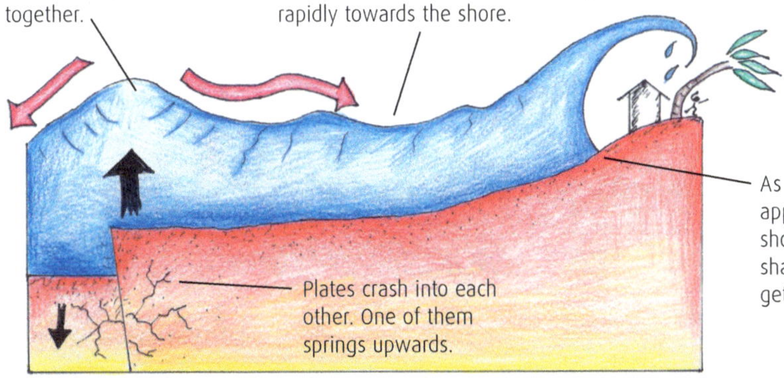

Diagram 21 – What causes a tsunami?

The water that has been lifted above the earthquake site collapses back downwards again. This then pushes fast-moving bodies of water outwards from the epicentre, and they then rush towards shorelines all around the ocean. They can travel as fast as a jet at 475 miles per hour!

Tsunami, Japan, 2011

When the water reaches the shore, it starts to slow down, but it also starts to increase in height. In fact, these waves can be as high as four houses on top of each other. They then crash into the shore – but, unlike a normal wave, they push inland, sweeping everything away in their path as they move.

In the last two decades, there have been two very famous, destructive killer tsunamis. One occurred on 26 December 2004 in the Indian Ocean. The second was off the coast of Japan on 11 March 2011.

Boxing Day Tsunami, Indian Ocean, 2004

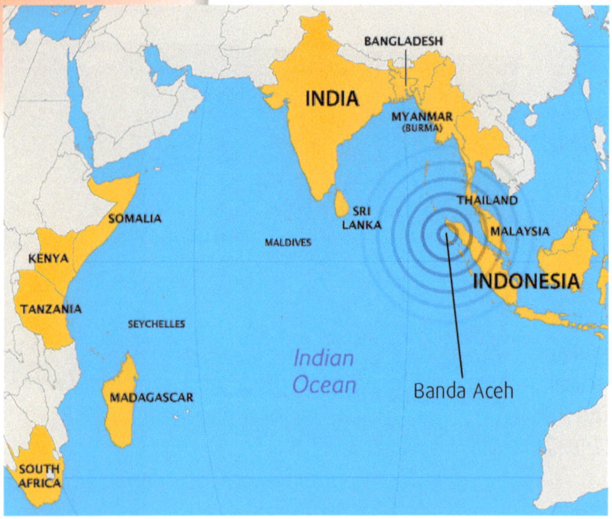

Countries affected by the Boxing Day tsunami, 2004

Boxing Day Tsunami Fact File

- Earthquake occurred at 7:59am local time.
- The energy released was the equivalent of 23 000 Hiroshima-type atomic bombs.
- It was so strong it made the whole planet wobble on its axis.
- The edge of the Indian plate was pushed under the Eurasian plate, making the Eurasian plate 'jump up'.
- It measured 9.2 on the Richter scale.
- It was located just off the north of Sumatra, Indonesia, in the Indian Ocean.
- There is no tsunami warning system there.
- Indonesia was hit first – Banda Aceh was particularly badly hit. Within hours, the waves had struck 11 countries.
- At least a quarter of a million people were killed.

Tsunami wave hits Thailand

Downtown Banda Aceh – devastation by the tsunami in Indonesia

A boat still lying inland where the tsunami wave of 2004 dumped it!

Even today, holidaymakers can still see the effects of the tsunami in Thailand

Classroom challenge

1. What does the word tsunami mean, and what language is it from?
2. Either trace or draw your own labelled diagram for your workbook of what causes a tsunami, using Diagram 21 on page 45. Carefully colour it in.

There is a template in our Teaching Notes to help with this.

3. Study the **Boxing Day Tsunami Fact File.**
   (a) What two plates crashed together to cause the Boxing Day tsunami in 2004?
   (b) Which country was hit first?
   (c) **Describe** the strength of the earthquake that caused this tsunami by stating how strong it was on the Richter scale and how many Hiroshima bombs this is equivalent to.
   (d) How many people were killed?
   (e) How many countries were affected?
   (f) Which Indonesian town was devastated?

Go Digital!

4. Watch the 'Fiji Emergency and Safety Procedures for Schools' film clip from the Homework Helpers. Make up a tsunami emergency plan for your school in your workbook.
5. Now, find out how difficult it is to deal with the effects of a huge natural disaster such as a tsunami. Collect a 'Tsunami Decision-Making Exercise' from your teacher. Work in a group to complete the exercise.

Tsunami emergency evacuation route

Question 4 could be set as a homework task if students have access to ICT.

TEACHING NOTES

Download the 'Tsunami Decision-Making Exercise' from our Teaching Notes bundle at www.brightredpublishing.co.uk

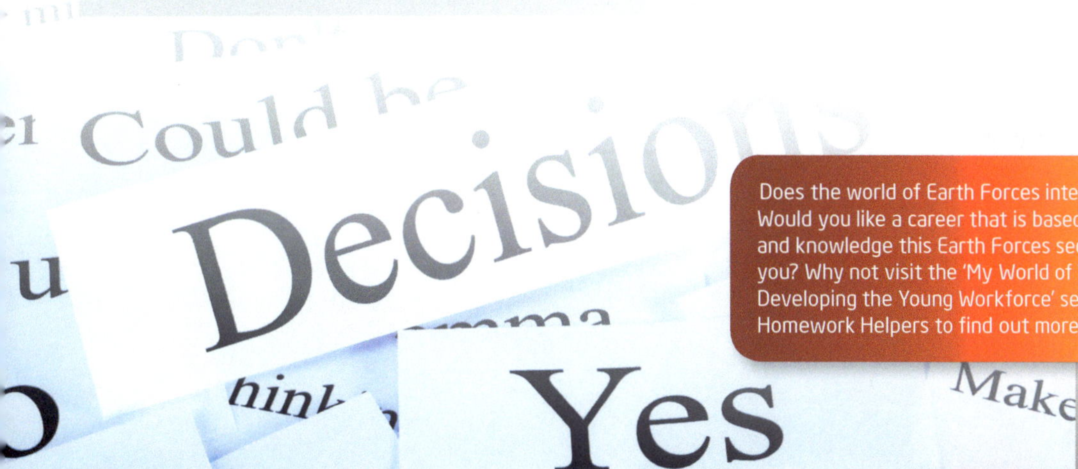

Does the world of Earth Forces interest you? Would you like a career that is based on the skills and knowledge this Earth Forces section has given you? Why not visit the 'My World of Work/STEM/Developing the Young Workforce' section of the Homework Helpers to find out more?

GLACIATION

Ice ages and glaciation – it's snow laughing matter!

GLACIATION

Having investigated processes which form and shape landscapes. I can explain their impact on selected landscapes in Scotland, Europe and beyond. SOC 3-07a

I can identify the possible consequences of an environmental issue and make informed suggestions about ways to manage the impact. SOC 3-08a

Benchmarks

- Identifies the processes which form landscapes across the world.
- Provides a simple explanation of at least three processes involved in the development of any chosen landscape, for example, coasts, volcanic, rivers or glaciated.
- Provides at least two explanations as to how landscapes influence human activity, using two contrasting areas.
- Reviews at least two simple graphical sources to interpret information and form a conclusion, for example, a map and a graph.
- Locates increasingly complex features such as different physical landscape features and human features on maps of Scotland, the UK, Europe and the wider world, for example, hills, mountains, valleys, population.
- Provides a simple explanation of at least three consequences of an environmental issue, and for each suggests how they could be managed.

What's coming up?

- What causes ice ages to begin?
- How can glaciers erode and change the shape of the land?
- What features are formed by glacial erosion?
- What do features of glacial erosion look like on a map?
- How can humans make use of glacial features?
- What conflicts arise between people who want to use glacial landscapes?
- How can we look after glaciated landscapes and protect them?

WHAT CAUSES ICE AGES TO BEGIN?

A **glacier** is a **moving river of ice**. Notice how this one in Georgia is flowing down from these mountain tops.

The word **glaciation** refers to a time when our landscape was covered in **glaciers** and ice sheets. Many people call these periods of time *the* '**ice age**'. Technically speaking, though, this is incorrect because we now know that there have been at least five great ice ages during the history of the planet.

Interact with the great links in the Homework Helpers to find out more on ice ages and glaciers.

What we imagine an ice age to look like

What Scotland would have looked like during peak ice-age conditions

For a glaciation to start, temperatures need to cool. However, surprisingly, they only have to drop globally by a mere 3°C to trigger an ice age! This could easily happen if we had a large volcanic eruption or if a meteorite struck the Earth, as so much dust and ash in our atmosphere would block the sun and start to cool the planet down.

When people discuss the 'ice age', they are usually referring to the one that started around 2 million years ago, peaked around 20 000 years before the present day and ended in Scotland around 10 000 years ago.

DON'T FORGET

You may be surprised to know that we are actually still living in an ice age called the **Quaternary ice age**. The Earth is in a warmer stage of this ice age at the moment, called an **interglacial period**.

Could a meteorite strike like this cause an ice age to begin?

Or could a major volcanic eruption cause an ice age?

Diagram 1 – How an ice age (glaciation) begins

The last glaciation started with winters getting colder and lots more snow falling – especially on mountain tops. In summer, because temperatures were colder, this snow did not melt (especially on the shaded northern sides of mountains). The following winter, more snow fell on top of this snow, which again did not melt in the summer. Gradually, layer upon layer of snow built up on the tops of mountains in western Europe. The weight of these layers of snow compressed and squashed down on each other, turning it into **firn** to begin with (firn is when snow starts to turn into ice and looks like sugar) and eventually into ice. The ice age had begun!

These rivers of ice, now called **glaciers**, started to ooze, like melted chocolate, down the mountainsides due to gravity, and into the valleys below, eventually filling them with ice. Very soon, parts of Britain were smothered in ice half a mile deep!

Did you know that the bones of a real polar bear were found in a cave in Inchnadamph in the Scottish Highlands? This is real proof that Scotland must have been like the Arctic in the past!

Classroom challenge

1. A glaciation is sometimes called by another name with two words. What is it?
2. How much does the global temperature have to drop by for glaciation to start?
3. Look at the photo of the glacier in Georgia at the beginning of this Chapter. **Describe** what a glacier is.
4. **Explain** why glaciers usually form on the northern sides of mountains.
5. The table below contains the beginnings and endings of sentences, but they have been mixed up. Match them correctly and write them out in your workbook.

The last ice age in Britain began..........	.......melted chocolate.
The main reason this ice age began was.......	.......are called glaciers.
When layers of snow gather on top of each other on a mountain...............	.......around 2 million years ago.
Moving rivers of ice..................	.......they compress to form firn and then ice.
Glaciers are said to move like............	.......because temperatures began to drop.

6. Study the map in Diagram 2. It shows the areas of Europe affected by the last ice age. Use an atlas to name as many countries as possible that had areas that were glaciated (**Hint** – these are the white areas on this map.)

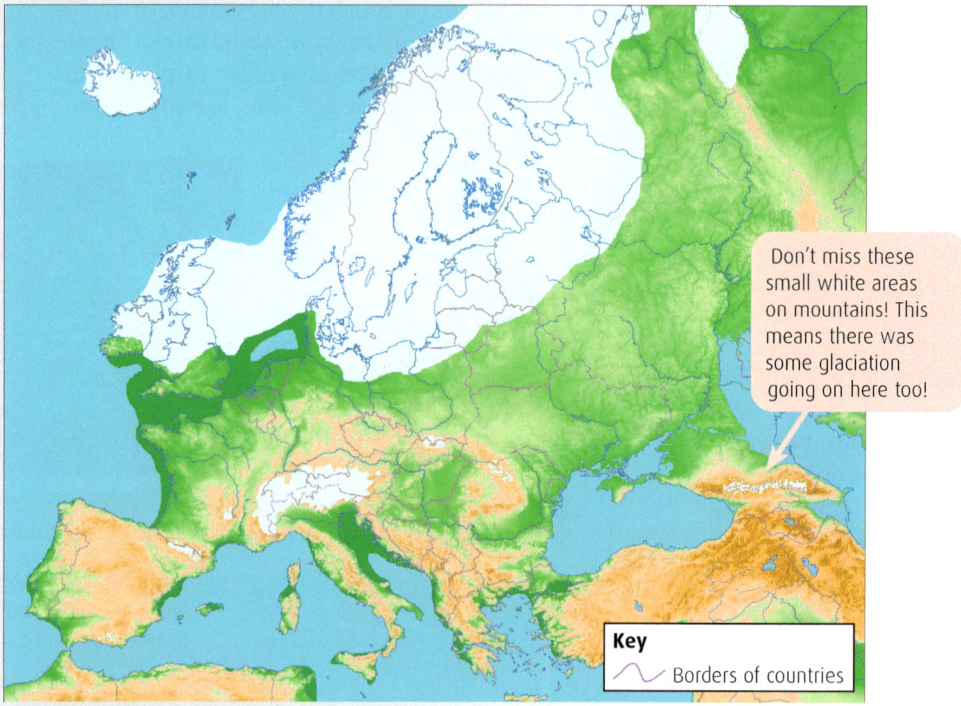

Diagram 2 – Map of areas of Europe affected by the last ice age (key: borders of countries)

7. You may need to hang onto that atlas for this activity! Once again using the map in Diagram 2, copy the paragraph below into your workbook and complete it by filling in the blanks with the correct names of countries, areas and mountains. Choose from the word box underneath.

> During the last ice age, a huge ice sheet spread from the north and covered large areas of ______ ________ E__________. In the UK, glaciers grew in the highlands of __________ as well as in the ______ __________. In Europe, two mountain areas still have glaciers to this very day. These are the ____ and the __________ between Spain and __________. Further east, glaciers existed in the __________ Mountains, which curve in an arch from Romania and form the border between Slovakia and ____________. In Russia, a large glaciated area existed in the ______ Mountains. There are also glaciers still to be found today on the border between Russia and Georgia in the _________ mountains.

Scotland	Caucasus	north-western Europe	Pyrenees		
Carpathian	Alps	Ural	Lake District	France	Poland

8. **Explain** why natural events such as volcanic eruptions and meteorite strikes can cause an ice age to start.
9. What proof do we have that Scotland was once like the Arctic is today?

HOW CAN GLACIERS ERODE AND CHANGE THE SHAPE OF THE LAND?

The fastest-moving glacier in the world is the Jakobshavn Glacier in Greenland, which is charging along at a speed of 40 metres a day!

The Fox Glacier in New Zealand plods along at the rate of only 1 metre per week.

Glacier – a river of ice!

As already mentioned, glaciers ooze across the landscape like melted chocolate. When it is warmer they move faster, and when it is colder they become more solid and slow down. They are also incredibly destructive! They act almost like a giant bulldozer, ripping the land to bits or wearing it away as they move. This is known as **erosion**.

As a result, there are three distinct ways in which glaciers are able to change the shape of our landscape – **plucking**, **abrasion** and **frost shattering**.

DON'T FORGET

Approximately 10% of planet Earth is currently covered by glaciers.

Experience what it is like inside a glacier with the video links in the Homework Helpers.

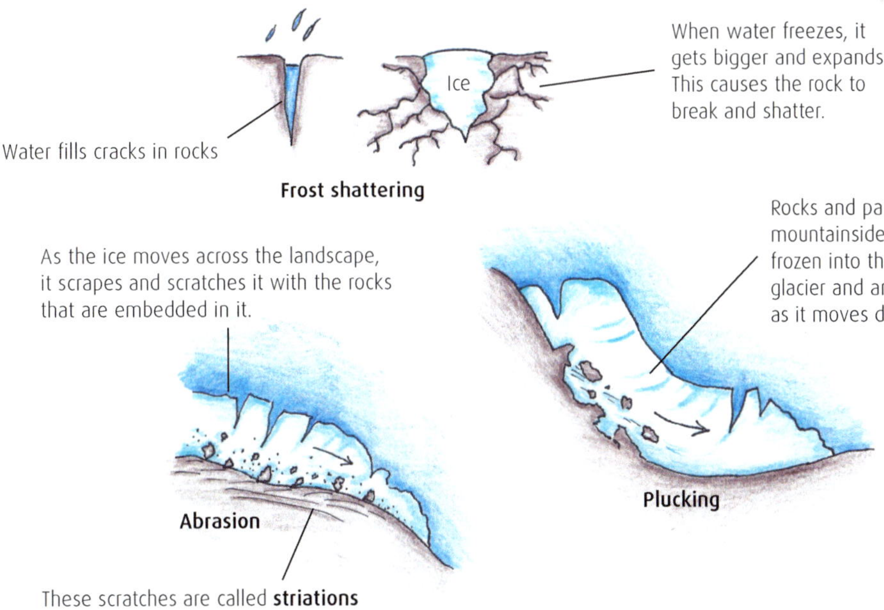

Diagram 3 – Three ways in which a glacier will erode the land

These processes completely changed the shape of the landscape during a glaciation.

The striations (scratches) on this rock show that a glacier once moved across this area

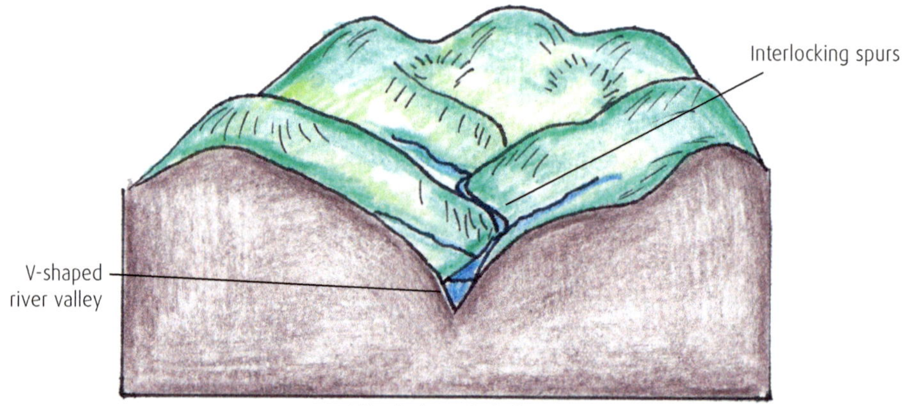

Valley before glaciation

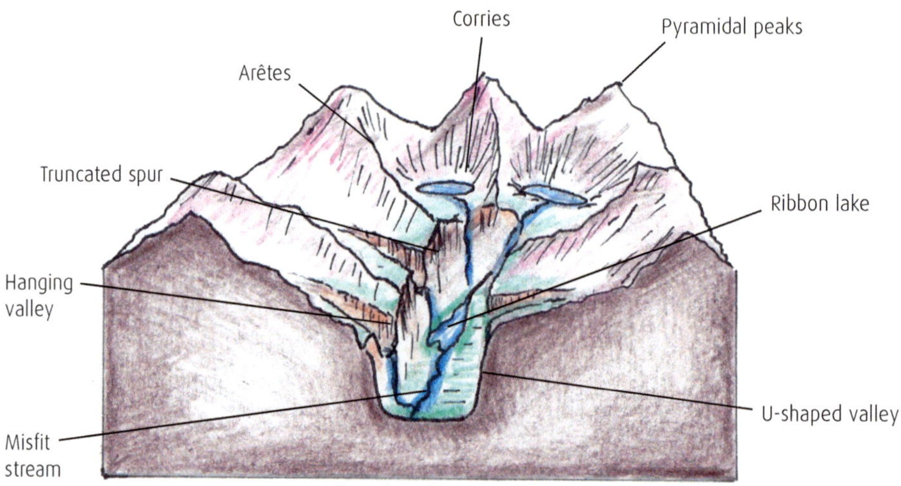

Valley after glaciation

Diagram 4 – How a landscape can be changed with erosion by glaciers

Classroom challenge

1. Study Diagram 3 on page 55. In your workbook, make your own coloured, labelled diagrams of the three ways in which glaciers erode the land.
2. **Describe** what glaciers are said to act like as they move across the land.

Check out the film clips on 'How glaciers shape the landscape' and the 'Glacier simulator' in the Homework Helpers bundle.

3. Study the images of the landscape before and after a glaciation in Diagram 4 on page 56.
   (a) **Describe** what shape valleys were before an ice age.
   (b) **Describe** what shape they were after an ice age.
4. Look at the names of erosion features formed by glaciation in Diagram 4. They are listed below but have become scrambled! Unscramble them and write them out in your workbook.

MR TIMSTAFSIE BLOB KEARIN RORICE REMADY PLAKIAP EATER DLASEY HEALVUP YANGLEH LIVAGN

WHAT FEATURES ARE FORMED BY GLACIAL EROSION?

We have already learned that glaciers are rivers of ice that can completely change the shape of the landscape, making it more dramatic. We have also found out that this happens as a result of plucking, abrasion and frost shattering. What we need to find out now is more detail about the features formed.

The formation of corries, arêtes and pyramidal peaks

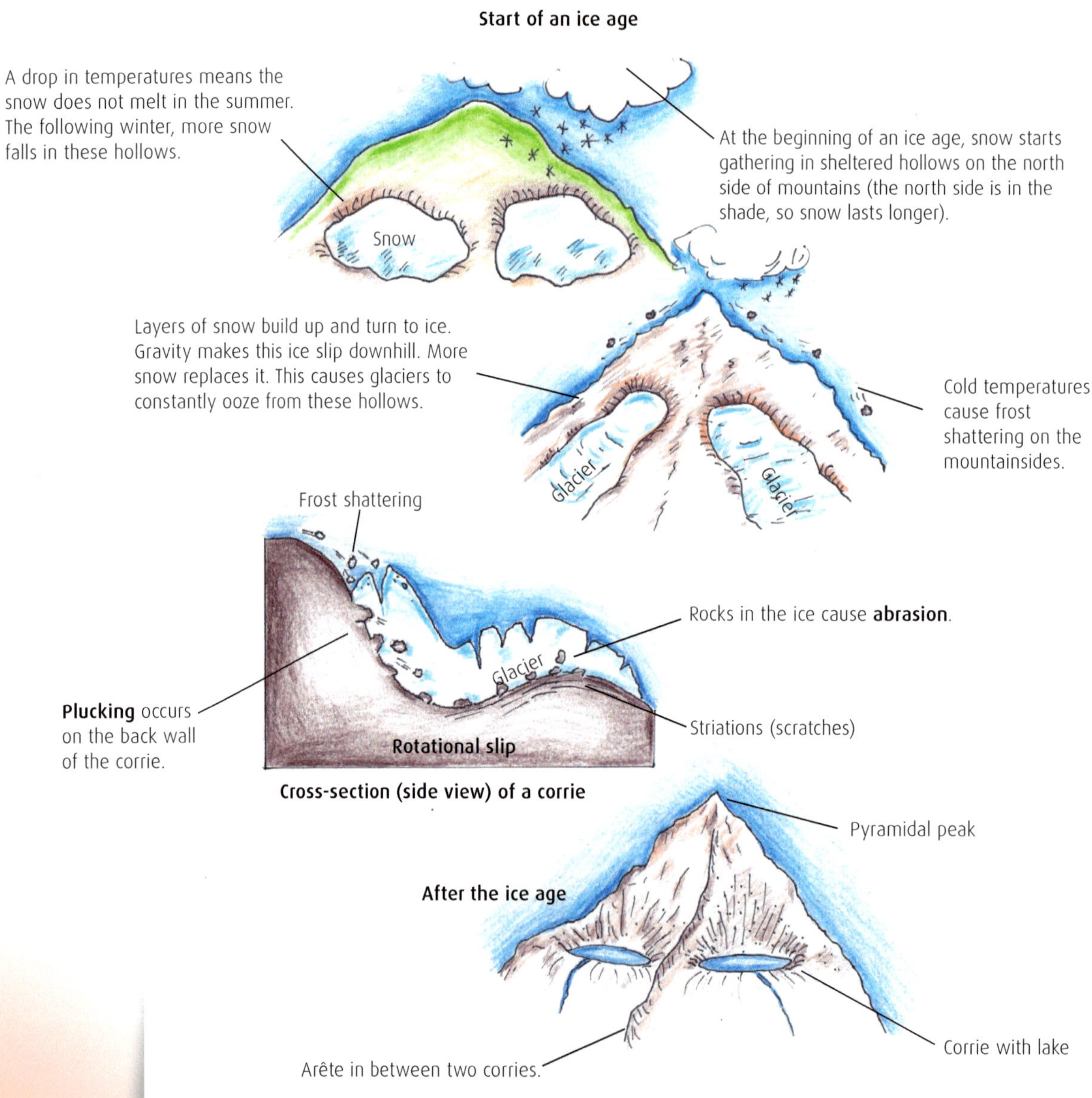

Diagram 5 – The formation of corries, arêtes and pyramidal peaks

A corrie with a lake on Lochnagar, Scotland

The Càrn Mór Dearg arête on the north side of Ben Nevis

Find out more on the Càrn Mór Dearg arête with the route description in the Homework Helpers.

The Matterhorn in the Alps – the ultimate pyramidal peak!

Striding Edge arête in the Lake District

Explore Striding Edge arête further by following the route description and maps in the Homework Helpers.

Classroom challenge

1. Write out the paragraph below in your workbook. You will have to study Diagram 5 on the formation of corries, arêtes and pyramidal peaks to be able to fill in the missing words. Choose them from the box below.

arête	shade	armchair	plucking	north	glaciers
ice	gravity	frost shattering	abrasion	temperatures	
pyramidal peak	corries				

Corries usually formed on the _______-facing sides of mountains. This is because they are usually in the ________. Snow gathered in hollows and did not melt because ______________ had dropped. Layers of snow eventually turned to ___ and began to slip down the mountainsides due to __________. These rivers of ice are called ___________. As they moved across the landscape, they ripped out rocks. This is known as ____________. These rocks became embedded in the base of the glacier and scraped and scoured the landscape as they were dragged across it. This is known as ____________. Any bare slopes were attacked by _______ ________________. Eventually, at the end of the ice age, the whole landscape had totally changed. The hollows where the snow first gathered had now been enlarged and are __________-shaped. These are known as ___________. If two corries formed side by side, a knife-edged ridge will be found in between them, called an __________. Dramatic frost-shattered mountain tops are called ________________ __________s.

2. Make your own labelled, colourful sketches to show how corries, arêtes and pyramidal peaks form.

Formation of U-shaped valleys, hanging valleys, misfit streams and ribbon lakes

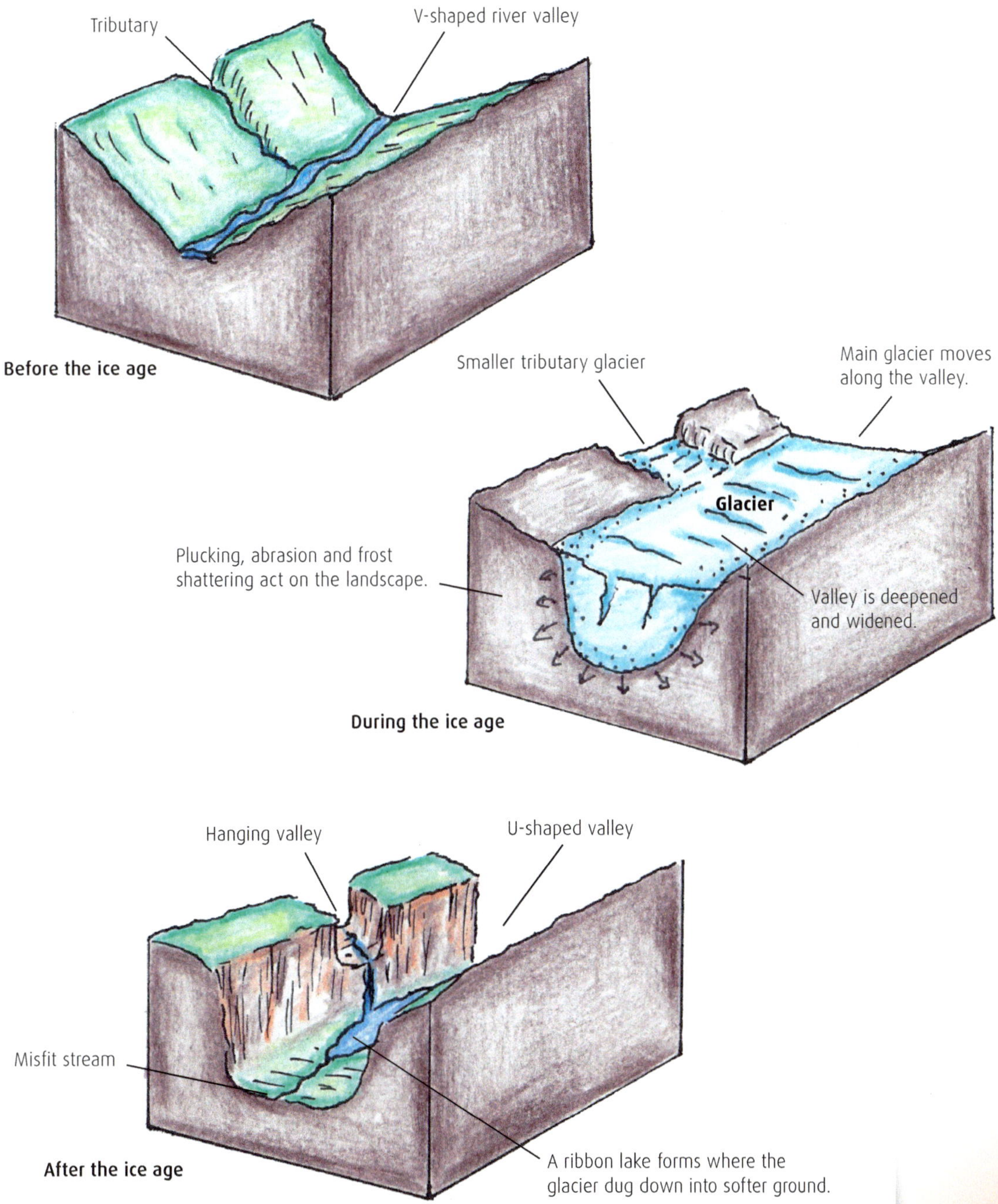

Diagram 6 – Formation of U-shaped valleys, hanging valleys, misfit streams and ribbon lakes

Classroom challenge

There are templates on the Teaching Notes to help with this.

Question 2 could be set as a homework task.

1. Study Diagram 6 on page 61. Draw or trace your own colourful labelled diagrams showing the formation of U-shaped valleys, hanging valleys, misfit streams and ribbon lakes.
2. Using these diagrams, **explain** in your own words how U-shaped valleys, hanging valleys, misfit streams and ribbon lakes were formed.
3. Study the sketch below of a glaciated landscape. Can you identify the missing features? Write them into your workbook.

4. Make up your own five questions on what you have learned about glaciation so far, and write them in your workbook. Now ask another student in your class these questions.

Go Digital!
Do you fancy being a detective? Carry out the investigation in the Homework Helpers on '**Ötzi** – the Ice Man' found preserved in a glacier in the Alps.

Ötzi – the Ice Man

WHAT DO FEATURES OF GLACIAL EROSION LOOK LIKE ON A MAP?

To be able to find glacial features on a map is an important skill in geography. There are certain shapes you must learn to recognise. To complete this section, you need to be able to read four-figure grid references using Ordnance Survey maps. If you don't know how to do this, visit pages 265–266 of this book.

Check out the 3D fly-through film clips and the link to the OS MapZone in the Homework Helpers to help with learning how to identify glacial features on maps.

Corries on a map

Red Tarn in the Lake District: a good example of a corrie with a lake (lochan)

When looking for a corrie on a map, the contour lines (brown lines on a map showing the height and shape of the land) will be close together and curve in a horseshoe shape. Look at square 3415 on the OS map (Diagram 7). There is a corrie with a lake in this square called Red Tarn. Notice the shape of the contours around the lake. There is another corrie above it (to the north-west) called Brown Cove. Can you see any other corries on this map?

Diagram 7 – OS map extract of Red Tarn

DON'T FORGET

Red Tarn is one of only three lakes in the Lake District that is home to the very rare and endangered Schelly fish.

Arêtes on a map

Arêtes are normally found where there are two corries next to each other. They will usually be found in between the corries. Sometimes there are black squiggly lines and dots on them on maps to show that there are rocks and crags here. On Diagram 7, there is a good example of an arête between Red Tarn and Brown Cove called Swirral Edge. There is another arête to the south of this, called Striding Edge.

Striding Edge arête

DON'T FORGET

Striding Edge claimed the life of Charles Gough in 1805. His body was found next to Red Tarn. His dog had remained by his side there for three months and even gave birth to a puppy during that time.

U-shaped valleys on a map

U-shaped valleys on a map should have steep sides and a very broad, flat valley floor. The steep sides on a map will be shown with the contour lines really close together. The flat valley floor will have no contour lines on it and will usually look like a white stripe on your map.

Borrowdale U-shaped valley

A good example of a U-shaped valley is in squares 2312 and 2412 on Diagram 8.

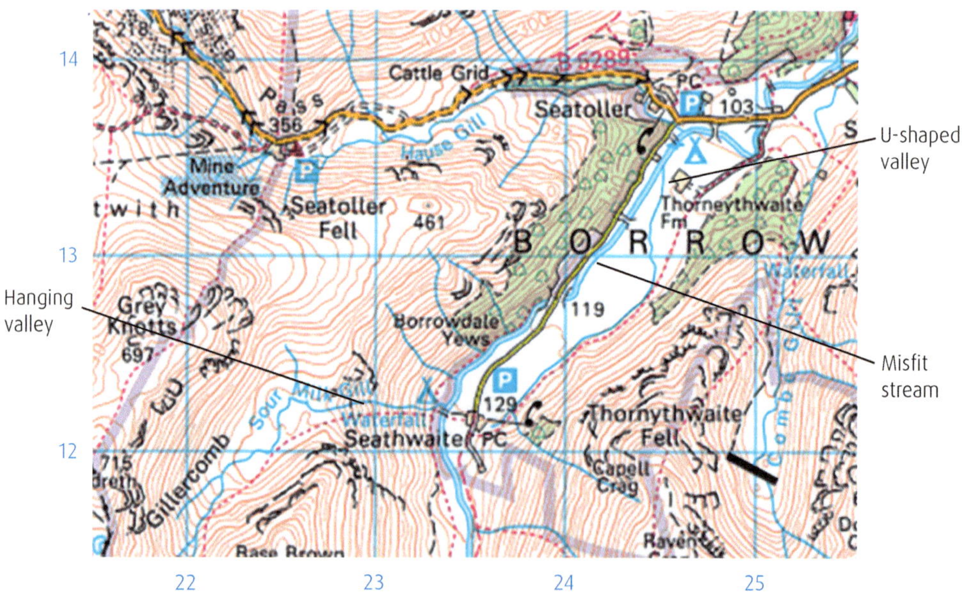

Diagram 8 – OS map extract of Borrowdale

Hanging valleys on a map

Hanging valleys are usually easy to spot on a map, as they will have a waterfall flowing out of the end of them. A waterfall on a map is simply marked with the word 'waterfall' in blue.

On Diagram 8, there is a good example of a hanging valley in squares 2212 and 2312, called Sour Milk Gill.

Hanging valley in the Lake District

Misfit streams on a map

Misfit streams flow along the bottom of U-shaped valleys. They are very small compared with the overall size of the valley, and hence they are given the name 'misfit'.

On Diagram 8, the blue river flowing along the floor of the valley (the white bit) is a misfit stream.

Misfit stream flowing in a very large U-shaped valley

Ribbon lakes on a map

Ribbon lakes formed in U-shaped valleys as a result of a glacier moving over an area of softer rock on the valley floor where it was able to erode more deeply. They appear on a map as a long, thin lake.

Lake Thirlmere on Diagram 9 is a ribbon lake.

Lake Thirlmere in the Lake District – an example of a ribbon lake

Diagram 9 – OS map extract of Thirlmere

Classroom challenge

1. You should now know how to identify features of glacial erosion on a map. Test this knowledge by trying to identify a CORRIE, ARÊTE, U-SHAPED VALLEY, HANGING VALLEY and RIBBON LAKE from the map below. Copy and complete this table in your workbook.

Feature	Name from map	Four-figure grid reference
Corrie		
Arête		
U-shaped valley		
Hanging valley		
Ribbon lake		

2. Read through all the pages on glaciation. Use the clues to complete this crossword.

Across

6. When rocks in a glacier scrape and scour the land.
7. An armchair-shaped feature.
8. The name of the world's fastest-moving glacier.
9. A knife-edged ridge between two corries.

Down

1. The name of the ultimate pyramidal peak.
2. When ice pulls rocks out of the landscape.
3. Used to be V-shaped.
4. A type of long, thin lake.
5. Comes out of the end of a hanging valley.

Check out the Homework Helpers for more fun-filled glaciation activities.

HOW CAN HUMANS MAKE USE OF GLACIAL FEATURES?

Like volcanic landscapes, glaciated areas can offer opportunities for humans. In fact, certain glacial features have proven to be extremely useful.

The diagram below shows some of these.

Diagram 10 – Uses of a glacial landscape

All these uses of glaciated landscapes mean that people are able to get jobs there and earn money. This means that people are happy to live and work in these places and not move away to nearby cities. When many people do leave a countryside area, we call it **rural depopulation**.

Follow the links on the Homework Helpers to find out more on how Scotland's glaciated landscapes can be used.

Some uses of glacial landscapes – rafting, hydroelectric power and skiing

There is money to be made from glaciation!

Rural depopulation

Classroom challenge

1. Study Diagram 10 on page 67. The sentences below have been jumbled up. Re-write them by fitting the correct beginning with the correct ending.

Beginnings	Endings
Ribbon lakes are good as...	...hold snow longer, which is good for skiing.
The basin shape of a corrie...	...for white-water rafting.
North-facing corries...	...for sheep farming.
Fast-flowing rivers can be used...	...holds water to make hydroelectric power from.
Steep slopes can be used...	...reservoirs for drinking water.

2. To complete this activity, you will have to go back to the 'Getting to know all things volcanic' (pages 22–32) section of this book.
You are now going to compare the human uses of a glaciated landscape with those of a volcanic landscape.
(a) Write the title 'Fire and Ice' in your workbook.

(b) Make your own larger copy of the diagram on the next page in your workbook. Cut out the land-use images. Decide if they are an image of a 'fire' land use or 'ice' land use, and stick them in the correct column. In the outside columns, describe what you think the land use is. One has been completed for you.

Print out the images of land uses from the Teaching Notes.

Human use	Fire	Ice	Human use
			Skiing – in corries that face north, as snow lasts longer because it is in the shade.

Choose your land uses for the table from those listed in the box below.

White-water rafting   Hydroelectricity in a corrie at Cruachan
Vineyards on rich volcanic soil at Vesuvius   Tourists visit Pompeii
Geothermal power in Iceland   Climbers in a Cairngorm corrie
Health and beauty treatment using a pumice stone

(c) Once you have completed your table, decide if you would rather live in a 'fire' or 'ice' landscape, and try to give at least two reasons for your choice. This means using your **evaluation** skills.

3. What is rural depopulation?
4. Give two reasons to **explain** why volcanoes and glaciers can be said to stop rural depopulation.
5. Look at the sets of numbers below. Use the table to write in your workbook the three words they are next to.

(a) Which word is the odd one out? Give reasons why.

Set 1 = 9 15 5
Set 2 = 1 3 7
Set 3 = 6 14 11
Set 4 = 8 3 1
Set 5 = 14 13 2

DON'T FORGET

Hint – they are phrases about volcanoes, earthquakes or glaciation.

1. Plucking	6. Corries	11. Arêtes
2. Tectonic plates	7. Frost shattering	12. Fold mountains
3. Shock waves	8. Epicentre	13. Pyramidal peak
4. Abrasion	9. Lava	14. Composite volcano
5. Focus	10 Ash	15. Volcanic bomb

WHAT CONFLICTS ARISE BETWEEN PEOPLE WHO WANT TO USE GLACIAL LANDSCAPES?

Location of Aviemore

People using the countryside should respect the fact that the people living there, the wildlife and the environment all need to be protected. However, so many different people would like to use glaciated landscapes for lots of different activities that it often leads to **conflict**. This means that groups of people start to have serious disagreements with each other about how the landscape should be used. Diagram 11 on page 71 sums up some of the arguments and conflicts that arise because of **tourism** in the Cairngorms National Park near Aviemore, Scotland.

TEACHING NOTES

Making valid conclusions about the impact of human activity on a chosen area is CfE Level 4 work.

The Cairngorms National Park

Farmers use the land in the Cairngorms.

Rare and endangered species such as the Scottish wildcat live in the Cairngorms.

The beautiful scenery is very fragile and easily damaged.

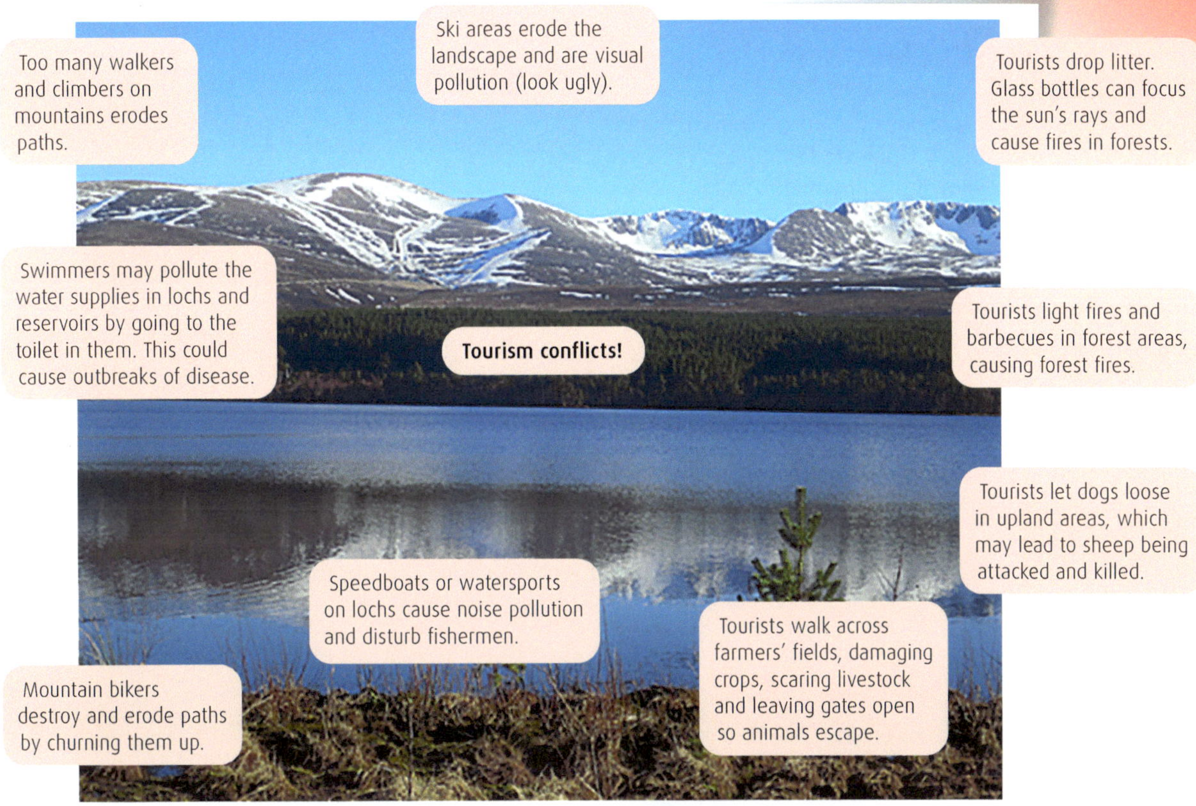

Diagram 11 – Conflict from tourism in the Cairngorms

Many think that skiing destroys the natural environment of Cairn Gorm mountain. What do you think?

Litter left by tourists

Mountain bikes erode the land

Wildfires like this can result from careless use of fires, barbecues and glass bottles

Classroom challenge

1. What does the word 'conflict' mean?
2. Study Diagram 11 on page 71 showing 'tourism conflicts'.
   (a) **Explain** two ways in which tourists cause problems in forests.
   (b) What problem do climbers and walkers cause on the mountains?
   (c) What type of pollution are ski areas on mountains said to be?
   (d) **Describe** another type of pollution tourists can cause, and **explain** what causes it.
   (e) **Describe** why farmers might be upset by visitors coming to a glaciated area.

3. It seems clear that sometimes people wanting to use glaciated landscapes for different activities clash and have arguments with each other.
   To understand why these disagreements happen, complete the Aviemore cooperative learning activity.

TEACHING NOTES

Visit www.brightredpublishing.co.uk and download the Teaching Notes for a cooperative learning activity on Aviemore.

HOW CAN WE LOOK AFTER GLACIATED LANDSCAPES AND PROTECT THEM?

One way to try to protect the countryside in a glaciated area from the conflicts brought by tourists is to educate visitors and have some basic rules or information to help people respect the countryside. In Scotland, this is called the **Scottish Outdoor Access Code**. In England, it is called **The Countryside Code**.

Scottish Outdoor Access Code

- Respect the interests of other people
- Care for the environment
- Take responsibility for your own actions

If we were to try to sum up how we should act in the countryside, we should consider the advice below.

Respect the Countryside!

- Enjoy the countryside but respect its life and work
- Fasten all gates
- Keep your dogs under close control
- Guard against all risk of fire
- Use gates and stiles to cross fences, hedges and walls
- Leave livestock, crops and machinery alone
- Take your litter home
- Help to keep all water clean
- Protect all wildlife, plants and trees
- Take special care on country roads
- Make no unnecessary noise
- Keep to public paths across farmland

Diagram 12 – Ways to respect the countryside.

TEACHING NOTES

Download the Teaching Notes for links to the Scottish Outdoor Access Code and The Countryside Code.

Another way to protect the environment in places that are really popular with visitors is to turn them into a **National Park**. The rules in National Parks can help find solutions to conflict in glaciated areas.

In the UK, there are now 15 National Parks. These are areas of countryside, wildlife and cultural heritage that are protected. People who live and work in National Parks, on farms and in villages and towns, are also protected. The main aims of National Parks are shown in the photograph here.

Aims of a National Park

Follow the online links for great National Parks info.

DON'T FORGET

The Cairngorm National Park is the largest in the UK and is 4528 km².

Diagram 13 – Location of the UK's National Parks

From Diagram 13, you will see that there are two National Parks in Scotland. They are Loch Lomond and the Trossachs National Park and the Cairngorms National Park. These are both glaciated areas which are extremely popular with visitors.

Classroom challenge

1. Name the two sets of guidelines for Scotland and England about how the countryside should be used.
2. **Describe** the aims of a National Park.
3. What two National Parks are found in Scotland?
4. The table below shows where visitors to the Cairngorms National Park come from.
   (a) Make up a bar graph in your workbook to show these figures. Make sure your graph has a title.
   (b) Most visitors to the Cairngorms come from Scotland. How many more visitors are Scottish compared to those from the rest of the UK, Europe and the rest of the world?

Where people come from	Percentage
Scotland	54%
Rest of the UK	26%
Europe	14%
Rest of the world	7%

5. Copy the diagram on the next page into your workbook. Complete it by choosing the solution from the table that you think would work best to solve each conflict. Colour it in when you have finished.

Walkers and climbers erode paths.

Speedboats cause noise pollution and disturb fishermen.

My solution is

Tourists leave farm gates open – animals escape.

Tourists light fires and have barbecues, which can lead to forest fires.

Possible solutions
Ban boats from lochs or have them zoned away from fishing areas.
Have safe areas set aside in forests where fires and barbecues can be in special stone pits.
Put gravel and rocks down to stop erosion.
Put self-closing gates where paths cross farmland.

This leaflet could be completed as a homework activity.

6. Make your own 'Respect the Countryside' leaflet to educate visitors about how they should behave. Use the list in Diagram 12 on page 73 to help you.

Dowload the Homework Helpers from the Bright Red website and check out film clips and activities for more on glaciation and land use.

Have you enjoyed learning about glaciation, land use and conflict? Would you like a career that uses the knowledge and skills you have gained from this unit? Why not visit the 'My World of Work/ STEM/Developing the Young Workforce' section of the Homework Helpers to find out more?

Sign using the Scottish Outdoor Access Code in Fife to educate visitors crossing farmland.

EMPTY LANDS

EMPTY LANDS

I can investigate the climate, physical features and living things of a natural environment different from my own and explain their interrelationship. SOC 3-10a

I can investigate the relationship between climate and weather and be able to understand the causes of weather patterns within a selected climate zone. SOC 3-12a

By comparing settlement and economic activity in two contrasting landscapes, I can reach conclusions about how landscapes influence human activity. I can explain my findings clearly to others. SOC 3-13a

I can identify the possible consequences of an environmental issue and make informed suggestions about ways to manage the impact. SOC 3-08a

I can use a range of maps and geographical information systems to gather, interpret and present conclusions and can locate a range of features within Scotland, the UK, Europe and the wider world. SOC 3-14a

Benchmarks

- Identifies the processes which form landscapes across the world.
- Provides a simple explanation of at least three consequences of an environmental issue, and for each suggests how they could be managed.
- Describes a natural environment different to their own, in terms of climate, physical features and living things.
- Provides a simple explanation of at least three links between climate, physical features and living things in that environment.
- Provides a simple explanation for a weather pattern within a selected climate zone; for example, convection rainfall in the rainforest.
- Provides at least two explanations as to how landscapes influence human activity, using two contrasting areas.
- Reviews at least two simple graphical sources to interpret information and form a conclusion; for example, a map and a graph.
- Uses relevant numeracy and digital technology skills to interpret at least two sources of data from maps and graphical information systems.

What's coming up?

- We can study planet Earth by looking at places where there are lots of people (**densely populated**) and areas where, for some reason, there are hardly any people (**sparsely populated**). Areas that are sparsely populated are sometimes referred to as 'empty lands' by geographers.
- We are now going to study three empty lands – rainforests, hot deserts and tundra. The environments of these areas are very different, and therefore the lives of humans who have chosen to live in them are also very different. Sometimes these areas are called **biomes**. These are giant **ecosystems** where the climate and landscape shape how plants, wildlife and humans live.
- We'll also learn about comparing and contrasting empty-lands biomes.

TROPICAL RAINFORESTS

Empty Lands – horrendously humid rainforests!

RAINFOREST CLIMATE

What's coming up?

- Where are the world's tropical rainforests?
- What is the rainforest climate like?
- How have the plants adapted to this climate?
- How do animals survive the humidity of the rainforests?
- How have humans traditionally survived in the rainforests?
- Why are rainforests being cleared?
- What are the impacts of rainforest clearance?
- How can we protect the rainforests?

Where are the world's tropical rainforests?

The Amazon rainforest – the largest rainforest in the world

Tropical rainforests are thick forests with very tall trees found around the Equator. They are sometimes referred to as 'jungles' or **equatorial forests**. Since they are **sparsely populated** (very few people live there), they can be classed as an 'empty land'.

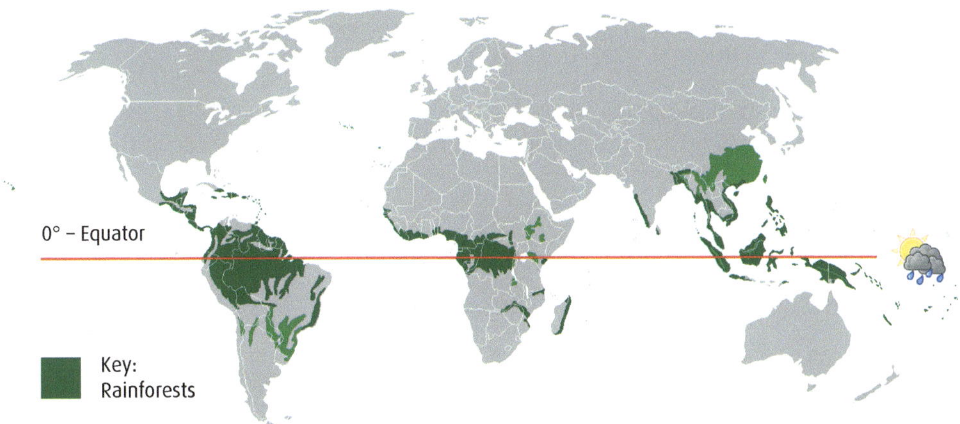

Diagram 1 – Location of the world's tropical rainforests

What is the rainforest climate like?

The rainforest climate is rather like being in a giant greenhouse and as a result is an ideal place for plants to grow. The strange thing is that there are no seasons. It is hot all year round, but there is also plenty of rainfall. In fact, more than 2000 mm of rainfall falls every year! You can perhaps appreciate how wet this is when you consider that Edinburgh in Scotland gets only around 700 mm of rain annually. The **rainfall graph** on the next page gives more information on the climate.

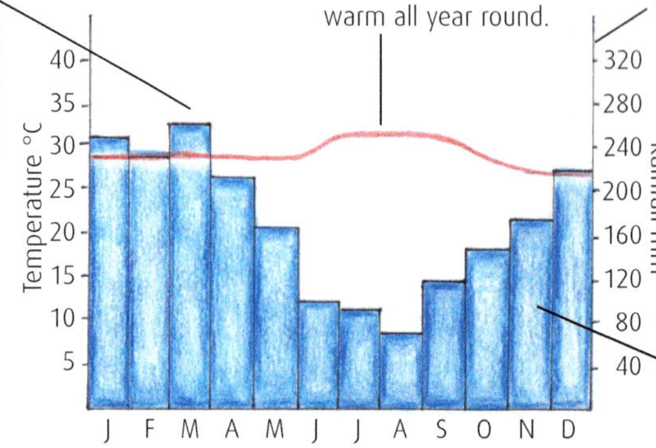

Diagram 2 – Rainfall graph for the Amazon rainforest

DON'T FORGET

Humidity is the amount of water in our atmosphere. The more humidity there is in the air, the more we sweat and feel uncomfortable.

My Rainforest Weather Diary

- Woke up at 8am. It is already roasting, and my phone says it is 25°C!
- Trying to walk in the forest. It feels so hot and sweaty, like being in a sauna. The sun is high in the sky, and my phone now says it is 28°C. When I look up, I can see clouds starting to form.
- 3pm – What a fright I just got! An enormous thunderstorm has just started. The thunder is like a booming explosion above my head, and the rain is coming down in buckets.
- It is 6pm and already dark. There are scary animal noises all around, but at least the storm has stopped.

The diary above describes a typical day of weather in the rainforest. The reason this daily weather pattern is repeated is explained in Diagram 3 below. It is due to the **heat, humidity** and **convection rainfall.**

5. Constant moist, rising air forms giant **cumulonimbus thunder clouds.** The rain that falls from these clouds is called **convection rainfall**.

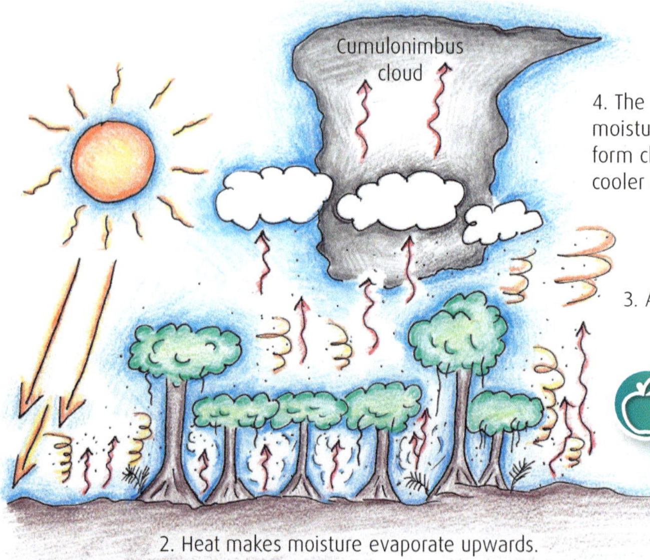

1. Intense heat from the sun warms the ground.
2. Heat makes moisture evaporate upwards.
3. Air becomes very humid.
4. The evaporated moisture starts to form clouds in the cooler atmosphere.

Diagram 3 – What causes convection rainfall?

TEACHING NOTES

Download the Teaching Notes at www.brightredpublishing.co.uk and follow the exciting links to find great ways of introducing rainforest learning.

Classroom challenge

1. Using a blank world map, make your own location map of the world's tropical rainforests, like the one below. Use an atlas to complete the names of the missing countries and add them onto your map.

TEACHING NOTES

A blank world map is available in the Teaching Notes.

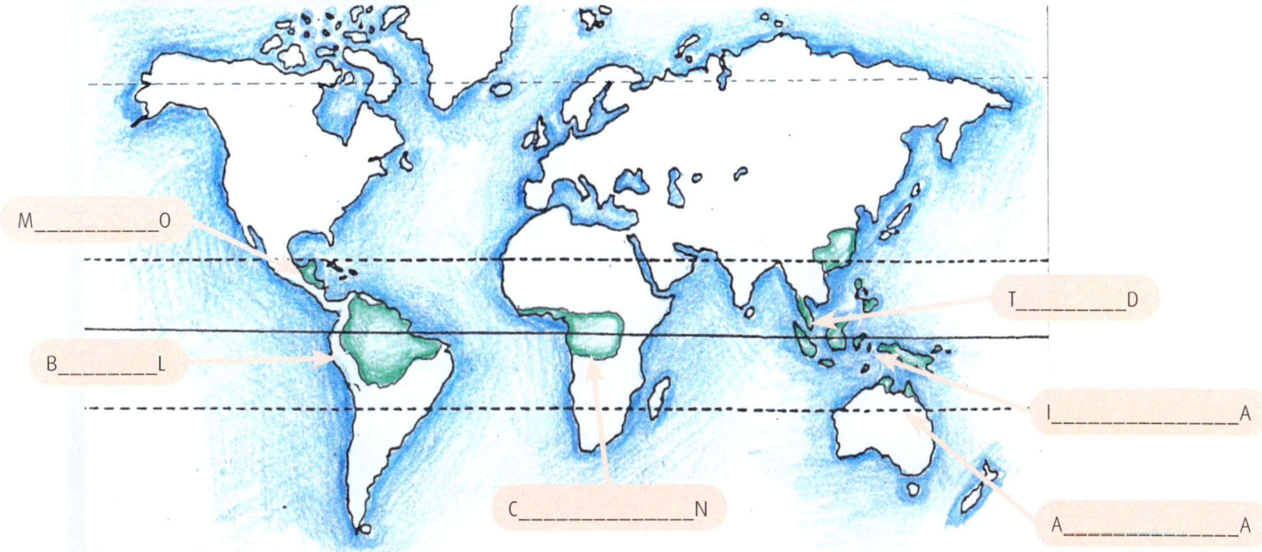

2. Study your map and Diagram 1 on page 81. Which line of latitude are rainforests located on or very close to?
3. Using the figures in the table below, make your own tropical rainforest climate graph.

TEACHING NOTES

Use the instructions and template from the Teaching Notes if you need help with this.

	J	F	M	A	M	J	J	A	S	O	N	D
TEMP. (°C)	26	27	28	28	28	28	27	27	27	27	27	26
RAINFALL (MM)	250	230	260	225	270	275	270	275	275	275	270	270

4. Study the climate graph you have just completed.
   (a) What is the average temperature in the rainforest? (To work this out, you will need to add together all the temperatures and divide your answer by the number of months there are in one year.)
   (b) What is the temperature range in the rainforest? (This is the difference between the highest and lowest temperatures.)
   (c) Again, looking at your climate graph, which month has the lowest rainfall, and how much was it?
   (d) Which month/s have the highest rainfall?

Why not go digital? Follow the instructions on the Homework Helpers on how to make your very own Excel rainforest climate graph.

5. Look at Diagram 3 on page 82 and 'My Rainforest Weather Diary'. Copy and complete the paragraph below by selecting the correct words from the word box.

HUMID	VAPOUR	CONDENSE	HEAVY	LIGHTNING	CONVECTION
EVAPORATE	MONOTONOUS	COLDER	CUMULONIMBUS		

The weather in the tropical rainforest is very __________. This is because the hot sun makes moisture e__________________ from the forest, making the atmosphere very sweaty. This water v___________ rises upwards above the trees. As it rises, it gets into _____________ temperatures, which makes the moisture c_____________ to form clouds. By afternoon, these clouds have grown into large, tall, _________________________ thunderstorm clouds. There will, therefore, often be h_________ rain, thunder and _______________ before the sun sets in the rainforest. Another name for these thunderstorms is ________________ rainfall. This happens almost every day, and so we can say that the weather in the rainforest is m___________________.

6. Make your own labelled diagram in your workbook to show what convection rainfall is.

TEACHING NOTES

You could make use of the template from the Teaching Notes for this.

ADAPTING TO THE RAINFOREST CLIMATE

How are plants adapted to this climate?

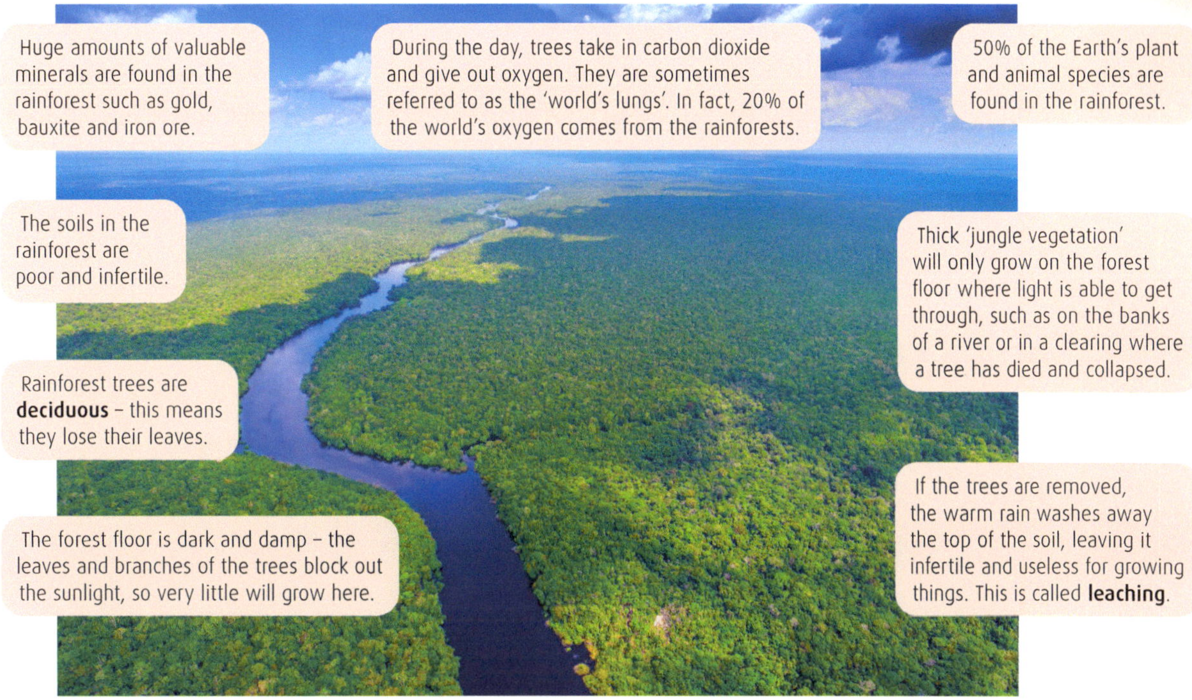

Diagram 4 – Important facts about the rainforest

Lack of light on the forest floor means no undergrowth. Thick jungle plants grow where there is light

Despite their poor infertile soils, rainforests are full of the most luxuriant vegetation found on our planet. This leads us to ask: how can this thick vegetation grow? Where are the **nutrients** (food from the soil for plants) coming from? The answer is that they are feeding on their own dead leaves, which are rotting on the forest floor!

The forest itself is made up of distinct layers.

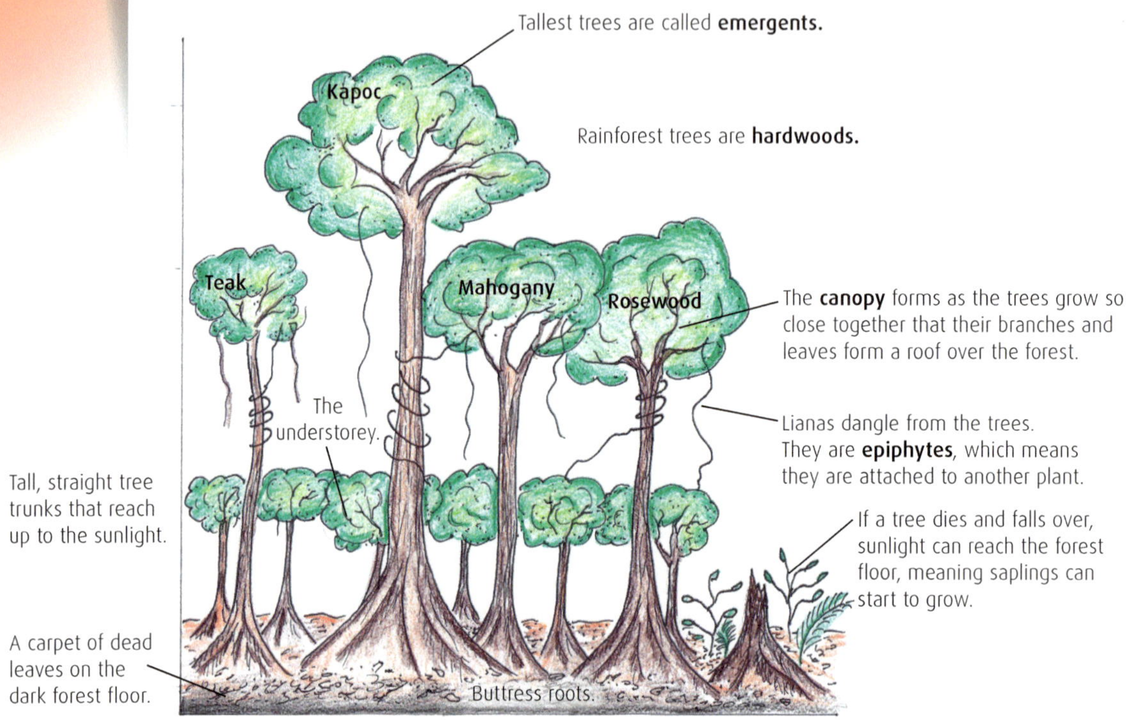

Diagram 5 – Layers within the rainforest

In addition, the plants are completely **adapted** to the climate and weather conditions found in the rainforest. These adaptations can clearly be seen in Diagram 5 and in sketches below.

- Some leaves have drip tips to help water run off leaves.
- Others have grooves in their leaves to help water drain off.
- Some leaves have holes in them for water to pass through.

How plants have adapted to the rainforest climate

Find out much more on rainforest plants with the links and activities on the Homework Helpers.

Trees have big buttress roots to help prop up these very tall forest giants.

Classroom challenge

There is a template in the Teaching Notes to help with this.

1. Draw or trace your own colourful, labelled diagram of the vegetation layers in the rainforest for your workbook.
2. Study Diagrams 4 and 5 on pages 85 and 86.
   (a) Name three examples of hardwood trees that grow in the rainforest.
   (b) Are rainforest trees **coniferous** or **deciduous**?
   (c) **Explain** why the forest floor is so dark.
   (d) **Describe** where you would find thick 'jungle' vegetation, and **explain** why it is found here.
   (e) **Explain** what might make a clearing appear in the forest.
   (f) **Explain** why rainforests are sometimes called the 'world's lungs'.
   (g) **Explain** what leaching is.
3. The sentences in the table below have been jumbled up. Match up the correct sentence beginnings with the correct endings and write them out in your workbook. Use Diagram 5 on page 86 to help you.

Beginnings	Endings
Lianas...	...help to support tall trees.
Emergents...	...are vine-like plants which climb up large trees.
The canopy...	...grow much taller than other trees.
The forest floor...	...are tall and grow straight up to reach the light.
Buttress roots...	...is a roof of leaves and branches over the forest.
Tree trunks...	...is very dark and damp with little sunlight or plant growth.

4. Rainforest plants are adapted to the hot, wet climate. The plant below has just started growing on the forest floor. Make up a checklist of four adaptations it might have to make in order to survive.

Plant checklist

Adaptation	Why is it needed?
______________________	______________________
______________________	______________________
______________________	______________________
______________________	______________________
______________________	______________________
______________________	______________________

5. Rainforests soils are infertile. **Explain** where plants get their nutrients from.

How do animals survive the humidity of the rainforests?

The rainforest is packed full of wildlife. An area the size of about 10 km^2 has around 400 different species of bird, 150 species of butterfly, 100 types of reptile, at least 20 types of animal, and around 60 types of **amphibian** (creatures such as frogs and toads). Some people estimate that there are up to 30 million different species of insects in the world's rainforests! Each of these different species has made its home in the different layers within the forest.

Sloth

Jaguar

Anaconda

Diagram 6 – Animal life in the rainforest layers, and percentage of sunlight reaching each layer

DON'T FORGET

An anaconda coils its body around a captured animal and squeezes until the animal eventually dies. It then opens its jaws wide enough to allow it to swallow the prey whole. A big meal will mean that the anaconda can go for months without feeding again.

There are some great activities, films and links in the Homework Helpers to enhance knowledge of rainforest animals.

Classroom challenge

1. Make up a page in your workbook detailing animal life in the rainforest. Pick at least one animal from each layer of the forest, sketch it and explain how it survives. You will have to do your own research to complete this.
2. Now that you have learned about the climate, plants and animals of the rainforest, copy the diagram below into your workbook. It shows an example of a rainforest ecosystem and how it works. Complete it by adding in the missing words. Choose from the word box below.

TEACHING NOTES

Print out or look online at the information sheets from the Teaching Notes to help with Question 1.

1. The hot sun ________ moisture from the forest floor and **trees**. This helps to make **thunderstorms** and **rain**.

2. Trees and **plants** in the rainforest enjoy the hot, ________, rainy **climate**.

3. Ranforest soil is very poor but **plants** and **trees** can grow because their own ________ leaves and stems provide nutrients in the soil.

4. Trees are adapted to the climate with ________ roots, drip tips and they grow very tall to reach the sunlight. Layers of tree growth are found in the forest.

5. The layers of the trees, such as the ________ and the understorey, provide homes for animals and insects.

6. Animals help to spread the ________ of plants and **trees** by eating them and then passing them out in their waste in other parts of the forest.

ECOSYSTEMS!

Keep calm and rely on each other

BUTTRESS	ROTTING	HUMID	CANOPY	SEEDS	EVAPORATES

STRETCH YOURSELF

3. Now, try to challenge yourself some more and think about what would happen if **trees** were taken out of the cycle above. Write a paragraph in your workbook about what would happen to the climate, the forest and animal life. This means using your powers of **analysis**.

TEACHING NOTES

Question 3 could be set as a homework task.

How have humans traditionally survived in the rainforests?

Amazon case study

The first people to populate the world's largest rainforest – the Amazon – were indigenous tribes. They lived in total harmony with the plants and animals. They took what they needed from the forest but did not destroy or damage it. This means their way of life was **sustainable** (in balance with nature and did not destroy it). This is very much how their tribal **descendants** try to exist today.

Location of the Amazon rainforest in South America

Today there are many rainforest tribes all over the world who still follow a traditional way of life, such as the Matis (Amazon), the Kayapo (Amazon), the Bora (Amazon), the Yanomami (Amazon), the Pygmies (Congo rainforest) and the Huli (Papua New Guinea). Many make use of body paints and head dresses to show their identity and importance.

These tribes practise a **subsistence** way of life, which means they hunt and gather all their food from the forest as well as growing their own crops. Members of the tribe usually live together in **longhouses.** These are made from wood and leaves from the forest, and often several families will share one house

Kayapo tribe from the Amazon rainforest

Tribal village in rainforest clearing

A typical rainforest longhouse made from wood and leaves

Tribes such as the Yanomami in the Amazon carry out a way of life called **shifting cultivation**. Diagram 7 below shows how this works.

DON'T FORGET

Around 400–500 different tribes call the Amazon their home. It is thought that at least 50 of these have never had any contact with the outside world!

Diagram 7 – Shifting cultivation: maize plants growing in the ash in a clearing made by 'slash and burn'

Manioc – a type of tropical potato

Poison-dart frog

In addition to growing food, the tribal people also hunt, gather and fish in the forest using spears, bows, arrows and poisoned darts. (They use the poison gathered from the poison-dart frog.)

They will hunt for such things as monkeys, tapirs, peccary and various birds. Daily life in the village consists of the men heading out into the forest to hunt while the women tend to the crops or weave baskets from roots and bark. The women also go out into the forest to collect edible insects, such as ants, as well as nuts and fruit.

The edible weaver ant is said to taste cheesy, spicy and crunchy! Yummm!

The howler monkey is said to taste like mutton or goat. It is tough and greasy but the rear end is said to be the best bit!

Using a blowpipe and poisoned darts

Some tribes have a medicine expert called a **shaman**. A shaman has an encyclopaedia-like knowledge of rainforest plants and knows exactly which ones can be used to cure certain illnesses. In fact, the modern world has learned a lot from the shamans, and 25% of all medicines prescribed by our doctors now come from the rainforests. In the USA, 70% of all plants that can be used in producing cancer-fighting medicines are from the rainforest. For example, the rosy periwinkle from the Madagascan rainforest can make a child's chances of surviving leukaemia rise from 10% to 95%! Sadly, however, many of these shamans are getting very old and, as they die, their great knowledge of rainforest cures dies with them.

Rosy periwinkle – the cancer-fighting rainforest plant

Find out more on rainforest tribes by using the links, film clips and activities in the Homework Helpers.

Tribal shaman

Classroom challenge

1. **Describe** what it means to live a subsistence way of life.
2. Study Diagram 7 on page 91. Copy the diagram below into your workbook. Complete it by slotting the phrases beneath it into the correct boxes.

* Ash a good fertiliser. Pumpkins, yams and manioc planted.
* Trees cut down with stone axes. Area set on fire to clear it.
* Tribe abandon clearing and move to another part of the forest to start again after 3 or 4 years.
* Constant rain leaches the goodness out of the soil.

3. **Describe** the weapons tribal people use to hunt with.
4. What animals do they hunt in the forest?
5. **Describe** other things the women may collect in the forest for the tribe to eat.
6. Study Table 1 below. **Explain** at least three ways in which the rainforest provides everything the tribe needs.
7. This subsistence way of life means you would never need money. The forest provides everything. Once again, study Table 1 below and imagine you lived this way of life. Would you like it? Write a paragraph in your workbook giving reasons why you would like this way of life and reasons why you might not like to live like this. This means using your **evaluation** skills.

Table 1 – Daily life of a rainforest tribe

Time of day	The daily life of men	The daily life of women
Early morning	Get up and wash in river.	Get up before sunrise. Collect water and light fires for warmth and cooking.
Breakfast	Eat cassava bread made from manioc, drink juice made from pineapples or bananas. Eat separately from the women.	Eat cassava bread made from manioc, drink juice made from pineapples or bananas. Eat separately from the men.
Morning	Choice of hunting monkeys, tapirs or peccary, or work on preparing another patch of forest as a village clearing by using slash-and-burn techniques.	Work in the fields in the clearing, planting, tending or harvesting crops. Collect fruit and nuts.
Lunch	Eat cassava bread made from manioc, drink juice.	Eat cassava bread made from manioc, drink juice.
Afternoon	Collect coca and tobacco leaves. Make baskets or poison darts for hunting.	Prepare cassava bread. Wash children and pots in the river. Weave baskets or make pots.
Dinner	Eat meat, fish, vegetables from the clearing and cassava bread. Drink juice.	Eat meat, fish, vegetables from the clearing and cassava bread. Drink juice.
Evening	Drink homemade beer, chew coca leaves which give hallucinations, smoke and play instruments.	Spend evening separate from men looking after children. May join men during special festivals.

7. Who or what is a shaman?
8. **Explain** one reason why it can be said that the traditional knowledge of the rainforest tribes and shamans is vital for our life in the modern world.

THE CLEARING OF RAINFORESTS

Why are rainforests being cleared?

When trees are cleared away on a large scale, we call it **deforestation**. This is happening to the world's rainforests at an alarming rate. Some estimates put the rate of destruction as being an area similar to the size of 50 football pitches being destroyed every minute since the year 2000. This means that rainforests will have completely disappeared in 40 years' time.

TEACHING NOTES

Explaining the impact of an economic activity in a chosen area and beyond is CfE Level 4 work.

STRETCH YOURSELF

Rainforests tend to be in countries that are not wealthy, such as Brazil, Cameroon and Papua New Guinea. However, they are also in places where there are a lot of valuable minerals to be found, such as copper, iron ore, gold and bauxite (for aluminium, which we use for things like cans for drinking fizzy drinks). As a result, starting in the 1960s and 1970s, countries like Brazil decided that they wanted to develop their rainforests.

What is the connection between this photo and rainforest destruction?

The big problem in a vast area such as the Amazon is how do you get into the forest in the first place to reach these valuable minerals? The answer lay in building lots of roads. Perhaps the most famous is one of the first roads built in the Amazon, called the **Trans-Amazonian Highway**.

Trans-Amazonian Highway as a dirt track

The Trans-Amazonian Highway opened in 1972, but because it was so long (4000 km) it was too expensive to pave all of it. As a result, a lot of it remained as a dirt track. However, it marked the beginning of the exploitation and destruction of the Amazon rainforest.

Once people could get into the forest on roads, it brought in lots of developers and different land uses. These are shown in the diagram below.

TEACHING NOTES

Identifying at least three threats facing main climate zones and analysing how these threats impact on the way of life is CfE Level 4 work.

STRETCH YOURSELF

A lot of forest clearance is still due to **tribes burning clearings** to grow their crops.

Many international companies have bought huge areas of the rainforest. They set fire to it to clear it. They then use the land to **graze cattle**, which are used to make cheap beef products such as burgers.

Since there are so many valuable minerals in the rainforest such as iron ore, gold and bauxite, many areas of forest have now been destroyed by **mining**.

Many **roads** have now been built into the rainforest. This means lots of trees have been cleared to make way for them.

Many poor, homeless people in Brazil were encouraged to move into the rainforest to set up **farms**. Trees were chopped down to clear land for this.

Rainforest trees such as mahogany, rosewood and teak are very valuable, and rich countries want to buy them. As a result, the **timber industry** is now destroying a lot of the Amazon rainforest. Some of this logging is illegal.

Sometimes large companies destroy huge areas of rainforest to grow **plantation crops** such as sugar, coffee and rubber.

Rainforest areas have large amounts of rain and very large rivers. This makes them ideal places to build large dams for the production of **hydroelectric power** (making electricity from water). However, the large reservoirs created drown and destroy large areas of forest.

Diagram 8 – Reasons why the Amazon rainforest is being destroyed

There are some superb film clips, reports, links and activities in the Homework Helpers on rainforest destruction and impacts.

Classroom challenge

1. What do we call it when we destroy forests on a big scale?
2. Give figures to show how fast rainforests around the world are being destroyed.
3. In how many years' time will there be no rainforest left?
4. What did the Brazilian government have to construct first so that people could get into the Amazon rainforest?
5. Study Diagram 8 on page 95. Below are the land uses in the Amazon. However, they have been mixed up. Unscramble them and write them in your workbook.

DRASO   BITLAR GLERACIN   YROHD WEPOR
SPINLATNATO   LETACT   GINMIN   BREMTI   MASFR

6. Now complete this 'Pointless' quiz using Diagram 8 on page 95 and the words above to help you.

Many trees in the forest have been cleared to make way for these. (R_______)

When companies grow large areas of coffee, sugar and rubber, we call these. (P____________)

When electricity is made from water. (H_____ ___________ ________)

When we dig valuable minerals out of the ground. (M___________)

This industry is chopping down valuable trees such as mahogany. (T___________)

Some poor homeless people in Brazil set these up in the rainforest. (F________)

These animals graze in the rainforest and are used to make cheap burgers. (C_______)

For many years, the forest has been traditionally cleared to make these. (T_________ C_______)

7. The table below gives the percentage of Amazon rainforest that has been destroyed since 1970. Use these figures to draw a line graph in your workbook. Give it the title 'Percentage of Amazon Rainforest Destruction since 1970'.

Year	1970	1980	1990	2000	2017
% of Amazon rainforest destroyed	3%	7%	10%	14%	20%

8. **Describe**, using figures from your graph, the destruction of the Amazon rainforest since 1970. To do this, try to use phrases such as 'risen rapidly' and 'substantially higher', and also say how much higher or lower the figures are from year to year.

STRETCH YOURSELF

What are the impacts of rainforest clearance?

The effects of deforestation have brought huge changes to areas such as the Amazon. However, believe it or not, some of these changes have been good for rainforest countries.

DON'T FORGET

Did you know that if you drink coffee, eat rice or tofu, or eat a burger, chocolate or ice cream, you could be contributing to the destruction of the rainforests? Visit the Rainforest Alliance link in the Homework Helpers.

TEACHING NOTES

Describing and making at least three valid conclusions about the impact of human activity on a chosen area is CfE Level 4 work.

Diagram 9 – Rainforest clearance has its benefits!

Download the Homework Helpers for a link using counters to show how quickly rainforests are disappearing around the world.

However, as with many stories covered in Geography, there are lots of bad effects of deforestation in the Amazon.

Modern life invading the Amazon beside a tribal village

Diagram 10 – The effects of deforestation in the rainforest caused by timber, mining, hydroelectric power, farming and ranching

The people who are suffering most because of deforestation in the rainforest are the tribal people. Their way of life is threatened and is dying out. In many places, they have been driven from their lands by developers constructing roads, dams, mines, farms and cattle ranches, and they have been forced to live in reservations. In some instances, if they have tried to resist, they have been killed. There are even gangs of illegal loggers with guns who have murdered tribal people who get in their way. There is no respect for their rights to tribal lands by governments or developers. As a result, entire tribes face **annihilation.** This should be a concern for everyone on our planet.

Diagram 11 – Tribal protest

Tribal people protesting over the Belo Monte dam in Brazil. Prior to construction, it was estimated it would flood and destroy 660km² of forest and wildlife and force 20,000 tribal people off their own land. It is now operational.

Classroom challenge

1. Study Diagram 9 on page 97. **Explain** how rainforest tribes have benefited from new developments in the forest.
2. (a) Read the information in Diagrams 9 and 10 on pages 97 and 98 carefully. Complete the table below by listing the good and bad points for each rainforest development activity.

Development activity	Good points	Bad points
Hydroelectric dams		
Mining		
Timber		
Farming and ranching		

   (b) Now that you have completed your table, do you think rainforests should be developed? Give at least three reasons to back up your judgement. This means using your **evaluation** skills.

TEACHING NOTES

Describing and making at least three valid conclusions about the impact of human activity on a chosen area is CfE Level 4 work.

STRETCH YOURSELF

3. Diagram 11 on page 98 shows tribal people protesting about a hydroelectric dam being built on their land. **Explain** two reasons why we should listen to their protests.

4. How many other words can you make out of **RAINFOREST DESTRUCTION**?

Find out more about the Belo Monte dam in the Homework Helpers.

Go Digital!

5. Study Diagrams 9 and 10 on pages 97 and 98 again. Also, watch the film clips in the Homework Helpers on 'uncontacted tribes' in the Amazon. Do you think that contact with the outside world is a good thing for rainforest tribes? You must back up your answer with at least **three** well-**explained** reasons why (or why not). Once again, this means using your **evaluation** skills.

Check out more on rainforest destruction, palm oil and the death of orang-utans in Indonesia in the Homework Helpers.

Uncontacted Amazon tribe in 1996

HOW CAN WE PROTECT THE RAINFORESTS?

The destruction of the Amazon rainforest

Sadly, we have now found out that the world's rainforests are disappearing at an alarming rate, destroying wildlife and the traditional way of life of tribal people. However, if enough people care about these problems, then perhaps we can save them. This will not be easy!

Perhaps a good starting point for taking steps towards saving rainforests is to remember the phrase TREES!

T = Teach others about the importance of rainforests and how they can help to save them.

R = Restore damaged areas by replanting trees in areas where they have been cut down.

E = Encourage people who live in the forest to do so in a way that won't damage it.

E = Establish parks to protect rainforests and wildlife.

S = Support companies that take care not to damage the environment in the rainforests.

Sustainable rainforest management

For us to have a rainforest in the future, it will take careful management. Rainforest countries do need to develop so that their citizens can have a better life, but people in richer countries need to help and encourage them so they can make rainforest development **sustainable**. This means developing in a way that won't damage the rainforests so that they are preserved for future generations.

Diagram 12 below shows some simple ways in which this might be done.

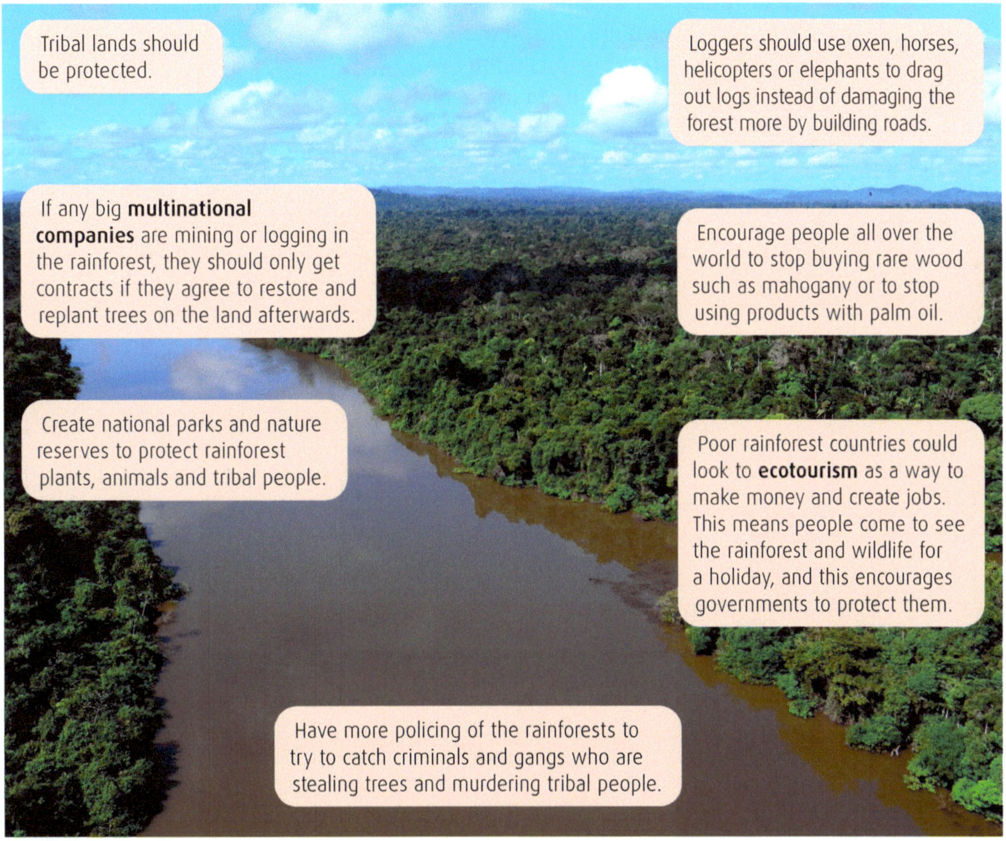

Diagram 12 – The protected environment of the Amazonia National Park, and ideas for saving the world's rainforests

Classroom challenge

1. Saving the rainforests must be **sustainable**. What does sustainable mean?
2. Study Diagram 12 on page 101. Which two solutions for saving the rainforest do you like most? Give reasons to **explain** why you have chosen these solutions.
3. Make a poster with the slogan **TREES**. It should tell the public what this means. Make it bright and colourful.
4. Imagine you are working for the gaming industry. Design and make up your own app idea about rainforests and present it using the format below so that it is ready for an app store. It could be about anything you have learned about rainforests such as:
   - survival
   - wildlife
   - tribes
   - battling illegal loggers
   - how to save the rainforest
   - daily life and survival of tribes
   - any other ideas!

TEACHING NOTES

The Teaching Notes have links to some great images of rainforest apps to investigate.

Image

Name of App
Summary of type of activity
GET

Insert screenshots of gameplay above

Description of game

Ratings and Reviews

Go Digital!

Visit the Bright Red website and download the Homework Helpers for more information and links on this.

STRETCH YOURSELF

5. Does the future of our rainforests lie with ecotourism?
   (a) Study Diagram 12 on page 101. What is ecotourism?
   (b) **Explain** three reasons why ecotourism is good for rainforests.
   (c) Can you see any problems that ecotourism can bring? Use the video link in the Homework Helpers to help you explain what these problems might be.

TEACHING NOTES

Contributing to a discussion on the development of sustainable systems is CfE Level 4 work.

6. Visit the '100 things to do in the Amazon rainforest' link in the Homework Helpers. Make up your own bucket list of at least ten things you would want to do in the rainforests.

TEACHING NOTES

Question 6 could be set as a homework task.

Check out other ways in which you can get involved in saving the Earth's rainforest in the Homework Helpers. After all, we all need them to survive!

Have you enjoyed learning about rainforests, ecosystems, destruction and conservation of rainforests? Would you like a career that uses the knowledge and skills you have gained from this topic? Why not visit the 'My World of Work/STEM/ Developing the Young Workforce' section of the Homework Helpers to find out more?

HOT DESERTS

Empty Lands – dreadfully dry, deserted deserts.

What's coming up?

- Where are the world's hot deserts?
- What is the hot desert climate like?
- What features do hot desert landscapes have?
- How are the plants adapted to this climate?
- How do animals survive in the hot, dry climate?
- How have humans traditionally survived in hot deserts?
- What changes are happening in hot deserts?
- What are the impacts of these changes?

DON'T FORGET

There are hot and cold deserts on our planet.
This section is about hot deserts only.

DESERT CLIMATE

Where are the world's hot deserts?

Life in hot deserts is difficult.
Temperatures can be so high you can fry an egg on the rocks, and the sun feels like it is drilling a hole into your skull. If that wasn't bad enough, hot deserts are also incredibly dry – less than 250 mm of rain a year. Strong winds can whip up sandstorms, meaning sand gets into your nose, mouth, ears and eyes.
However, because the sky hardly ever has any clouds, it can get really cold at night.
Would you like to live in these conditions?

Death Valley and Lake Disappointment do not sound like places that many people would want to visit. Their names come from the fact that they are found in hot deserts and therefore this makes them difficult places for any life to survive. The Atacama Desert in South America is one of the most difficult places for life to exist, as it is the driest desert on the planet. Some parts of it have never had rainfall, ever, and scientists have stated that overall the Atacama never experienced any significant rain from 1570 to 1971 (that's 400 years)!

Death Valley, California, USA

Atacama Desert, Chile

From Diagram 1 on page 106, we can see that most hot deserts are either on, or close to, the Tropics of Cancer and Capricorn (between 10° and 30° latitude north or south of the Equator). They also tend to be found on the western sides of continents, especially if a **cold ocean current** exists there.

The **Sahara** is the largest and most famous hot desert on Earth. It covers an area of 9 200 000 square kilometres! Located in the north of Africa, it crosses many countries, including Egypt, Libya, Morocco and Sudan.

DON'T FORGET

20% of the land surface on our planet is hot desert!

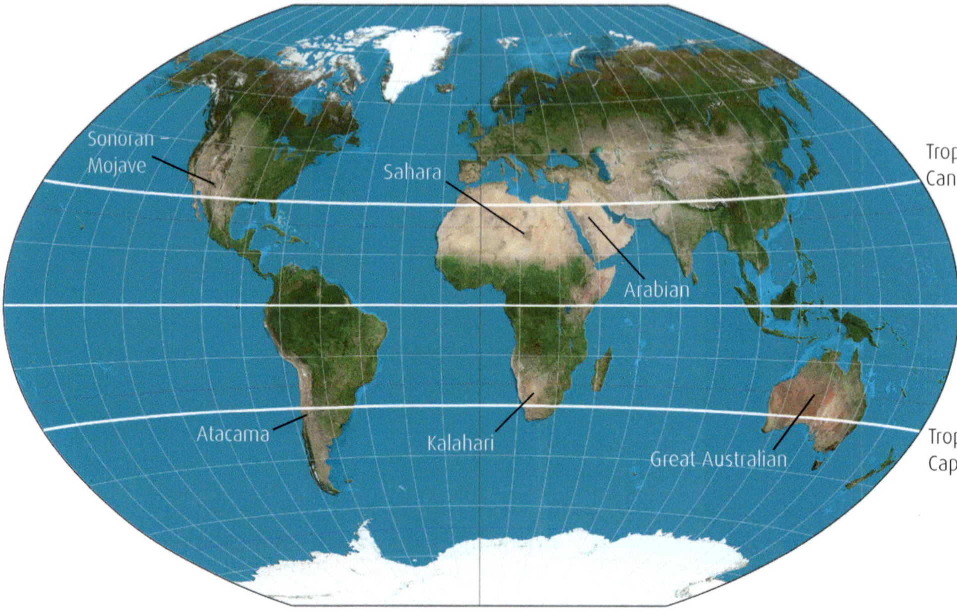

Diagram 1 – Location of the world's hot deserts

TEACHING NOTES

Follow the great links, activities and film clips in the Teaching Notes as a great way to introduce hot deserts.

Classroom challenge

1. Hot deserts can be so hot. **Describe** what you can do with an egg.
2. (a) Give the names of a valley and a lake found in hot deserts.
   (b) Can you think of the reasons why they have been given these names?
3. (a) What is the name of the driest hot desert on the planet?
   (b) What continent is this desert found in?
   (c) For how many years did part of this desert have no rainfall?
4. Read the statements below. Five are true and the others are false. Write out the statements that you think are true in your workbook.

- The Australian desert is the largest hot desert in the world.
- Some hot deserts are found on the west side of continents.
- Some hot deserts have hot ocean currents on their coasts.
- Some hot deserts have cold ocean currents on their coasts.
- The Sahara is the world's largest desert.
- Hot deserts are found on the Equator.
- Hot deserts are found close to, or on, the Tropics of Cancer and Capricorn.
- There are no hot deserts in Europe.

5. Name two hot deserts found in the continent of Africa.

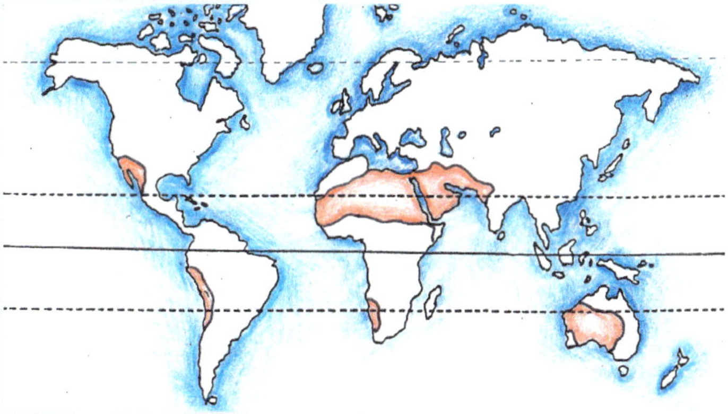

TEACHING NOTES

A blank world map is available in the Teaching Notes.

6. Use a blank world map (like the one above) to make your own location map of the world's hot deserts for your workbook. Look at Diagram 1 on page 106 and complete your map by adding the correct names of hot deserts to it.

What is the hot desert climate like?

Temperatures in hot deserts

On average, we can say the **climate** of a hot desert is hot and dry. However, the **weather** in the world's hot deserts can in fact vary greatly from day to day. In one week, it can change from hot, sunny days with cold nights, to intense dust storms which blow for two or three days. Temperatures can reach higher than 50°C in the summer. In fact, the world's hottest temperature of 56.7°C was recorded in Death Valley, California, USA. This is a significant temperature because these conditions will almost definitely cause heat stroke in humans. People very quickly become dehydrated, as they can easily lose a litre of water rapidly just from sweating during the day. This makes life in hot deserts very difficult.

What many people don't realise about hot deserts is that it can get very cold at night – it might even drop below 0°C. This happens because there are no clouds in the sky to keep the heat in.

It is also important to point out that winter can be much cooler in hot deserts, as Diagram 2 on page 108 shows.

Remember – anywhere that gets less than 250 mm of rainfall in a year is classed as a desert.

The hot desert climate makes life very difficult

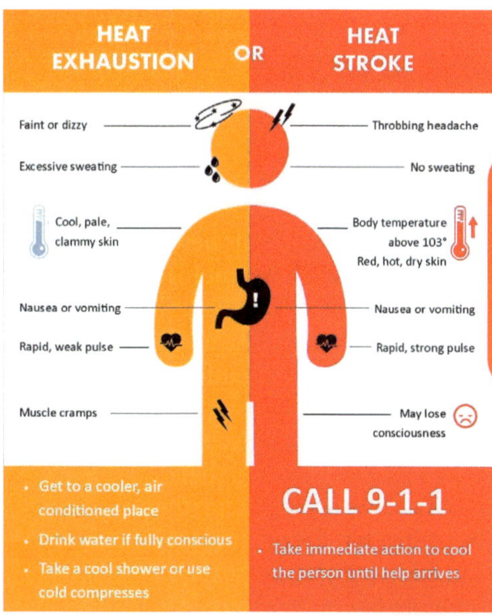

Health advice given in the USA on problems caused by heat

Check out the NHS link in the Homework Helpers for some more information on heat stroke and how to treat it.

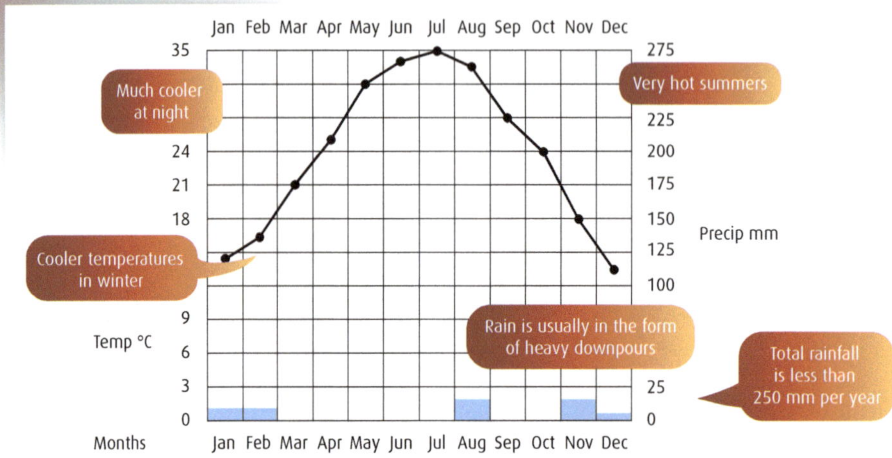

Diagram 2 – Hot desert climate graph

Rainfall in hot deserts

During one year in the desert, it might rain, and then there might be no rain at all for three or four years! It is this uncertainty of how much rain will fall that makes life so difficult. Even when it does rain, it comes as very heavy, violent downpours, which cause **flash floods**. Once again, this makes life very difficult in hot deserts.

Flash floods can arrive with no warning and sweep you away.

Flash flood in Libya

Dust storms are killers! They can last over 48 hours, and people have been known to suffocate during them.

Desert dust storm approaching

Why are deserts so dry?

The reason that hot deserts are so dry is because air here sinks and causes constant high pressure and lack of clouds. This is the complete opposite of what happens to air in the rainforests! Another reason that contributes to these deserts being so dry is the fact that the wind that usually blows across them (the **prevailing wind**) comes from land and not from the sea, and therefore has no moisture in it.

The lack of clouds in desert skies means the stars and the Milky Way can be seen clearly at night

Classroom challenge

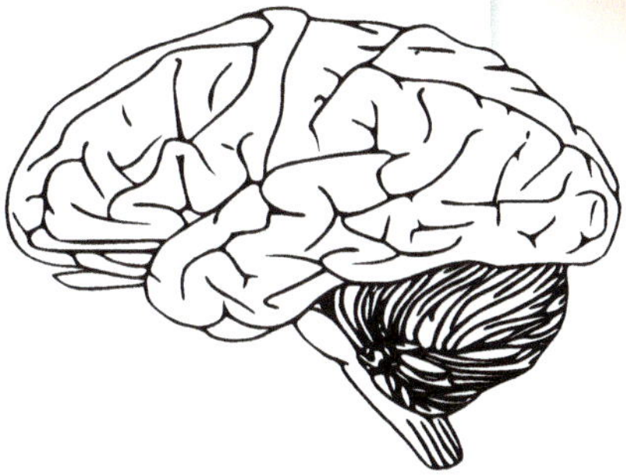

1. (a) Make a copy of this brain drawing in your workbook. Add onto it words that come into your mind when you think of the climate of a hot desert.
   (b) Can you **explain** why you have chosen these words?
2. What is the hottest temperature ever recorded in a hot desert, and where was it recorded?
3. (a) Study Diagram 2 on page 108. What is the hottest temperature, and in which month does it occur?
   (b) What is the coolest temperature, and in which month does it occur?
   (c) What is the temperature **range** for this hot desert? (Note – this is the difference between the hottest and coolest temperatures.)
   (d) Deserts have rainfall that is less than how many millimetres in a year?
4. **Explain** two reasons why life is so difficult in hot deserts.
5. **Explain** two reasons why it is so dry in hot deserts.
6. **Explain** why it can be so cold at night in hot deserts.
7. Make your own hot desert climate graph for your workbook using the figures in the table below.

TEACHING NOTES

There is a template on the Teaching Notes that can help with this.

Month	J	F	M	A	M	J	J	A	S	O	N	D
Temperature in °C	12	16	21	25	30	34	35	34	27	24	18	13
Rainfall in mm	10	11	0	0	0	0	0	25	0	0	20	5

Go digital!

Want to go digital? – Follow the instructions on how to make your own Excel climate graph available in the Homework Helpers at www.brightredpublishing.co.uk

FEATURES

What features do hot desert landscapes have?

TEACHING NOTES

Explaining in some detail how at least two landscape types from across the globe are formed is CfE Level 4 work.

STRETCH YOURSELF

Many people imagine that a hot desert landscape is a huge area of nothing but sand dunes. This is not true. The Sahara Desert is the world's sandiest desert, and yet only 25% of it is covered in sand!

Have you ever wondered why hot deserts have sand in the first place? The answer is partly due to a type of **weathering** (breaking up of rocks) called **exfoliation**. Diagram 3 below shows how this happens.

Diagram 3 – Exfoliation weathering of rocks (sometimes called onion-skin weathering)

When sand exists in a desert, it can be a very powerful means of **erosion**. This is the wearing away of rocks and the landscape. Erosion happens a lot in deserts, thanks to the wind picking up sand and blasting it against objects. It is like scrubbing them with a piece of sandpaper. This type of erosion is called **aeolian erosion**, and it can create some very bizarre features such as mushroom rocks.

Wind and sand have been constantly blasting the base of this rock, resulting in this very odd shape.

Mushroom rocks – formed by aeolian erosion

Exfoliation makes a rock peel apart like the layers of an onion

Desert landscapes are not as boring, therefore, as you might imagine. There are quite a variety of different landscape features that are very unusual and interesting. Diagram 4 below summarises some of these.

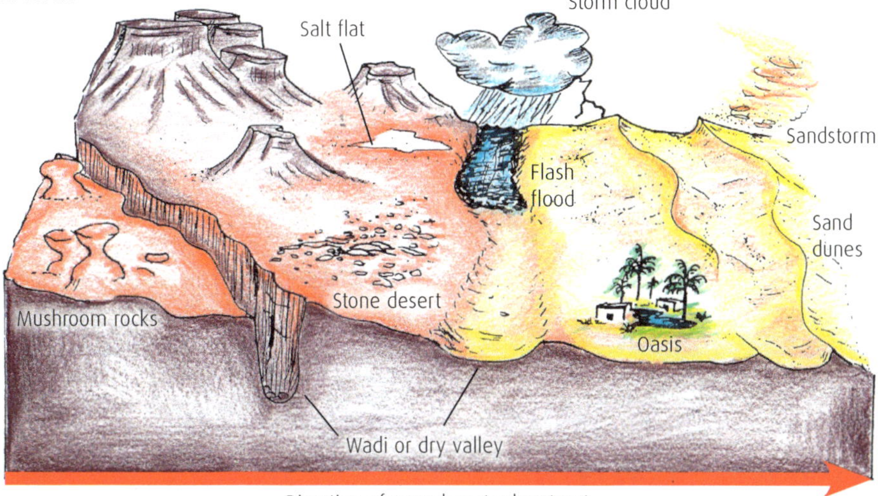

Diagram 4 – Hot desert landscapes

Lake Disappointment in Australia – a large salt flat

Aron Ralston gives a talk about his ordeal

DON'T FORGET

Did you know that Lake Disappointment in Australia is actually a large salt flat?

This wadi is very famous because in 2003, adventurer Aron Ralston was exploring it. Unfortunately, he dislodged a boulder, which fell on his arm, trapping him. Eventually, after 5 days, he cut off his own arm to escape. His story features in the movie *127 Hours*.

Blue John Canyon, Utah, USA (inside a wadi)

Explore canyons in Arizona with the BBC YouTube clip in the Homework Helpers.

Classroom challenge

1. Draw or trace your own diagram of hot desert landscapes (using Diagram 4 on page 111) in your workbook. Colour it and carefully label all the different landscape features onto it.

There is a template in the Teaching Notes to help with this.

2. What percentage of the Sahara Desert is covered in sand?
3. Study Diagram 3 on page 110. **Explain** fully, in your own words, the reasons why there is sand in hot deserts.
4. What does weathering mean?

5. These images show features caused by erosion in a hot desert. What does erosion mean?
6. What is the name of the type of erosion caused by sand and wind in hot deserts?
7. **Explain** how mushroom rocks form.
8. On Diagram 4 on hot desert landscapes, on page 111, an arrow has been drawn across the base of the image. Imagine you were travelling on a desert adventure along this arrow. Describe each desert landscape you pass through, and list any difficulties or dangers you might experience in them.

TEACHING NOTES

Some of the film clips and links in the Teaching Notes will help here.

Question 8 could be set as a homework task.

TEACHING NOTES

There are some great activities, film clips and links in the Teaching Notes to bring desert landscapes to life in the classroom!

ADAPTING TO THE HOT DESERT CLIMATE

How are the plants adapted to this climate?

The biggest problem for any living thing in hot deserts is the lack of water. This means they have to find ways of adapting to living in **drought** conditions. Only plants with the best adaptations will survive. Plants that are adapted to living with very little water have a scientific name – they are called **xerophytes**. A cactus is a good example of a xerophyte. It can survive drought because it is able to store water in its stem.

Cactus – the ultimate xerophyte

Some plants remain **dormant** for long periods of time. This means they lie in the ground and wait for any rain to come. They then suddenly burst into life – with some plants, you can almost watch this happening before your eyes! They will grow, flower, produce seeds and die back within a few days. These types of plants also have a scientific name – they are called **ephemerals**.

Desert ephemerals flowering after a rainstorm

Diagram 5 below shows examples of the different ways that plants survive.

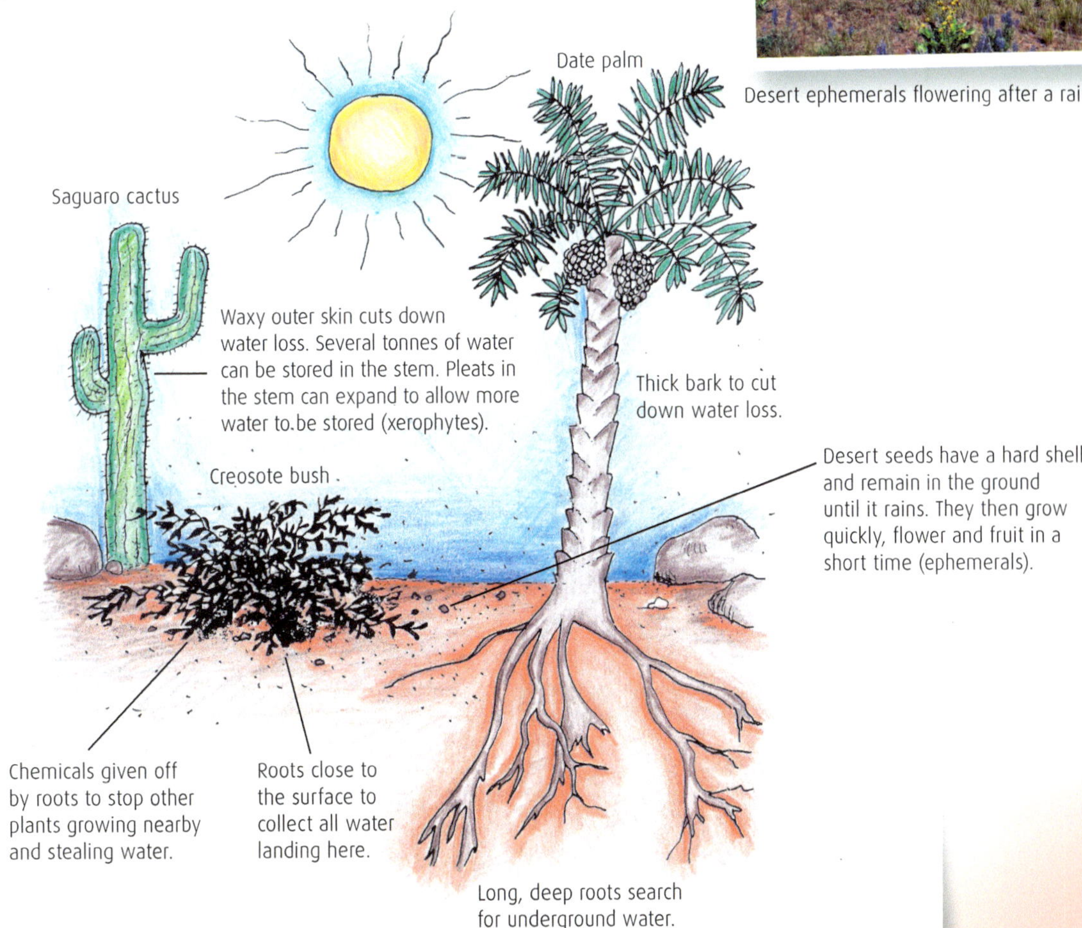

Diagram 5 – How desert plants survive the hot, dry conditions

How do animals survive in the hot, dry climate?

Since very little or no rain falls in hot deserts, the animals have to manage with hardly any water. They also have to try to exist in sizzling temperatures – especially in the summer months. Many of them are **nocturnal** – which means they only come out at night. During the day, they burrow under the sand and sleep. While they sleep, the moisture from their breath makes the air humid. Any seeds and food stored in their burrow will absorb this moisture, which will then be taken back into the animal when it eats those seeds and food.

Many desert creatures try to save moisture as much as possible by not sweating. They produce very little urine, and their dung is as dry as powder.

Other creatures such as lizards are cold-blooded. They will only become active when the intense heat warms their blood.

Some other examples of how animals survive are shown in Table 1.

Name of animal		How it is adapted to the desert?
Kangaroo rat		All the water a kangaroo rat needs comes from its food. It does not need to drink water. It can literally go its entire life without ever having to drink a single drop!
Rattlesnake		The rattlesnake hides in the cool of the sand waiting for its prey. It has waterproof skin, so it cannot sweat. It can only lose moisture through its mouth.
Fennec fox		Animals such as the jackrabbit and the fennec fox have very large ears. These have lots of blood vessels in them, which means their blood cools as they wave their ears in the air.
Kangaroo		Creatures such as kangaroos constantly lick parts of their bodies when the temperatures are really high. This cools them down because as their saliva evaporates, it draws heat out of their bodies.
Tortoise		Tortoises very sensibly spend 90% of their time underground in burrows to avoid the intense heat during the day, and cold temperatures at night.

Table 1 – How desert animals survive

Of course, the ultimate desert survival machine is the camel. It has many adaptations to the climate and the environment of hot deserts, as we can see in Diagram 6 below.

Diagram 6 – The camel, the ultimate desert survival machine

There are plenty of links and film clips in the Homework Helpers to enhance your knowledge of desert animals and plants.

Classroom challenge

1. Study Diagram 5 on page 113. Complete the paragraph below by slotting in the words from the word box into the correct spaces. You will need to unscramble the words first!

SICACHELM	AUGASOR	TEAD	ETMS	FURCEAS
RATEW	SLEEPMERAH	YAXW	GOLN	HEPEXROTY

Desert plants have many different ways of surviving the hot, dry climate. ______ palms are drought-resistant, which makes them a type of x__________. They have very _______ roots to get to underground water. They also have very thick bark to cut down _________ loss. The ___________ cactus has a ________ outer skin to stop water loss and can store tonnes of water in its ________. The creosote bush has c____________ given off by its roots to stop other plants growing nearby. Its roots are close to the ___________ to collect water landing there. Other plants and seeds are ______________. This means they lie dormant in the ground and burst into life when it rains.

2. Choose three desert animals from Table 1 on page 114. Either draw or trace them into your workbook and annotate (label) them with ways in which they survive in the hot, dry conditions.

TEACHING NOTES

There are templates in the Teaching Notes that can help with this.

3. Pointless Camel! Study Diagram 6 on page 115. Complete the missing words below in the 'Pointless' quiz.

Nostrils are like this to keep out sand. (M____________)

Feet are like this to stop the camel sinking into the sand. (B________)

This is what is found in a camel's hump. (F___)

Eyelashes are like this to keep sand out. (L_______)

Camels can drink 136 of these, of water in 13 minutes. (L_________)

The number of months a camel can survive for without drinking water. (S____)

Which of the answers above do you think would be 'Pointless'? This means the answer that the least amount of people would know. Write it in your workbook and explain why you think people would not know this fact.

4. Now, use your knowledge of the hot desert environment to create your very own desert plant or animal.
   - Produce a drawing of what your plant or animal looks like.
   - Label it with at least three ways in which it is adapted to the desert environment.
   - Colour it in and give your plant or animal a name.

TEACHING NOTES

Question 4 could be set as a homework task.

How have humans traditionally survived in hot deserts?

The people who live in hot deserts have to cope with the daily issues of hunger, heat, thirst and sandstorms. However, like the tribes of the rainforests, they have found their own unique ways to adapt and survive in this harsh environment. These ways of life are very different, depending on which desert area they live in. Three very different traditional ways to survive in hot deserts are shown in Diagram 7 below.

DON'T FORGET

There are 1 billion people in the world who live in desert environments.

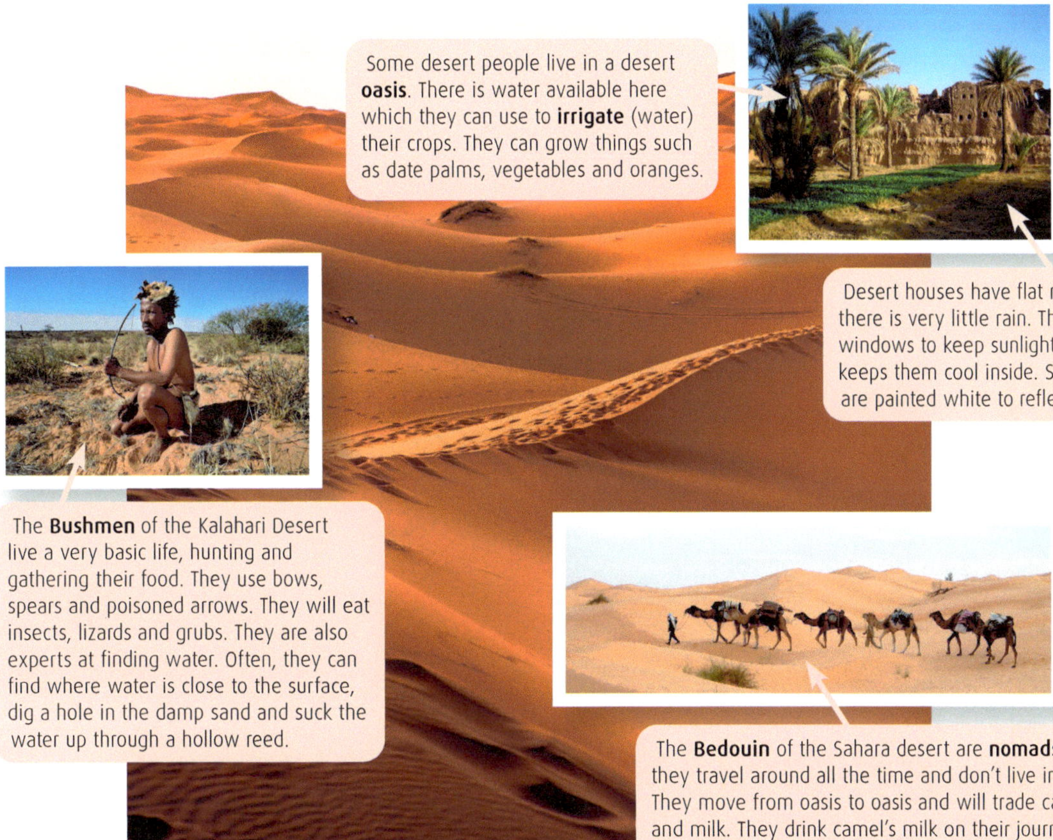

Some desert people live in a desert **oasis**. There is water available here which they can use to **irrigate** (water) their crops. They can grow things such as date palms, vegetables and oranges.

Desert houses have flat roofs since there is very little rain. They have small windows to keep sunlight out, which keeps them cool inside. Some houses are painted white to reflect the sun.

The **Bushmen** of the Kalahari Desert live a very basic life, hunting and gathering their food. They use bows, spears and poisoned arrows. They will eat insects, lizards and grubs. They are also experts at finding water. Often, they can find where water is close to the surface, dig a hole in the damp sand and suck the water up through a hollow reed.

The **Bedouin** of the Sahara desert are **nomads.** This means that they travel around all the time and don't live in fixed houses. They move from oasis to oasis and will trade camels, goats, rugs and milk. They drink camel's milk on their journeys. Their long clothes protect them from the sun. At night they sleep in tents.

Diagram 7 – Traditional human life in hot deserts

What you wear in a hot desert is very important! There are very good reasons why the people who live there are not running around in their swimwear!

Take a look at the Tuareg man in Diagram 8 on page 118. The **Tuaregs** are nomads who inhabit the Sahara Desert in countries such as Libya, Algeria, Niger, Mali and Burkina Faso (see Diagram 9 on page 118). The name Tuareg means 'abandoned by God', but they prefer to refer to themselves as Imohag, which means 'free men'. Due to the colour of the robes the Tuareg wear, they are sometimes also called the 'blue people'. What is unusual about the Tuareg is that women often don't wear veils, as the men want to see their beautiful faces, and the family name and inheritance comes through the woman's side of the family.

Investigate the links and film clips in the Homework Helpers for much more on the peoples of hot deserts.

Diagram 9 – Distribution of Tuareg people in north Africa

Diagram 8 – Tuareg clothing

Classroom challenge

1. Study Diagram 7 on page 117.
   (a) **Explain** the reason why some desert people choose to live at an oasis.
   (b) What does the word **irrigate** mean?
   (c) **Explain** why desert houses have flat roofs.
   (d) Why might you paint your house white if you lived in a hot desert?
   (e) **Describe** how Bushmen of the Kalahari get their food.
   (f) What sort of things do they eat?
   (g) Why is a hollow reed useful to the Bushmen?
   (h) What is a nomad?
   (i) **Describe** the way of life of the Bedouin people.
2. Study Diagram 8 above.
   Make up a missing-persons poster for a Tuareg tribe member.

TEACHING NOTES

Check out the Teaching Notes for a template for this activity.

3. Humans across the world have learned much from the people of the hot desert regions – especially survival skills. Do you think you could survive in a hot desert? Now, work in pairs to complete the table below, listing what you would put in your own hot desert survival kit, and **explain** why each item is needed.

TEACHING NOTES

Watch the YouTube clips, and visit the links on the Teaching Notes to help the class with this.

Hot desert survival kit item	Description of why it is needed

Go Digital!

4. (a) Now test out your survival kit by using the 'Hot Desert Survival Scenarios' from the Homework Helpers.
   (b) Having completed this activity, is there anything else you would add to your survival kit?

WHAT CHANGES ARE HAPPENING IN HOT DESERTS AND WHAT ARE THE IMPACTS OF THESE CHANGES?

Tourism

TEACHING NOTES

Explaining the impact of an economic activity in a chosen area and beyond is CfE Level 4 work.

STRETCH YOURSELF

Hot deserts are an incredibly important part of the world's wealth. This is because there are valuable resources found in them, such as oil, just like in the rainforest.

Increasingly, hot desert countries are also becoming tourist destinations, such as Dubai, Bahrain, Tunisia, Egypt, Jordan and Morocco. They have also become a playground for the rich and famous. This is because they offer guaranteed sunshine and heat, which are often the main things people want when they go on holiday.

There are also lots of activities that tourists like to do in hot desert areas. Have a look at Diagram 10 below. Can you identify the different activities that people can do?

Desert oilfield

Diagram 10 – Tourist activities in hot deserts

The popular beach area of Dubai and the 7-star Burj Al Arab hotel

More and more people travelling to hot deserts for their holidays have brought benefits for the people who live there. It means more jobs for local people and more money for the country. However, the growth of tourism has also brought problems for both travellers and the desert environment. Diagram 11 below shows the impact that 'dune bashing', a very popular desert activity, is having on the local area and environment.

Check out the Homework Helpers for film clips and guides to popular hot desert locations.

Experience 100% Pure Adrenalin! Come Dune Bashing!

Are you an off-road addict?
Fancy driving at extreme speed roaring up and down desert sand dunes? Then book with us.
purebashingthedunes.geog.brightred.com

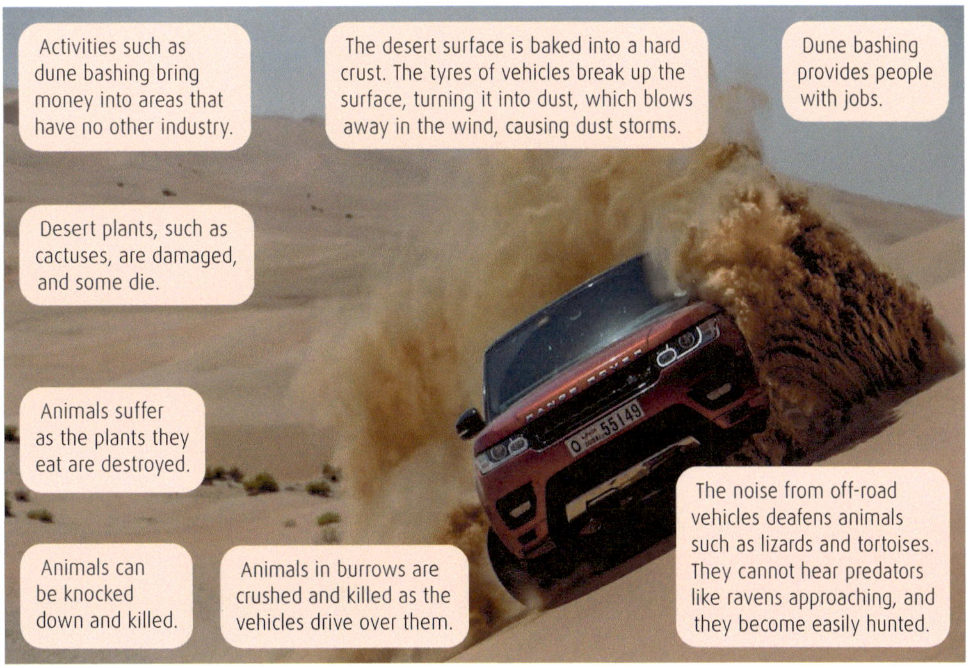

Diagram 11 – The impact of dune bashing on desert areas

Ecotourism

However, there are other ways that hot desert countries can encourage tourism, provide jobs and make money to boost their economies without damaging the fragile environment. Once again, the answer, as in the rainforests, could lie with **ecotourism**. This means that activities can be **sustainable** (not damaging the local area, and preserving it for the future); and the only thing that the tourists leave behind, after their visit, are footprints in the sand.

Some examples of things people can do are shown in Diagram 12 on page 122.

STRETCH YOURSELF

Diagram 12 – Ecotourism activities in the desert

TEACHING NOTES

Contributing to a discussion on the development of sustainable systems is CfE Level 4 work.

Classroom challenge

The film clips in the Teaching Notes could help with this.

1. Give two reasons why you think tourists want to go to hot deserts for their holidays.
2. Tourism can bring great benefits to hot desert countries, but can also introduce some problems.
   (a) Study Diagram 11 on page 121 on dune bashing, and complete the table below.

Benefits brought by dune bashing	Problems caused by dune bashing

(b) Now that you have completed the table, do you think people should go dune bashing in deserts? Give at least three reasons to back up your judgement. Remember, this is you using your **evaluation** skills.

STRETCH YOURSELF

3. Look at Diagram 12 on page 122 on ecotourism activities in hot deserts. Pick two that you might like to do, and **describe** why you would like to do them.
4. Imagine that you are working for a marketing company and have been given the job of promoting **ecotourism** in hot deserts. With a partner, make up a poster, slide show or film telling people about the problems caused by activities such as dune bashing, and give information on ecotourism activities that people can do instead.

TEACHING NOTES

Describing and making at least three valid conclusions about the impact of human activity on a chosen area is CfE Level 4 work.

The links and film clips in the Teaching Notes could help with this.

Go Digital!

5. In some parts of the world, the impacts of development are destroying the traditional way of life of desert-dwellers. This is happening in the Kalahari Desert in Botswana and is affecting the Bushmen very badly. Read the report in the Homework Helpers very carefully and **explain** at least three reasons why there is a call for a boycott (telling people to stop going there) of tourism in Botswana.

TEACHING NOTES

Identifying at least three threats facing main climate zones and analysing how these threats impact on the way of life is CfE Level 4 work.

Lots of people are concerned about rainforest destruction. However, hot deserts are also an important biome that is under threat. Do you care about hot deserts? Why not set up your own group in your school to alert people to the issues facing hot deserts, their environment, their wildlife and their people?

Have you enjoyed learning about hot deserts? Would you like a career that uses the knowledge and skills you have gained from this topic? Why not visit the 'My World of Work/STEM/Developing the Young Workforce' section of the Homework Helpers to find out more?

THE TUNDRA

Empty Lands – brrrrrrrrrutally chilly tundra!

What's coming up?

- Where is the tundra?
- What is the tundra climate like?
- What features do tundra landscapes have?
- How are the plants and animals adapted to the tundra environment?
- How have humans traditionally survived in the tundra?
- What changes are happening in the tundra?
- What are the impacts of these changes?
- What is the future for the tundra?

TUNDRA CLIMATE

Where is the tundra?

There are some places on Earth where it is very difficult for people, plants and animals to live. Humans need sufficient warmth, water and nourishment in order to stay alive. Without them they cannot survive. The tundra biome is one of these places.

The word **tundra** comes from the language of the Sami people and means flat, treeless plain. It has been given this name for very good reason, as trees would find it extremely difficult to survive in the harsh environment.

The tundra is located in the far north of the continents of the northern hemisphere, in places such as Alaska, northern Canada, Greenland, northern Scandinavia and Siberia (see Diagram 1 below). It occurs mostly between 65° and 70° north and is found around the edges of the Arctic Ocean. Please note – the tundra is not found at the North Pole! The North Pole is actually in the middle of the frozen Arctic Ocean.

The frozen wasteland of the tundra

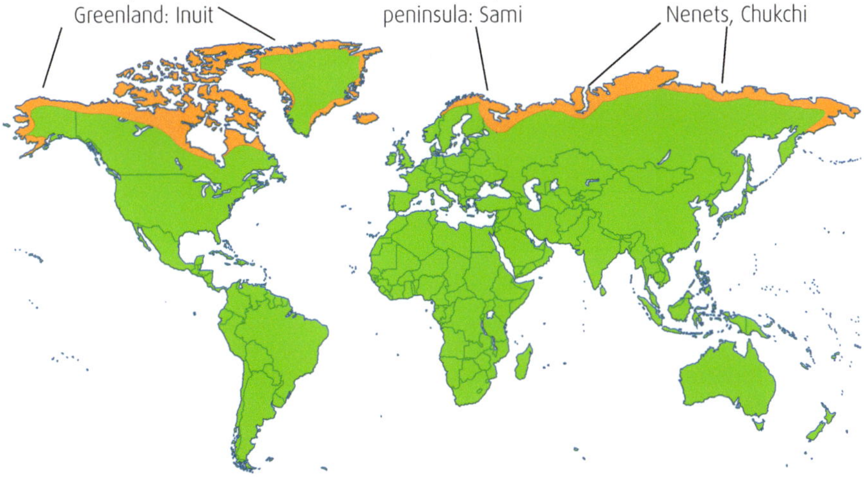

Diagram 1 – Map showing the location of the tundra and the names of some of the **indigenous** (native) people living there

DON'T FORGET

Did you know that Alaska used to belong to Russia? It was sold to the United States for the meagre sum of $7.2 million in 1867 because the Tsar (leader) of Russia needed the cash!

Classroom challenge

There is a blank world map in the Teaching Notes.

1. Use a blank world map to make up your own location map of the tundra similar to the one below for your workbook. Complete the labels.

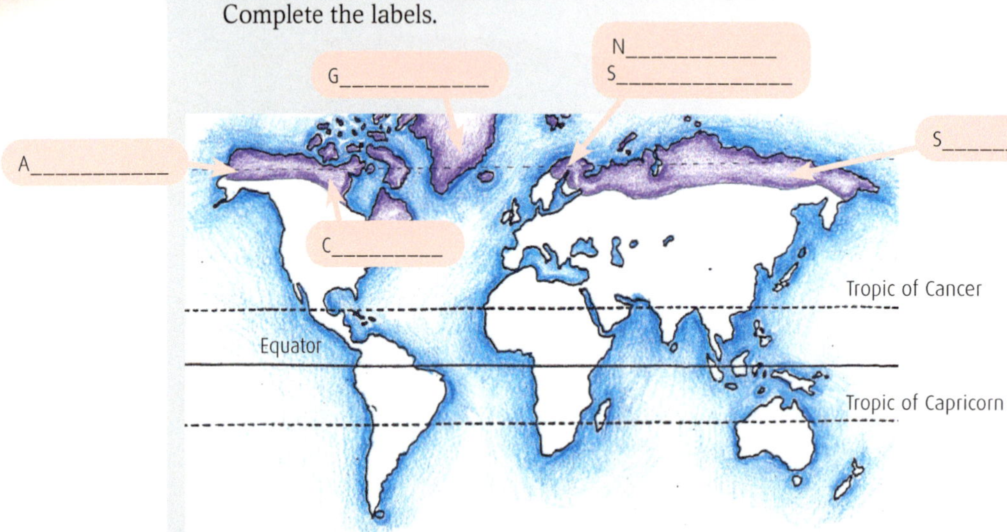

You might need an atlas to answer the next two questions.

2. Give the names of the countries that you would find in northern Scandinavia.
3. Which country is Siberia a part of?
4. Which country does Alaska belong to today?
5. How much was Alaska sold for?

You could use the link in the Homework Helpers to access an online atlas.

Go Digital!

6. Now that you know which countries have areas of tundra in them, make up a poster with the title 'Tundra Territory Flags'. Use the 'World Flag Database' on www.flags.net to help you with this.

What is the tundra climate like?

Winter in the tundra

The tundra climate makes survival extremely challenging for all living things (see Diagram 2 on page 127). In January, the average temperature is –28°C, but it can get much colder than this. In Siberia, it once dropped to a thermometer-shattering –68°C in Oymyakon in 1933. In temperatures such as this, you can throw a pot of boiling water into the air and it will instantly turn into snow! Survival time outside in such cold conditions can be measured in minutes, because you would very quickly start to suffer hypothermia and frostbite.

Watch the film clip in the Homework Helpers to witness boiling water turning into snow.

Tundra landscape as snow melts in summer

Frostbite can easily occur in these conditions. Frostbite is when exposed flesh freezes, especially fingers, toes and noses. They will start to turn black, your blood can become infected, and affected areas may even drop off or have to be amputated. Explorers in cold regions have reported that when they took their socks off, some toes came off with them!

One thing that can break up the cold dark nights is the **aurora borealis**. This spectacle is caused by electrons released by solar winds from the sun. They occur in the tundra a lot because they are attracted to the magnetic field found at the North Pole.

The aurora borealis (northern lights)

If the cold temperatures weren't bad enough, there are also often fierce winds, which whip up the snow into blinding blizzards. Finally, to make winters even more bleak, tundra areas in the far north may not have any daylight for up to three whole months. These conditions can literally make people go insane!

Summer in the tundra

In summer, however, things become a bit better. Summer doesn't last long, though – on average only around three months. Temperatures do rise above freezing, so any snow and ice will melt. The highest temperature will average around 10°C. Crucially, this means that the temperatures rise above 6°C, which is the **growing point** for plants. Daylight hours are long – in some places, it may not get dark for three months. This is why the tundra is sometimes called the 'land of the midnight sun'.

Follow the link on the Homework Helpers to find out more about the aurora borealis.

Precipitation in the tundra

There is not a great deal of **precipitation** (anything that falls from the sky – rain, hail, sleet, snow – is precipitation) in the tundra. The surprising thing is that, despite the fact this biome is covered in snow for most of the year, it only gets around 250 mm of precipitation. This means it is classified as a cold desert.

Notice that, even in the summer, temperatures do not get very high.

Notice how bitterly cold the average temperatures are in winter.

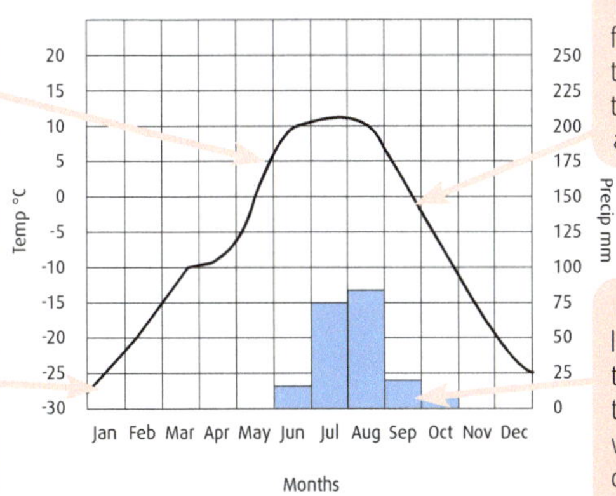

Notice how few months there are when temperatures rise above 0°C.

Notice how little precipitation there is in the tundra. This is why it is often called a cold desert.

Diagram 2 – Tundra climate graph for Barrow, Alaska

Brooks Range, Alaska, in the summer

TEACHING NOTES

There are some great links in the Teaching Notes to help introduce the tundra environment.

Classroom challenge

1. Use graph paper or the template available in the Homework Helpers to make your own tundra climate graph using the figures below.

Month	J	F	M	A	M	J	J	A	S	O	N	D
Temperature °C	-28	-24	-17	-10	-2	7	10	9	5	0	-15	-20
Precipitation mm	5	6	16	26	30	50	30	20	20	10	0	0

2. Study the tundra climate graph you have just completed. What is the temperature range of the tundra (remember this is the difference between the coldest and warmest temperatures)?
3. What is the record coldest temperature in the tundra, and where did it occur?
4. What can you do to impress your friends using a pot of boiling water in these temperatures?
5. How long does summer last in the tundra?
6. Why is the tundra sometimes referred to as the land of the midnight sun?
7. **Describe** what precipitation means.
8. **Explain** why the tundra can be called a cold desert.

TEACHING NOTES

Want your class to go digital? You could use the instructions in the Teaching Notes to create Excel climate graphs for this.

Go Digital!

9. (a) What dangers to your health can occur in cold temperatures?
   (b) Follow the NHS links in the Homework Helpers and describe what you would do if you were suffering from these health issues.

What features do tundra landscapes have?

Since tundra lands are cold for a good nine months of the year, the ground remains permanently frozen. This is appropriately called **permafrost,** and it means the ground is as hard as concrete. In the three-month summer period, the top layer of the ground will thaw out and, because the melting snow and ice can't drain into the rock-hard permafrost below, the ground becomes very waterlogged and boggy. Lots of small lakes form, and this sodden landscape is called **muskeg**.

Ice wedge in the permafrost

Bog-covered surface of the tundra in summer

An ice-age remnant

The permafrost of the tundra can hold some fascinating secrets. A brilliantly preserved body of a woolly mammoth from the last ice age was found in the Siberian permafrost in 2013. It even still had its woolly coat! Scientists believe it had been lying in its icy tomb for around 39 000 years. Some have even suggested that a blood sample found at the scene would be enough for us to be able to create a woolly mammoth clone in true Jurassic Park style.

Muskeg landscape

Woolly mammoth

Go online to the Homework Helpers for more exciting activities and links on the tundra landscape.

STRETCH YOURSELF

Diagram 3 below shows some of the features found in a tundra landscape.

Diagram 3 – The tundra landscape

TEACHING NOTES

Explaining in some detail how at least two landscape types from across the globe are formed is CfE Level 4 work.

Classroom challenge

There is a template in the Teaching Notes that can help with this.

1. Draw or trace your own labelled diagram of a tundra landscape like Diagram 3 above.
2. Look at the table below. The sentence beginnings and endings have been mixed up. Match the correct sentence beginning with the correct ending, and write it out in your workbook.

Beginnings	Endings
Permafrost is.......	.......a waterlogged landscape with lots of small lakes.
A pingo is.........	.......have many rivers of ice called glaciers.
Muskeg is........	.......are called dwarf willows.
Mountains in the tundra.....	.......permanently frozen ground.
Small trees growing in the tundra..	.......a dome-shaped feature with an icy centre.

3. **Describe** what was found in the permafrost of the Siberian tundra in 2013.
4. How long had it been buried for?
5. What might scientists be able to do with a blood sample found at the scene?
6. Make your own tundra landscape word search. Ask another student in your class to try to complete it.

ADAPTING TO THE TUNDRA CLIMATE

How are the plants and animals adapted to the tundra environment?

Plants

Tundra plants are very tough and are adapted to the permafrost, the cold, the strong winds and waterlogged soils. As soon as average temperatures rise above 6°C (the growing point), and the winter coating of snow and ice melts, the tundra will burst into life.

Most of the plant life exists very low to the ground and has a very quick life cycle, to make the most of the very brief period when temperatures are above the growing point. The vegetation is not lush and consists of such things as herbs, grasses, mosses and lichens. Although the name 'tundra' means land without trees, some very small dwarf trees will live close to the ground away from the wind, such as **dwarf willows**.

Tundra plants – dwarf willow on the left and tundra lichens on the right

These low-lying plants are important food for tundra animals to graze on during the summer months.

DON'T FORGET

Lichens are very slow-growing due to the lack of warmth. A bunch of lichens the size of a cabbage may have taken hundreds of years to grow!

Animals

As with other biomes across the planet, animals in the tundra have adapted in different ways to help them deal with the extreme climate. Some of these different adaptations are shown in Diagram 4 below.

Many tundra creatures do not stay there all year. Animals such as the caribou (reindeer) **migrate** to the forests of the south for the harsh winter months. When temperatures start to rise, they travel northwards in enormous herds, to graze and have their young in the tundra over the summer months. When winter starts to set in, they migrate southwards again.

The caribou herd is often followed by arctic wolves. There is an obvious reason why they do this – it is their food supply!
It is said, though, that being hunted by the wolves keeps the caribou herd healthy. This is because the wolves are more likely to take the old, injured, diseased members of the herd, leaving the young strong animals to breed.

Some animals stay in the tundra all year round. Probably the most famous example of an animal that does this is the polar bear. It has very thick fur and a layer of fat underneath it, to keep it warm. Its fur looks white to help camouflage it in the snow. However, the fur fibres are actually hollow and simply reflect the light. The fur is also oily, which means that after the bears have been hunting in the sea, water just runs off them and they won't freeze. Polar bears hibernate in snow caves over winter.
Their noses are so sensitive they can smell a seal 20 miles away!

The tundra is found on the edges of the Arctic Ocean. Many sea creatures live in its icy waters, such as seals, walruses and whales, and are able to do so because they are adapted to it. Perhaps one of the most unusual creatures is the narwhal. It looks a bit like a cross between a whale and a unicorn! It has a long tusk, which is actually a tooth that can be 10 feet long. Some scientists now believe this tusk has something to do with sensing things.
All Arctic Ocean creatures survive due to having a thick layer of blubber (fat) under their skin. The narwhal uses cracks in the sea ice to come up for air.

Do not miss checking out the Homework Helpers for brilliant links, games and clips on plant and animal life in the tundra. There is even the chance to track real polar bears in the Arctic.

Diagram 4 – Tundra animals are adapted to the harsh environment

Classroom challenge

1. Tundra Plant Code Words!
The codes below spell out the names of tundra plants. Use the code-buster and swap each number for the correct letter to find out their names.

A	B	C	D	E	F	G	H	I	J	K	L	M
1	2	3	4	5	6	7	8	9	10	11	12	13
N	**O**	**P**	**Q**	**R**	**S**	**T**	**U**	**V**	**W**	**X**	**Y**	**Z**
14	15	16	17	18	19	20	21	22	23	24	25	26

(a) 13, 15, 19, 19
(b) 12, 9, 3, 8, 5, 14
(c) 4, 23, 1, 18, 6 23, 9, 12, 12, 15, 23
(d) 2, 5, 1, 18 2, 5, 18, 18, 25
(e) 20, 21, 6, 20, 5, 4 19, 1, 24, 9, 6, 18, 1, 7, 5
(f) 12, 1, 2, 18, 1, 4, 15, 18 20, 5, 1

2. Copy the spider diagram below, showing how tundra plants are adapted to the environment, into your workbook. Complete it by answering the questions in the boxes.

At what temperature will tundra plants start to grow?

Why do tundra plants have shallow roots?

POLAR PLANT POWER!

Why do tundra plants have a quick life cycle?

Name a type of small tree found in the tundra.

3. Make up a page in your workbook that includes sketches of the tundra animals. Beside each animal, **explain**, in your own words, how they are adapted to their environment in the tundra. Choose three animals to focus on from Diagram 4 on page 132.

Question 3 could be set as a homework task.

TEACHING NOTES

You may wish to look at the links in the Teaching Notes for extra information as well as using the animal templates to help with sketches.

How have humans traditionally survived in the tundra?

In a harsh, frozen, barren wasteland such as the tundra, it is very hard to imagine any humans existing. The people who do live there have done so for thousands of years and have completely adapted to the environment. Traditionally, tundra people lived off the land, often by **migrating** (being on the move) all the time, usually following animal herds such as the caribou. This is a bit like desert nomads.

Traditional tundra life

Eskimos or Inuit?

Usually, when people in the UK are asked who lives in the tundra, they will reply 'Eskimos'. They will then go further and state that they also live in igloos. These ideas are incorrect, and in most tundra areas using the word 'Eskimo' is considered racist and is frowned upon. This is because it was a word used by people from lands to the south of the tundra, in North America, and means 'eaters of raw meat', suggesting that they were uncivilised savages. It is much better to refer to the people of the tundra by their proper names, such as the **Inuit** or the **Nenets**. Also, these people did not, and do not, live permanently in igloos. Igloos are used only as temporary shelters in the winter.

Traditional Inuit clothing

In the past, the people of the tundra lived in cheerful societies, where being a good hunter to help the community was more important than being rich.

Like the animals, people such as the Inuit of Alaska, northern Canada and Greenland have developed adaptations to help them deal with the Arctic cold (see Diagram 5 below).

Diagram 5 – Traditional Inuit clothing

Traditional Inuit houses

The Inuit lived in different shelters according to the season. In winter, they lived in stone houses, while in the warmer, lighter days of summer, they lived in a tent (see Diagram 6 below). Igloos were used as temporary shelters when they were out on hunting trips, and they travelled using huskies and sledges in winter, and **kayaks** in summer.

Diagram 6 – Traditional houses in the tundra

Hunting and food

The Inuit hunted and gathered all their food from the tundra environment. They only ever caught as many animals as they needed, and they cannot understand why people would want to just kill an animal for fun. This meant that tundra wildlife was never threatened with extinction.

Diagram 7 – Uses of a seal

DON'T FORGET

A delicacy in the Arctic is kiviak. This is a type of sausage. The outside of it is seal skin lined with blubber, and it is stuffed with little auks (small birds). It is buried underground for 6 months to rot and then eaten, and it smells like rancid cheese! Yum!

Classroom challenge

1. What does the word **migrating** mean?
2. **Explain** why it is not correct to call the people of the tundra 'Eskimos'.
3. Study Diagram 5 on page 134 on traditional Inuit clothing.
   (a) Use it to make your own labelled diagram showing traditional Inuit clothing.
   (b) Now, complete the passage below by copying it into your workbook, filling in the missing words as you go. Choose the words from the word box underneath.

> Inuit people in the past had no need for ________. They took everything they needed from the e________________ they lived in, including their clothing. Their outer tunics were made from sealskin. The fur around their hoods was trimmed with ____________ fur, because moisture from _________ won't freeze on it. Trousers were made from ____________ or polar bear skin. The Inuit name for boots is __________. Socks are made from sealskin and are stuffed with dried ____________ for comfort and ____________.

ENVIRONMENT	BREATH	MOSS	SHOPS
REINDEER	WOLVERINE	WARMTH	KAMIKS

4. Study Diagram 6 on page 135. Make your own labelled diagrams of the Inuit summer and winter houses. You may wish to make use of the template in the Homework Helpers to help you with this.
5. **Describe** what the Inuit used to travel on in winter and summer.
6. **Explain** why it can be said that the Inuit did not threaten tundra animals with extinction.
7. Study Diagram 7 on page 135 on uses of a seal.
   Copy the speech bubbles below into your jotter. If they are 'true', colour them blue. If they are 'false', colour them red.

Bones are used as windows.

Skins are made into toilet roll.

Sinews are used for sewing.

Blubber is used to heat homes.

Sinews are used as dental floss.

Skins are made into clothes.

Bones are used for tools.

Bladders are made into windows.

8. Study Diagram 8 below showing how to make an igloo.

Diagram 8 – How to make an igloo

TEACHING NOTES

Question 8 could be set as a homework activity.

There are also some video links in the Homework Helpers showing how to do this.

Now write out an instruction sheet on how to make an igloo correctly. This could come in very handy the next time you have a snow day!

9. We have now learned all about the climate, landscape, plants, animals and humans of the tundra. What is clear is that they all have a big influence on each other. When living things and the non-living environment interact with each other, we call it an **ecosystem**. Use your knowledge of the tundra ecosystem to complete the table below. You will need your powers of **analysis** to complete this!

Name three ways that the climate affects the tundra landscape.	1. Permanently frozen ground (permafrost). 2. 3.
Name three ways that the tundra animals have adapted to surviving in the tundra climate.	1. 2. 3.
Name three ways that tundra plants have adapted to the tundra climate and landscape.	1. 2. 3.
Name three ways that tundra people make use of the landscape, plants or animals.	1. 2. 3.

Don't forget to look at the great links, film clips and activities in the Homework Helpers to view the reality of traditional ways of life on the tundra.

WHAT CHANGES ARE HAPPENING IN THE TUNDRA AND WHAT ARE THE IMPACTS OF THESE CHANGES?

STRETCH YOURSELF

Fossil fuel extraction

At present, the world still relies on **fossil fuels** (coal, oil and gas) for things such as transport, industry and generating power. As these become scarcer, governments are starting to look more and more at areas such as the tundra to extract these fuels. Some of the resources found in the tundra are very valuable, such as gold, copper, uranium, oil and gas. The problem is that, although mining for these provides jobs and money for the locals, it destroys the environment and the traditional way of life of the tundra people. As in the other biomes we have studied, the local, **indigenous** people, such as the Inuit, are losing their knowledge, skills and lands.

TEACHING NOTES

Explaining the impact of an economic activity in a chosen area and beyond is CfE Level 4 work.

TEACHING NOTES

Identifying at least three threats facing main climate zones and analysing how these threats impact on the way of life is CfE Level 4 work.

Oil extraction at Prudhoe Bay; and caribou herd

This huge ship is an oil tanker. Ships like this are used to transport oil around the world.

Case study 1 – oil in Alaska

One of the most famous discoveries of oil was in Alaska in 1963. The largest oilfield in North America was discovered at Prudhoe Bay on Alaska's northern coastline.

The trouble with Prudhoe Bay is that it is an area where the sea remains frozen for at least 10 months of the year. There is no way that tankers could sail into this area to collect oil. However, in the south of Alaska there is a port called Valdez, which never freezes thanks to a warm ocean current.

Location of Prudhoe Bay and Valdez in Alaska

The problem was how to get the oil from Prudhoe Bay to tankers at Valdez. The obvious answer was to build a pipeline. However, this was not as straightforward to do in Alaska as it is in other parts of the world!

Diagram 9 – Trans-Alaska Pipeline System (TAPS) features

In addition, any work to get at resources in the tundra faces huge problems thanks to fierce blizzards, temperatures below –50°C, total darkness in winter months and **isolation** from the outside world.

Buildings and structures, like the pipeline, have to be built on stilts to stop heat escaping from their foundations into the ground, since this would melt the permafrost, making the building collapse. Roads also have to be raised up on gravel beds to stop them sinking in the summer muskeg.

Building on stilts

Conservationists (people who want to protect the environment) were totally against the construction of the pipeline, but, despite protests, construction went ahead.

The Trans-Alaska Pipeline System (TAPS) has its very own website. Find the link to it in the Homework Helpers to find out more.

Exxon Valdez disaster

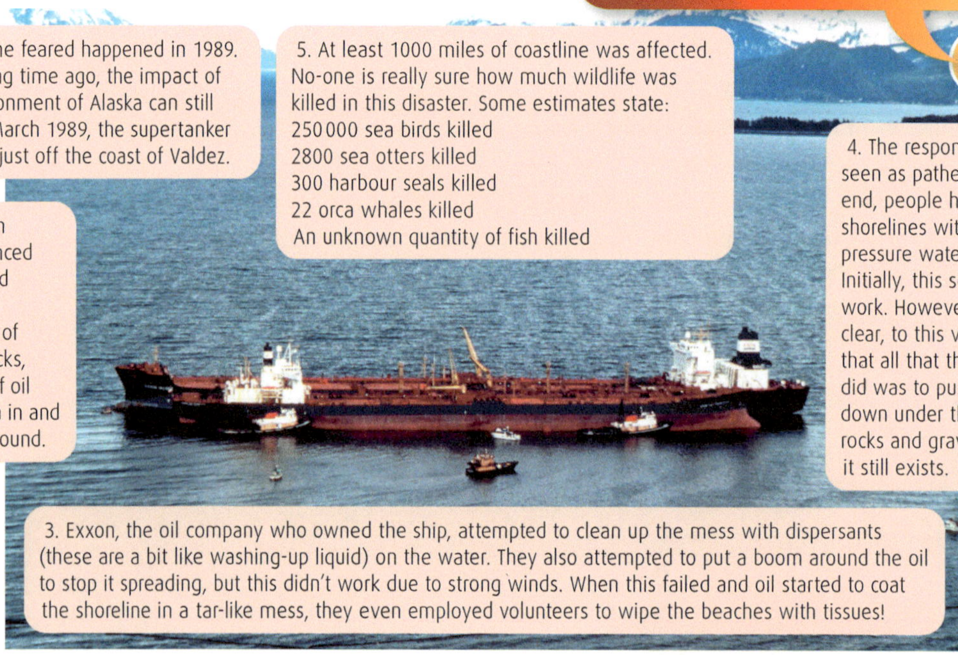

Diagram 10 – The *Exxon Valdez* oil disaster

There are many links and film clips on the Exxon Valdez disaster to investigate in the Homework Helpers.

The effects of the *Exxon Valdez* disaster

Oil in Alaska today

Today, the oil supplies at Prudhoe Bay are running out. However, oil companies have found another area of Alaska where there are at least 10 billion barrels of oil, and where it would be easy to reach. The problem is that it is in the **Arctic National Wildlife Refuge** (ANWR). At present, the main indigenous group of people living here are called the Vuntut Gwitchin. They hunt caribou and live a traditional life. The area is also home to very rare wildlife, such as grizzly bears, wolves and many different species of bird. Oil companies have so far been blocked from going into the area by the US Government. However, this may change in the near future. Should this be allowed to happen?

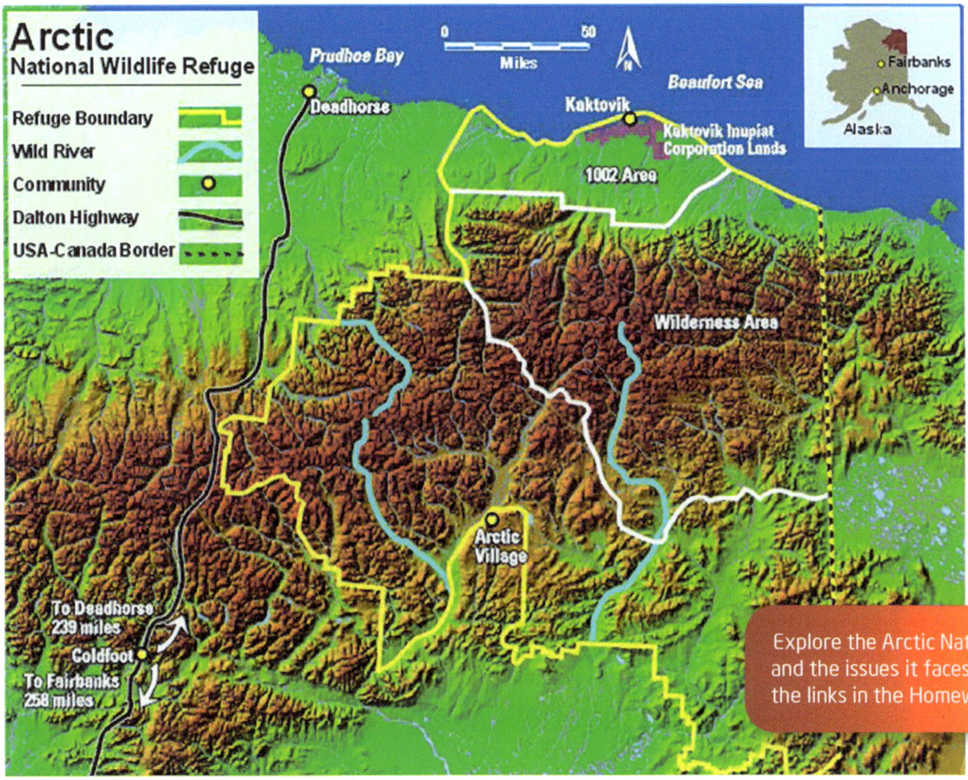

Area of the Arctic National Wildlife Refuge

Explore the Arctic National Wildlife Refuge and the issues it faces further, by following the links in the Homework Helpers.

Arctic National Wildlife Refuge

Arctic village – home to the Vuntut Gwitchin

Classroom challenge

There is a map template in the Teaching Notes to help with this.

1. Make your own map of Alaska like the one below, showing where the Trans-Alaska Pipeline System is located. Complete it by adding colour and the missing labels from the box below.

BROOKS RANGE	CANADA	BERING STRAIT	ANCHORAGE
PRUDHOE BAY	ALASKA RANGE	RUSSIA	VALDEZ

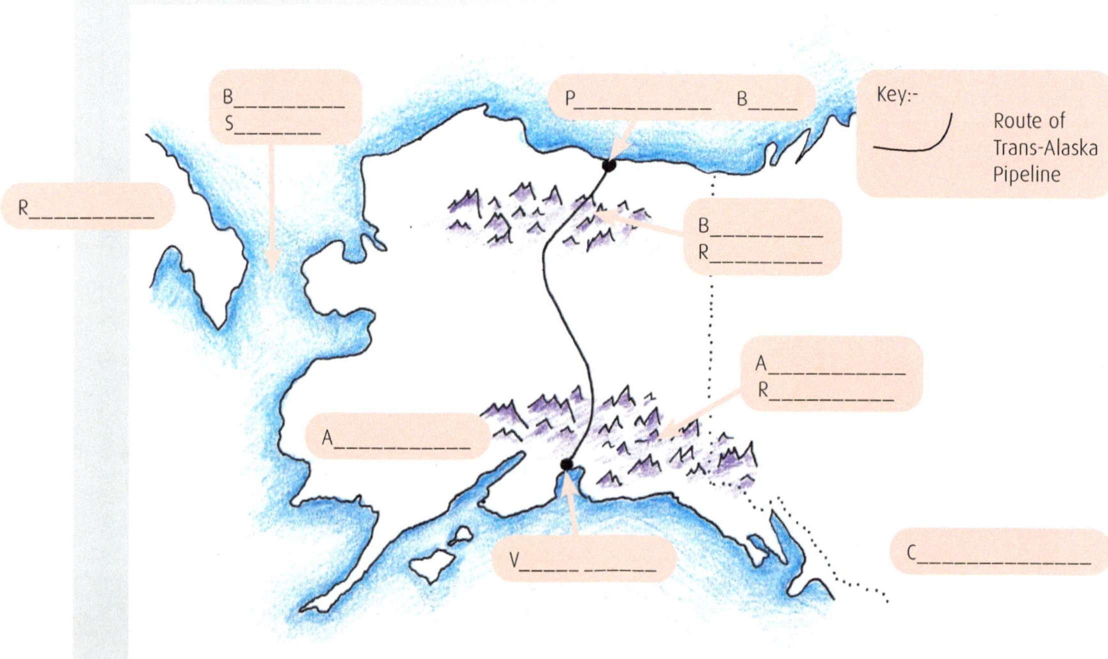

Map of Alaska and the Trans-Alaska Pipeline System

2. The sentences below about the features of the Trans-Alaska Pipeline System have become mixed up. Unscramble them and write them out correctly in your workbook.

Fibre glass...........................so that caribou herd can run underneath.

On stilts...............................to help it slide in an earthquake.

Encased in concrete..........to keep it up above the permafrost so it won't melt.

Raised up in areas..............to keep the oil warm.

On support beams.............under rivers.

3. Study Diagram 10 on page 140 on the *Exxon Valdez* disaster. Now make a flow diagram, like the one below, detailing the events as they happened, in your own words.

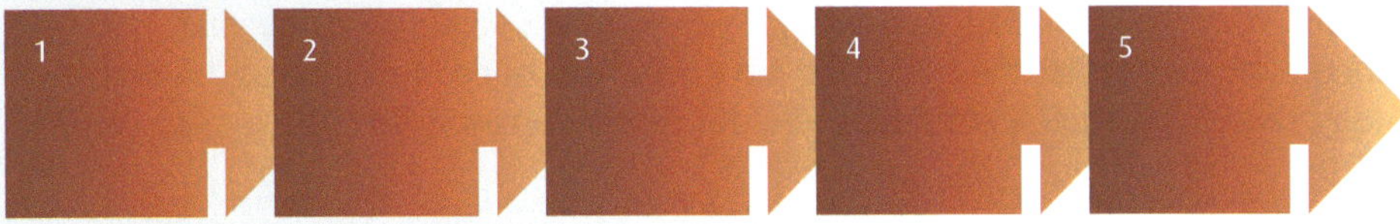

4. In which other area in Alaska have oil companies found 10 billion barrels of oil?

STRETCH YOURSELF

5. Do you think oil companies should go into this area to get oil? Give at least three well-**explained** reasons why (or why not). This involves using **evaluation** skills to make your judgement.

TEACHING NOTES

There are film clips and links to websites in the Teaching Notes to help with this.

TEACHING NOTES

Explaining the impact of an economic activity in a chosen area and beyond is CfE Level 4 work.

Tourism

Case study 2 – Tourism in the tundra

Tundra areas are becoming increasingly popular tourist destinations, especially places such as Alaska! This may seem strange to people in the UK, as we tend to like holidays in the sun and heat. However, wouldn't you like the opportunity to see glaciers, go skiing, climb mountains, go dog-sledding, ride a snowmobile, and watch sea otters, whales, polar bears, seals and other wildlife? Plenty of people do. In fact, Alaska records almost 2 million visitors every year.

Tourists snowmobiling in the tundra. Would you like to do this?

Tourism benefits

However, once again, tourism brings benefits and problems. One in every eight jobs in Alaska is to do with tourism. It brings in more than $1.8 billion every year to the economy. It means that the local Inuit have been introduced to a modern life with shops, schools and medical centres, and they live in houses with triple glazing, central heating and hot water.

Anchorage, Alaska – a modern settlement

Iqaluit town – a modern Inuit settlement in northern Canada

Tourism problems

However, the traditional skills, knowledge and lifestyle of the tundra people, that were in tune with the environment, are dying out. The people of the tundra have also been introduced to some of the less healthy aspects of modern life, such as alcohol and drugs. In fact, alcoholism among the tundra population is now a big problem. In addition, some tourists seek out the ultimate holiday photo by leaving out bait for grizzly or polar bears to come close to them. This brings obvious dangers. Other people also pay a lot of money so that they can hunt and kill wildlife in Alaska.

Tourists want to take selfies with polar bears and their young.

Ecotourism

Organisations such as the World Wildlife Fund have now become involved due to the increasing number of people arriving in the fragile tundra environment. They promote ecotourism (remember, this means activities are **sustainable** by not damaging the local area, thus preserving it for the future) and have issued a code of conduct for tour operators. This code includes the list in Diagram 11 on the next page.

Ten Principles for Arctic Tourism

1. Make tourism a part of looking after the environment.
2. Support protecting the wilderness.
3. Use natural resources in a sustainable way.
4. Make very little waste and pollution.
5. Respect local cultures.
6. Respect historic and scientific sites.
7. Arctic communities should benefit from tourism.
8. Trained staff are the key to responsible tourism.
9. Make your trip an opportunity to learn about the Arctic.
10. Follow safety rules.

Diagram 11 – Ecotourism in the Arctic

Classroom challenge

1. How many tourists visit Alaska every year?

STRETCH YOURSELF

2. Tourism brings benefits and problems.
   (a) Complete the table below with at least three benefits and three problems.

Tourism in the tundra: benefits	Tourism in the tundra: problems

   (b) Now, decide if you think tourists should go to the tundra. Give reasons for your decision. Remember, this means using your **evaluation** skills.

TEACHING NOTES

Explaining the impact of an economic activity in a chosen area and beyond is CfE Level 4 work.

3. Study Diagram 11 on page 145 and read the section on ecotourism to play 'Ecotourism Blockbusters'! The aim of this game is to get from one side of this puzzle to the other by saying what the initial in each 'block' stands for.

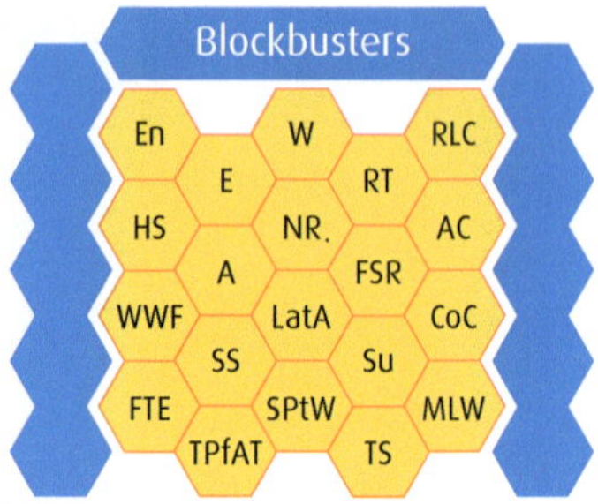

Clues!

En – What needs to be protected.	WWF – Organisation involved in Arctic tourism.
E – Tourism that does not damage the tundra.	SS – These need to be respected.
W – Make very little of this.	LatA – What you are doing just now
RT – Trained staff are the key to this.	Su – When things are preserved for the future
RLC – We should be considerate towards this.	CoC – Issued to tour operators.
HS – Be considerate of areas from the past.	FTE – Under threat from tourism.
A – The region.	TPfAT – What all tourists should follow.
NR – Use these sustainably.	SPtW – What we should all do in the tundra.
FSR – Avoid danger.	TS – These should take care of tourists.
AC – These should benefit from tourism.	MLW – Don't leave anything behind.

Answers

En – Environment E – Ecotourism W –Waste RT – Responsible Tourism RLC – Respect Local Cultures HS – Historic Sites A – Arctic NR – Natural Resources FSR – Follow Safety Rules AC – Arctic Communities WWF –World Wildlife Fund SS - Scientific Sites LatA – Learn about the Arctic Su – Sustainable CoC – Code of Conduct FTE – Fragile Tundra Environment TPfAT – Ten Principles for Arctic Tourism SPtW – Support Protecting the Wilderness TS – Trained Staff MLW – Make Little Waste

Go Digital!

4. Type in http://arctickingdom.com/ on a tablet, mobile device or computer, or follow the link provided in the Homework Helpers. Once into the site, click on the three-line menu in the top left corner. Click on 'See Our Trips'.
   (a) Choose a trip that you would like to go on – there are two pages to select from. Click on the trip link.
   Look at the 'Trip itinerary' and list the things you will do in your workbook.
   (b) How many people will be allowed in your group?
   (c) What are the average temperatures for your trip?
   (d) How many hours of daylight will there be?
   (e) What will your transport be?
   (f) How much will your trip cost?
5. Now, go back to the home page and click on the three-line menu button again. Click on 'Values and sustainability'.
   (a) What sizes of groups are allowed to travel to the Arctic?
   (b) What do travel groups do with their waste and water?
   (c) What are the rules with drugs and alcohol?
   (d) How does this tour company make sure Arctic communities get something back?
   (**Hint** – what charities do they support?)

STRETCH YOURSELF

6. Now, imagine you actually work for an Arctic travel company. Your job is to market (get people to buy) a holiday to the tundra. Create a leaflet that tells people all about the trip you have selected in Question 4. Make it bright and colourful with lots of pictures that would make people really want to buy this holiday. You may wish to do this digitally using Publisher or another suitable app.
   Don't forget to tell people that this is ecotourism and should not damage the environment!
   Make sure your trip follows the code of conduct listed in Diagram 11 on page 145.

TEACHING NOTES

Contributing to a discussion on the development of sustainable systems is CfE Level 4 work.

STRETCH YOURSELF

The future for the tundra

Unfortunately, for the tundra and the Arctic area as a whole, global warming is having a big impact. Sea ice in the area is melting. This could make sea levels rise around the world.
My hunting areas are changing because I like to go out onto the sea ice to catch seals. I now have to swim much bigger distances to do this because the ice has melted. This is exhausting, and many of my fellow polar bears have been found drowned.

Polar bear exhausted after swimming long distances

Arctic ice is melting!

Have you enjoyed learning about the tundra? Would you like a career that uses the knowledge and skills you have gained from this topic? Why not visit the 'My World of Work/ STEM/Developing the Young Workforce' section of the Homework Helpers to find out more?

TEACHING NOTES

Suggesting the impact and possible outcomes of climate change on a chosen region and proposing reasoned strategies to slow or reverse the impact is CfE Level 4 work.

EMPTY-LANDS BIOMES

COMPARING AND CONTRASTING EMPTY-LANDS BIOMES

I can investigate the climate, physical features and living things of a natural environment different from my own and explain their interrelationship. SOC 3-10a

By comparing settlement and economic activity in two contrasting landscapes. I can reach conclusions about how landscapes influence human activity. I can explain my findings clearly to others. SOC 3-13a

Benchmarks

- Describes a natural environment different to their own, in terms of climate, physical features and living things.
- Provides a simple explanation of at least three links between climate, physical features and living things in that environment.
- Provides at least two explanations as to how landscapes influence human activity, using two contrasting areas.

Classroom challenge

You have now learned a lot about three of the world's great biomes. Use this knowledge to complete this Venn diagram. Work in pairs to help each other complete this.

In each circle, select words and phrases from the word box which describe that biome. If it is a word or phrase that is shared between two biomes, write it in the appropriate overlapping area. If it is a word or phrase that all three biomes share, write it in the middle of the diagram.

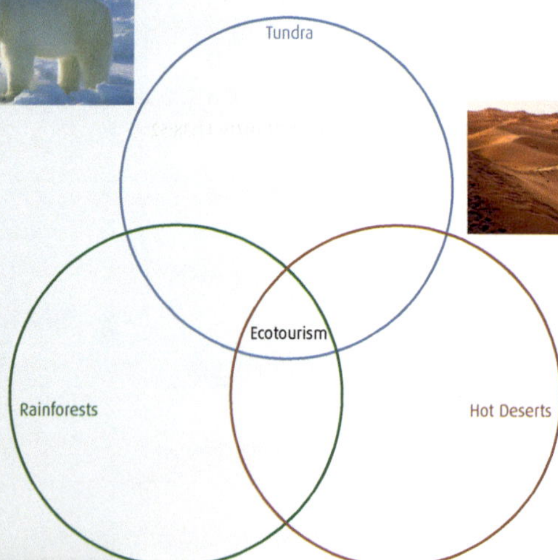

Word/Phrase Box Ecotourism Humid On the Equator Traditional life threatened Hot Nomads Mushroom rocks Cold Pingos Yanomami Animals endangered Inuit Canopy Muskeg Sparsely populated Desert Oil Mosquitoes Dry Oasis Fennec fox Environment threatened Between 65 and 70° north Affected by global warming Deforestation Dune bashing Permafrost On Tropics of Cancer and Capricorn Tuareg Sloths Wadis Convection rain Flash floods Land of the midnight sun Camels Biome Lichens Sandstorm Frost

Produce a large poster that compares two empty-lands biomes. You can choose which biomes you want to compare from rainforests, hot deserts or tundra. You should use the layout below to help you design your poster. Be creative and make it bright, interesting and informative. Add in any extra diagrams, graphs, sketches, maps or pictures that you think would give more information about your two biomes.

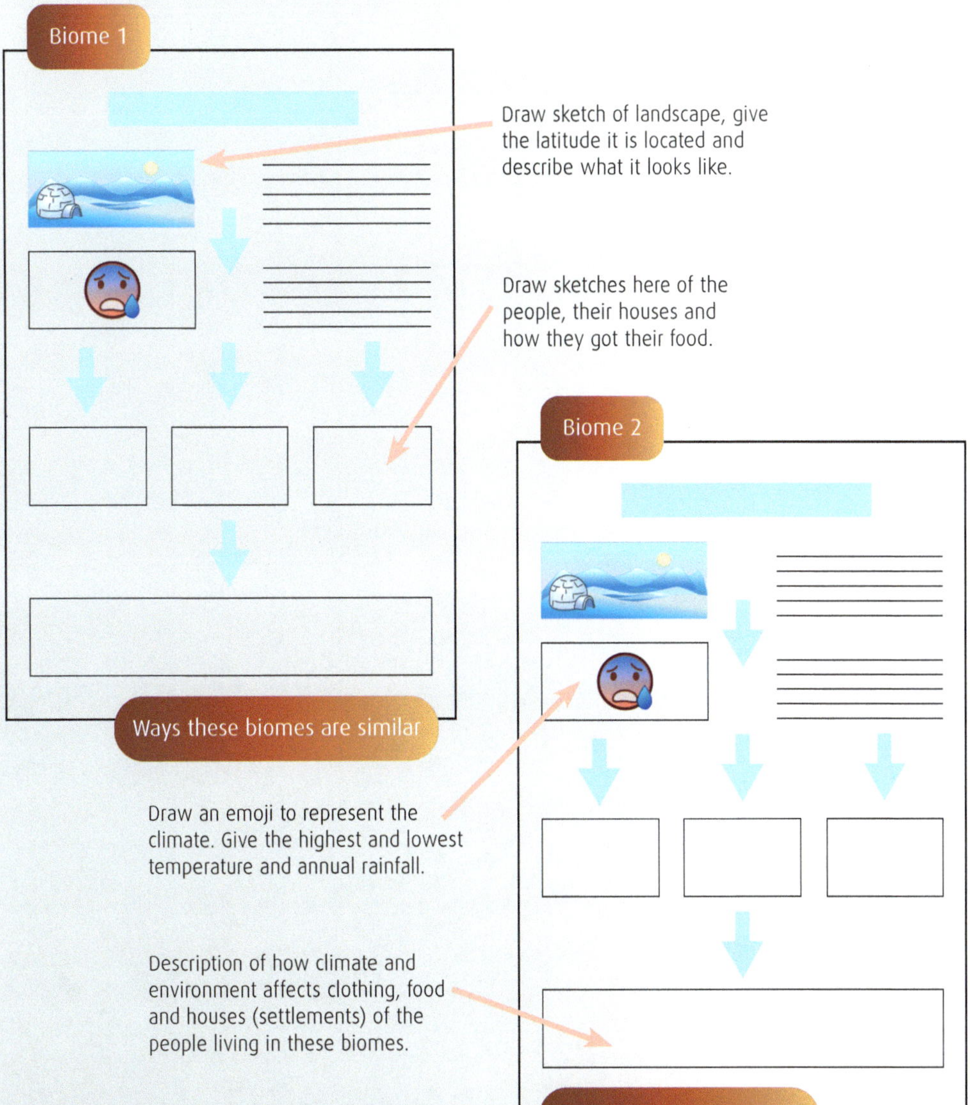

Now state at least two ways these biomes are similar and two ways in which they are different.

WEATHER

Wonderfully weird weather!

WEATHER

I can investigate the relationship between climate and weather and be able to understand the causes of weather patterns within a selected climate zone. SOC 3 - 12a

Benchmarks

- Demonstrates a basic understanding of the relationship between weather and climate.

What's coming up?

- What is the difference between weather and climate?
- What are the weather elements?
- The 'Beast from the East'.
- How do we measure the weather?
- Where should we site a weather station?
- Forecasting the weather using nature.

WHAT IS THE DIFFERENCE BETWEEN WEATHER AND CLIMATE?

In our Empty Lands unit, we learned a lot about the different climates of rainforests, hot deserts and the tundra.

Remember, though, that climate is not the same as weather!

The **weather** is what happens from day to day and has elements that you can measure, such as temperature and rainfall.

The **climate** is the average weather for a place over a long period. For example, we would say that a hot desert's climate is hot and dry.

Classroom challenge

Can you tell the difference between weather and climate?

1. Copy the sentences below into your workbook and, after each one, write in the brackets if the statement is about weather or climate. The first one has been done for you.

> Today, in London it was wet and windy. (**weather**)
> Tomorrow, I hope it is going to be hot and sunny. ( )
> At the Equator, it is hot all year round. ( )
> On holiday in Blackpool, it was sunny all week. ( )
> At the North Pole, it is usually cold and dry. ( )
> School closed yesterday because there was too much snow. ( )

2. There is a saying in Scotland that 'If you don't like the weather – wait a minute'. **Explain** what you think this means.
3. How would you **describe** the climate of Scotland?
4. What would you like the weather to be like tomorrow where you live? **Explain** why.
5. What is the weather like where you are now? Have a look out of the window and try to think of four descriptive weather words to put into the table below.

Four weather words for today

6. **Explain**, in your own words, what the difference is between weather and climate.

What are the weather elements?

Floods, droughts, the 'Beast from the East', or just hot, sunny afternoons – there aren't many days that go by without the weather being in the headlines. This is very much part of the British way of life. We talk about weather all the time and even like to blame it when things go wrong!

However, there is a serious side to the weather. It can actually kill. Events such as thunderstorms, tornadoes, hurricanes and blizzards can all lead to people losing their lives. For some people, the weather has an impact on their work and even on their safety, such as farmers, pilots, fishermen and builders. That is why it is important that we get weather forecasts right.

The 'Beast from the East' – February 2018

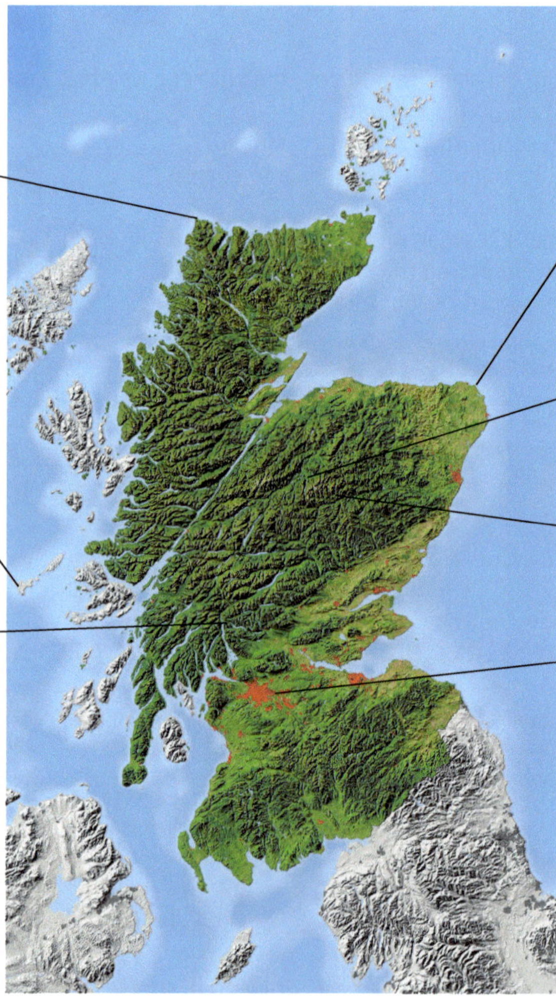

Diagram 1 – Scotland's weather extremes

There are great, entertaining links to help you understand weather and climate on the Bright Red website: just visit www.brightredpublishing.co.uk and download the Homework Helpers bundle.

Classroom challenge

1. The beginnings and endings of the sentences below have been mixed up. Match them up correctly and copy them into your workbook.

Worker	How their job is affected by the weather
Fishermen	...may have their crops destroyed in storms, or animals could get stuck in snow.
Builders	...may have their plane struck by lightning, and it could crash.
Pilots	...may be hit by storms and winds at sea, and their boat sinks.
Farmers	...may be blown off scaffolding in strong winds.

Sheep farm in the snow

Fishing boat in a storm

2. Study Diagram 1 on page 154 showing the weather extremes of Scotland. Answer the following questions in sentences in your workbook.
   (a) Which royal town holds the record for the lowest Scottish temperature on record, and what was that temperature?
   (b) Which west-coast island holds the record for the most sunshine in one month, and how many hours was it?
   (c) How many miles per hour was the strongest gust of wind at low level, and where was it recorded?
   (d) Which town near Glasgow recorded the highest temperature, and how hot did it get?
   (e) Where was the highest amount of rainfall in one day recorded, and how wet did it get?
   (f) Where was the strongest gust of wind at high level recorded, and what was the strength of this gust?
3. The weather is made up of elements that we can measure using instruments. These elements are listed below, but the letters are mixed up. Unscramble them and write them out in your workbook.

SCUDLO ____________
RIA REPESURS ___ ____________
NLARILAF ________________
NUSINESH __________________
TEREMRPTEAU _______________
YILTSIVIBI ________________
INDW SDEPE NDA CRENITODI __________ __________
______ ______________

4. Now, try to match up the seven weather elements above with the correct definitions.

_________________ = The weight of the air pushing down on us.
_________________ = How clear or foggy it is.
_________________ = All the moisture that lands on the ground.
_________________ = The direct heat from the sun's rays.
_________________ = A measure of how hot or cold it is.
_________________ = The movement of air.
_________________ = Tiny water droplets high up in the sky.

How the weather affects us – dressing for the weather

5. The images above show clothing advice given in the USA for cold weather. Produce your own unique Scottish clothing advice images for the weather experienced at Motherwell, Sloy and Braemar in Diagram 1 on page 154. Put a Scottish slant on your ideas!

The 'Beast from the East'

Schoolchildren enjoying a day off

Blizzards in Edinburgh

The weather can have a huge impact on our lives. At the end of February and the start of March 2018, Great Britain and Ireland were hit by unusually cold temperatures and vicious snow blizzards, when freezing conditions swept across from Russia. Weather systems such as this are nicknamed; this one was called the 'Beast from the East'. Conditions were so bad that the Met Office was forced to issue a 'Red Weather Warning'.

Use the links in the Homework Helpers to investigate what happened during the 'Beast from the East 2018' and what UK Met Office Weather Warnings mean.

50p

Weather World

1 March 2018

The Beast from the East causes Weather Chaos!

Scotland ground to a halt as the first-ever Red Weather Warning for snow was issued. Schools, government offices and courts shut down, and thousands of employees were sent home.

Train and bus travel services were axed, with ScotRail cancelling all services in the Red Weather Warning area. Flights have also been cancelled.

Drifting snow caused chaos on the roads, with closures or traffic grinding to a standstill on the M8 and Edinburgh City Bypass. Hundreds of people were trapped overnight in their cars on the M80, with local people having to bring food to them. Delivery lorries were also unable to get supplies to shops.

Drifting snow and the severe wind chill meant that temperatures felt like –10°C for much of the day.

Drifting snow - Kirkcowan

Tractor clearing snowdrift on road

More Beast from the East stories inside!

Diagram 2 – The 'Beast from the East' news!

Met Office Red Warning

Dangerous weather is expected and, if you haven't already done so, you should take action now to keep yourself and others safe from the impact of the severe weather. It is very likely that there will be a risk to life, with substantial disruption to travel and energy supplies, and possibly widespread damage to property and infrastructure. You should avoid travelling, where possible, and follow the advice of the emergency services and local authorities.

Diagram 3 – Empty shelves in a Hamilton supermarket

@shoppingnightmare

By the way, don't bother heading to your local supermarket as the shelves have been cleaned out! Selfish people stockpiling again! #beastfromtheeast #nobread

2nd March 2018   1,000 Retweets   20 Likes

Classroom challenge

1. Read the paragraph on the 'Beast from the East' and study Diagram 2 on page 157. Complete these 'Pointless' clues to find the correct answer. Use the initials in brackets to help you.

These were closed, along with Government offices and courts. (S)

The country these weather conditions came from. (R)

The reason bus and rail services were axed. (RWW)

This caused chaos on the roads. (DS)

These were unable to get to shops. (DL)

This made the temperature feel like –10°C. (WC)

This is likely during a Red Weather Warning. (RtL)

Advice given to people during a Red Weather Warning. (AT)

People should follow the advice of these. (ES and LA)

2. Study Diagram 3 on page 157 and the Twitter feed.
Explain two reasons why the supermarket shelves ended up empty.
3. **Describe** up to five ways in which the 'Beast from the East' affected you. Write them in your workbook as a Twitter feed. Use the template below to help you organise this.

Your own title photo/image
Your profile picture

Title of Twitter Account – for example - Beastly News!
@name of handle? - @beastblitz?
Number ?? Following ?? Followers

Now tweet how the Beast from the East affected you up to five times.
Add # hashtags at the end of each tweet. #noschoolyes!
You can add comments, number of retweets and loves.

HOW DO WE MEASURE THE WEATHER?

We have now found out that there are different elements of the weather that we can measure. We need to use special instruments for this.

Measuring temperature

In science, you might have used a thermometer to measure temperature. For weather, we need to use a very special type of instrument called a **maximum–minimum thermometer**. It measures temperatures in **degrees Celsius** (°C).

Maximum–minimum thermometers are put in a special box called a Stevenson screen so that they can measure air temperature accurately.

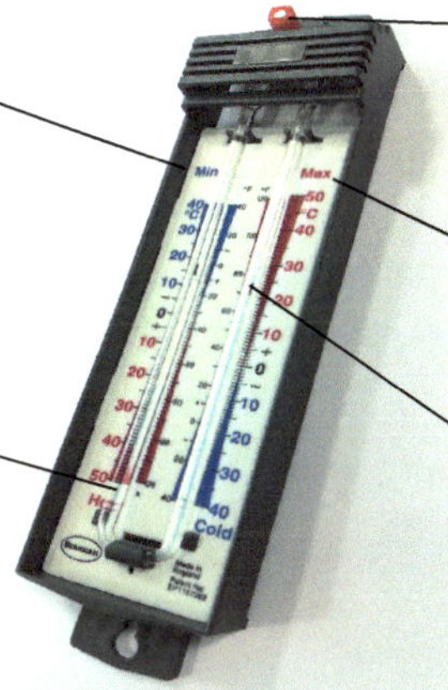

Diagram 4 – Maximum–minimum thermometer

Measuring precipitation

Precipitation, as we have already found out in our Empty Lands unit, is anything that falls from the sky. This includes rain, hail, sleet and snow. To measure these on a daily basis, we use a **rain gauge**.

This is basically a collecting bottle with a funnel on the top of it. However, because it has to be outside all the time in a weather station, it needs to be carefully placed to make sure accurate measurements can be collected from it. The rain gauge measures precipitation in **millimetres**.

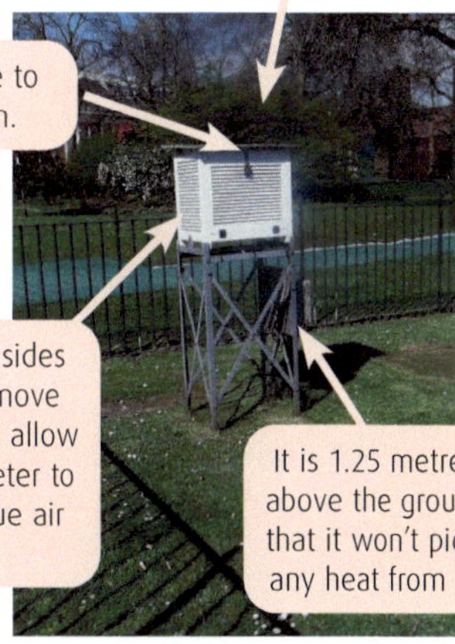

Diagram 5 – Stevenson screen – the perfect place for a maximum minimum thermometer

Diagram 6 – Measuring precipitation with a rain gauge

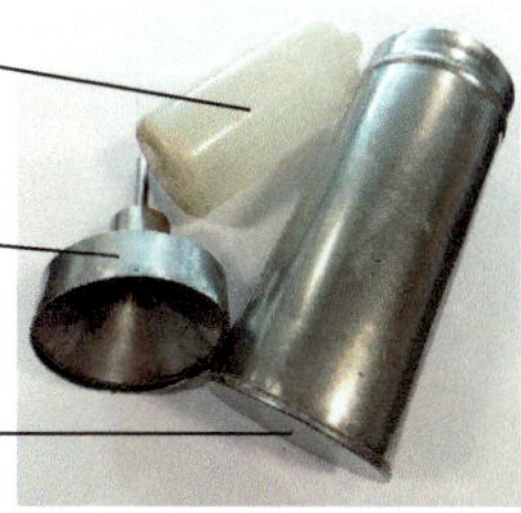

Rain guage

Measuring wind

Measuring wind speed

To measure wind speed, we use a special instrument called an **anemometer**. This has three hollow cups on it. When wind blows into them, they start to spin round. The speed at which they spin is recorded on a speedometer underneath the cups. The stronger the wind, the faster the cups will spin.

The unit we measure wind speed in can be a bit confusing. On British weather forecasts, we talk about wind speed in miles per hour. However, the normal unit of measurement of wind speed is **knots**.

DON'T FORGET

In the UK, the wind mostly comes from the south-west. We call this the **prevailing wind**.

Diagram 7 – Measuring wind speed with an anemometer

Measuring wind direction

In Diagram 7 above, we can clearly see an instrument called a **wind vane** next to the anemometer. This instrument measures wind direction. You may well have seen one before, on the roof of a building. Wind vanes measure wind direction using **compass points**.

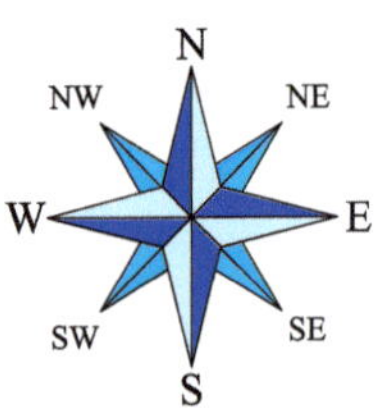

Compass points

Wind vane in a weather station

Wind vane on a roof

When we keep a weather record of wind direction, we use a special graph called a wind rose.

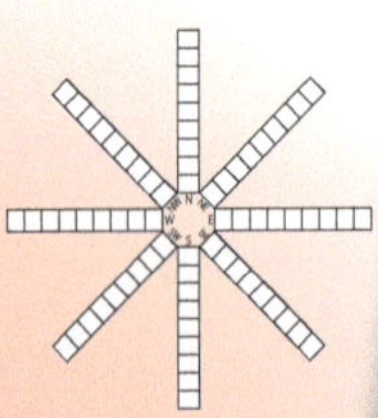

Wind rose

There are some fantastic links, activities and film clips in the Homework Helpers detailing how to measure the weather and even on how to make and set up your own weather station.

Classroom challenge

1. Copy the table below into your workbook. Use the information you have just read through to help you complete this table.

Name of instrument	What it measures	What unit it measures in	Where it should be placed
	Precipitation		
			In a Stevenson screen
Anemometer			
		Compass directions	

2. Read the sentences below. Some are true, while others are false. Write out only the true sentences in your workbook.

* We read temperatures on a maximum–minimum thermometer from the top of the metal marker.
* We use a magnet to reset a maximum–minimum thermometer.
* A wind vane measures wind direction.
* A rain gauge should be placed under trees.
* A rain gauge should have grass around it because raindrops will not bounce and splash up into it, making the reading too high.
* A wind vane measures wind speed.
* An anemometer needs to be placed on top of a 10-metre-high pole to catch the wind.
* A wind vane uses knots as a measurement.
* A maximum–minimum thermometer measures air temperature.
* A wind vane measures precipitation.
* An anemometer measures air temperature.
* An anemometer measures wind speed.

3. (a) In your class, keep a record of the wind direction measured at your school for two weeks. If you don't have a wind vane, don't worry. You can get the information from weather apps on your phone, your local airport website or the Met Office website. Complete a wind rose of your results.
   (b) When you have completed your wind rose, **describe** and **explain** what it tells you about wind direction in your area. For example, where did the wind come from most of the time? Why did this happen?
4. Make your own sketch of a Stevenson screen in your workbook. Complete it by adding labels, and, in your own words, describe how it is adapted to measure air temperature.

TEACHING NOTES

There is a template and instructions to help with this in the Teaching Notes.

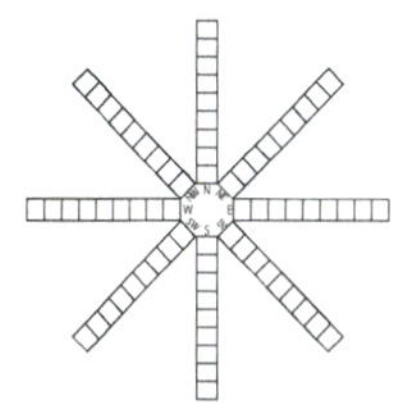

Stevenson screen

Measuring air pressure

Air pressure is the weight of the atmosphere pushing down on us. Apparently, the weight of the atmosphere pushing down on each square kilometre of land is the equivalent of two large elephants!

STRETCH YOURSELF

If there is less weight in the atmosphere above us, it is called **low pressure**. If there is more weight in the atmosphere above us, it is called **high pressure**. We can use pressure readings to help us forecast the weather. Low pressure usually brings us wind and rain. High pressure will bring us clear skies and sunshine.

TEACHING NOTES

Explaining links between weather and air pressure is CfE Level 4 work.

The instrument used to measure air pressure is called a **barometer.** As Diagram 8 below shows, this looks a bit like a clock – and you may even have one of these hanging on a wall at home. Weather stations use a special type of barometer called a **barograph**. It measures air pressure in **millibars**. Average air pressure at sea level should be 1013.25 millibars (mb).

DON'T FORGET

Did you know that the sun is so huge, one million planet Earths could fit inside it?

If pressure drops below 1013.25 mb, it is low pressure and rain is likely.

If pressure rises above 1013.25mb, it is high pressure and it is likely to be sunny and dry.

Diagram 8 – Barometer

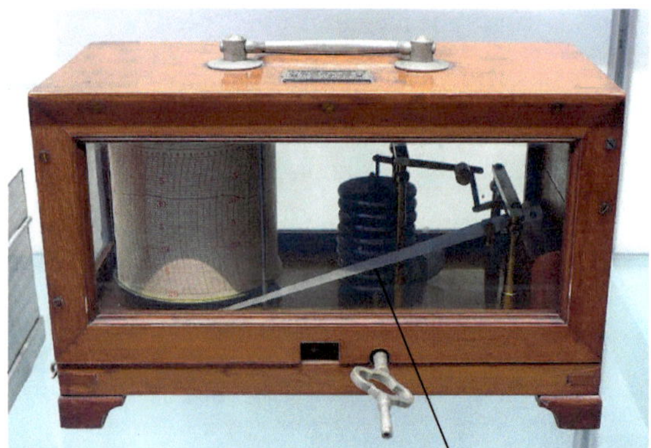

Barograph

In a weather station the barograph is often placed inside the Stevenson screen.

Measuring sunshine

Sunshine is measured using a special piece of equipment called a **sunshine recorder**. It is made up of a stand that sits at an angle, and a very large glass ball. There is a place behind the glass ball to slot a piece of card marked out in **hours**. It must be placed so that it faces south (where the sun is) and away from any buildings and trees that might shade it. When the sun shines, the glass ball magnifies the rays onto the card, causing burn marks. These burn marks can be counted up at the end of the day, and the amount of hours and minutes of sunshine can be recorded.

Burn marks can be counted up to find out how many hours of sunshine there have been.

Sunshine recorder: card with burn marks showing hours of sunlight

Measuring cloud cover

For this weather element, a very special piece of equipment is needed. **Your own eyes**! To do this, you must find somewhere where you can see the whole sky. You must then imagine that the sky is divided up into eight sections (**oktas**). To record cloud cover, you must estimate how much of the sky is covered in clouds. This takes quite a bit of practice! If there are no clouds, it would be 0 oktas. If the whole sky is covered in clouds, it would be 8 oktas.

We mark out our okta measurements in circles as shown in Diagram 9 here.

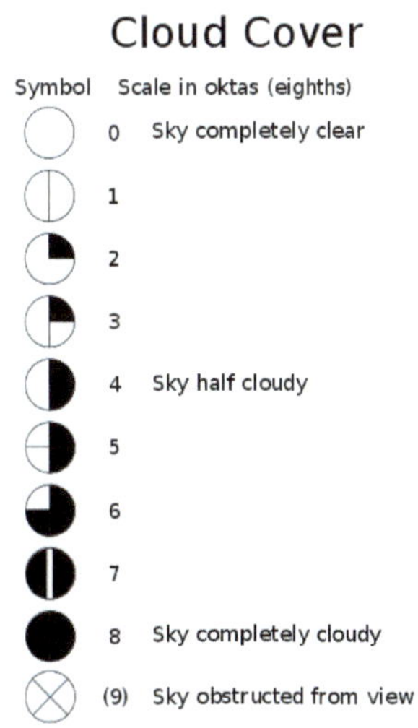

Sky obscured means that you can't see the sky because it is foggy.

Diagram 9 – Okta symbols

8 oktas

4 oktas

Sky obscured

Clouds can also be studied according to cloud type. Diagram 10 below shows how clouds come in all sorts of shapes and sizes and exist at different levels of our atmosphere.

If you see cirrus clouds in a blue sky, it often means it is going to rain!

Thunderclouds

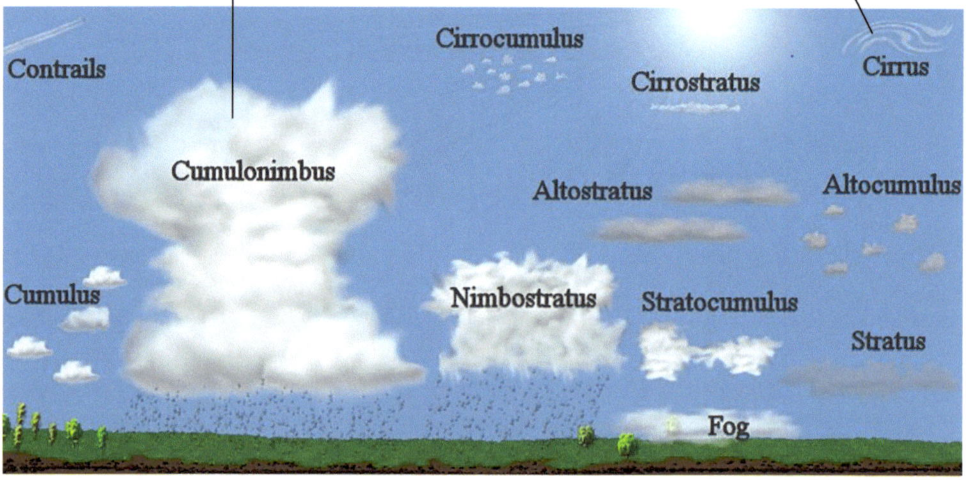

Diagram 10 – Different cloud types in different levels of the atmosphere

Cumulonimbus cloud

Cumulus clouds

Nimbostratus cloud

Classroom challenge

1. Copy the table below into your workbook. Use the information you have just read through to help you complete this table.

Name of instrument	What it measures	What unit it measures in	Where it should be placed
		Millibars	
			In an open space with nothing to block the view of the sky
Sunshine recorder			

STRETCH YOURSELF

2. Study Diagram 8 on page 162 and Diagram 11 below.
   (a) **Describe** what happened to air pressure between Monday 7th and Sunday 13th.

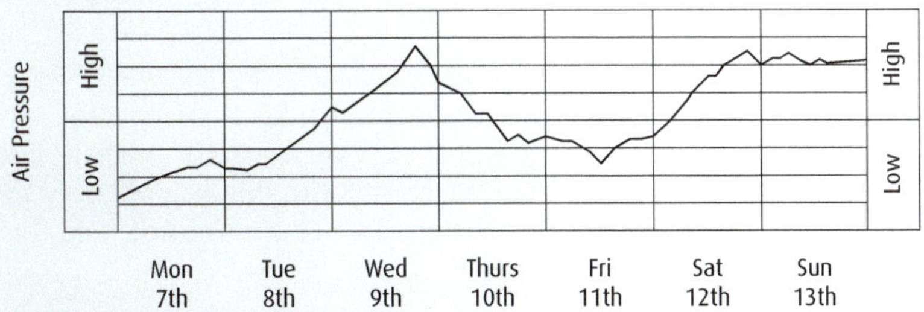

Diagram 11

   (b) **Describe** what the weather would have been like on Monday, and **explain** why.
   (c) **Describe** what the weather would have been like on Wednesday, and **explain** why.
   (d) **Describe** what the weather would have been like on Sunday, and **explain** why.

TEACHING NOTES

Explaining links between weather and air pressure is CfE Level 4 work.

3. **Explain** the reason why a sunshine recorder must face south.
4. Look out of your classroom window. For the area of sky you can see, how many oktas of cloud cover are there? Draw these oktas onto a circle in your workbook using Diagram 9 on page 163 to help you.
5. Again, looking out of your window, can you identify the types of clouds that are in the sky, using Diagram 10 on page 164?
6. Again looking at Diagram 10 on page 164, what name is given to thunderclouds?
7. If you were lying sunbathing in your garden on a lovely summer's day and some cirrus clouds appeared in the sky, what would that mean?
8. How many other words can you make out of **WEATHER INSTRUMENTS**?

Cirrus clouds

Keep a weather diary for the next week. Don't worry, you don't need any fancy weather instruments for this – just use the template in the Homework Helpers!

FORECASTING THE WEATHER

Weather stations

A weather station sounds like it should be something very technical. However, a weather station is simply a collection of weather instruments. As geographers, we must be very careful about where we set up a weather station in order for the instruments to take accurate readings.

Weather station

Classroom challenge

1. Examine the photos on the next page. They are all possible places to locate a weather station. However, we must check carefully that each site is suitable for all the instruments.
   (a) It is your job to select the best site. To help you with this, you will need to complete the 'Site Evaluation Checklist' for each photo. This will help you to develop **evaluation** skills.

Instrument	Suitable location? Y/N	Explain why
Max-min thermometer (Stevenson screen)		
Rain gauge		
Anemometer		
Wind vane		
Sunshine recorder		

Site Evaluation Checklist

Use the link in the Homework Helpers on setting up a weather station to help you with your decision.

Site No. 1

Site No. 2

Site No. 3

(b) Having completed your evaluations, **explain** which site would be the best for a weather station, and clearly give the reasons why.

Now try going around the grounds of your own school looking for the ideal site for a weather station. Use the site evaluation checklist in the Homework Helpers!

Forecasting the weather using nature

Do we really need fancy weather equipment to measure the weather? Apparently, all we need to do is watch animals and they will tell us about weather changes. In fact, there are even some sayings that state that watching animals means we can actually forecast the weather! Often this is dismissed as an 'old wives' tale, but there is some evidence that animals are more likely to react to air-pressure changes than we are.

Diagram 12 – Animals help us forecast the weather

Classroom challenge

1. Here are two weather sayings based on how animals behave:

Now, work with a partner and make up a weather saying for each of the animals in Diagram 12 on page 168.

2. Think of some questions of your own on what you have learned in this Weather unit. Now use these questions to help you make up a weather crossword.

Have you enjoyed learning about the weather? Would you like a career that uses the knowledge and skills you have gained from this topic? Why not visit the 'My World of Work/ STEM/Developing the Young Workforce' section of the Homework Helpers to find out more?

DEVELOPED AND DEVELOPING COUNTRIES

A world of difference

DEVELOPED AND DEVELOPING COUNTRIES

I can compare the social and economic differences between more and less economically developed countries and can discuss the possibilities for reducing these differences.
SOC 3 - 11a

I can use a range of maps and geographical information systems to gather, interpret and present conclusions and can locate a range of features within Scotland, the UK, Europe and the wider world. SOC 3 – 14a

Benchmarks

- Identifies at least three social and economic differences between developed and developing countries, for example infant mortality rate, % adult literacy rate, Gross National Product per capita.
- Suggests possible ways these differences would be reduced, and provides valid opinions as to their likely success.
- Provides at least two explanations as to how landscapes influence human activity, using two contrasting areas.
- Reviews at least two simple graphical sources to interpret information and form a conclusion, for example, a map and a graph.
- Uses relevant numeracy and digital technology skills to interpret at least two sources of data from maps and graphical information systems.
- Locates increasingly complex features such as different physical landscape features and human features on maps of Scotland, the UK, Europe and the wider world, for example, hills, mountains, valleys, population.

What's coming up?

- What do we mean by developed and developing countries?
- How do we know if a country is developed or developing?
- How can we reduce differences between developed and developing countries?
- Where does the world's population live, and why do they live there?
- What population differences are there between developed and developing countries?
- What differences are there in rural life between developed and developing countries?
- What differences are there in urban life between developed and developing countries?
- What differences are there in health between developed and developing countries?

INDICATORS OF DEVELOPMENT

WHAT DO WE MEAN BY DEVELOPED AND DEVELOPING COUNTRIES?

As geographers, it is clear to us that all countries in the world are very different.

We can measure the wealth of a country through studying how developed a country is. However, what does this actually mean?

In general, countries with a high standard of living are classed as **developed**, and countries with a low standard of living are classed as **developing**.

What this generally means is that developed countries are able to provide the people who live in them with basic things such as clean water, **sanitation** (sewage systems), housing, jobs, health care and a reliable supply of food. These are things that we take for granted. Unfortunately, people in the developing world often have no access to these things.

However, we must be very careful not to generalise. There are many rich people in developing countries, and there is poverty to be found in developed countries.

The Favelas in São Paulo, Brazil – people lack basic facilities

This part of Brazil certainly does not look poor!

Copacabana Beach, Rio de Janeiro, Brazil

Where are developed and developing countries?

Diagram 1 below shows us where the developed and developing countries are in the world. It shows that developing countries tend to be **located** in the south, and developed countries in the north.

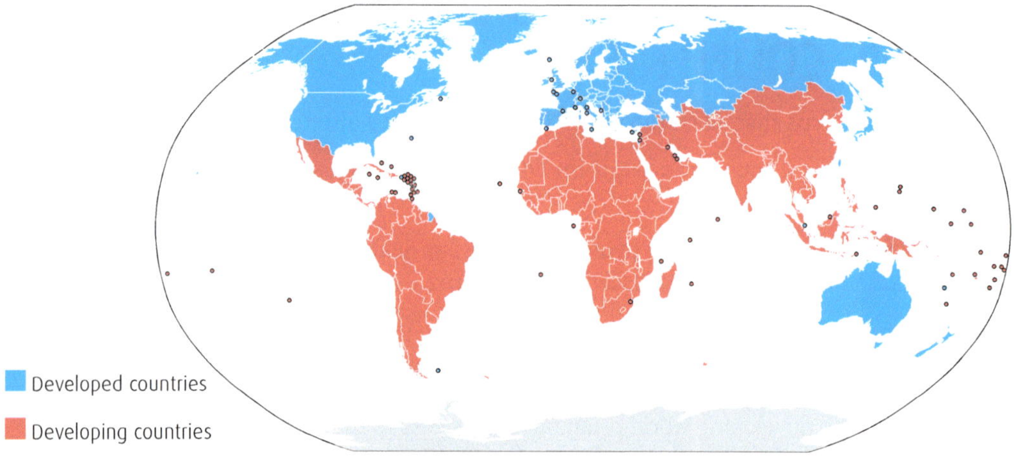

Diagram 1 – Locations of developed and developing countries

Classroom challenge

1. What basic things can developed countries provide for the people living in them? Copy the 'Pointless' phrases below into your workbook, and write the word that the initial at the end stands for.

   - What we eat (F)
   - Sewage systems (S)
   - What we live in (H)
   - What we drink (CW)
   - What we need when we are ill (HC)
   - How we earn money (J)

2. (a) Study Diagram 1 above. Where are most of the developed countries located?
   (b) Name two countries that are in the south of the world but are not developing.
3. You are now going to make up a map of your own to show the differences between developed and developing countries.
   (a) Using a blank world map, take the phrases from the next page and write them in boxes on your map. If it is a phrase about a developed country, it should go in a box in the north. If it is a phrase about a developing country, it should go in a box in the south.

There is a template on the Bright Red website to help with this.

- More than 60% of all Americans are overweight
- Less than half the population are educated in schools
- 80% of the world's total population
- People live, on average, to 64 years old
- 85% of the world's wealth
- These countries use 86% of the world's resources
- These countries waste vast amounts of food every day
- One in four young people are unable to read and write
- Diarrhoea kills around 525 000 children aged under 5 every year
- 6 million children under age 5 die from hunger every year
- These countries eat more than 67% of the world's cereal crops
- Only 12% of the world's spending on health care
- People live, on average, to 79 years old

(b) Using Diagram 1 on page 174, complete your map by colouring developed countries in green and developing countries in red.

4. Copy out the paragraph below into your workbook. Complete it by adding the correct words from the box into the spaces.

> In a developed country, people have a ________ standard of living. They have h________, s__________, j____ and _________ c_____. Developed countries are mostly found in the ______ of the world.
>
> In a developing country, people have a _____ standard of living. As a result, they have less _____ to eat. There is more disease and many children die from _________. There are fewer schools, so many people cannot r_______ and _______. Developing countries are mostly found in the _______ of the world.

DIARRHOEA	HIGH	READ	FOOD	LOW	HEALTH CARE
HOUSES	WRITE	NORTH	JOBS	SOUTH	SCHOOLS

TEACHING NOTES

Try some of the fun activities on the Bright Red website to learn more about developed and developing countries.

HOW DO WE KNOW IF A COUNTRY IS DEVELOPED OR DEVELOPING?

We now know that our world can be divided into developed and developing countries. However, how can we tell if a country is rich or poor? The answer lies in using what are known as **indicators of development**.

One of the most commonly used indicators of development is a measurement called **Gross Domestic Product (GDP).** This is the value of all the goods and services produced in a country in one year, divided by how many people live in the country (**per capita**). It can instantly tell us if a country is developed or developing.

DON'T FORGET

Geographers used to use a measurement called GNP (or gross national product) to decide if a country is developed or developing. However, it is a bit old-fashioned to use this now because it includes in its calculation money earned by a country's residents abroad. GDP just measures the value of everything produced **within** a country and is seen as being more accurate. Developed countries usually have quite a high GDP, and developing countries tend to have a lower GDP.

Countries of the world showing GDP per capita

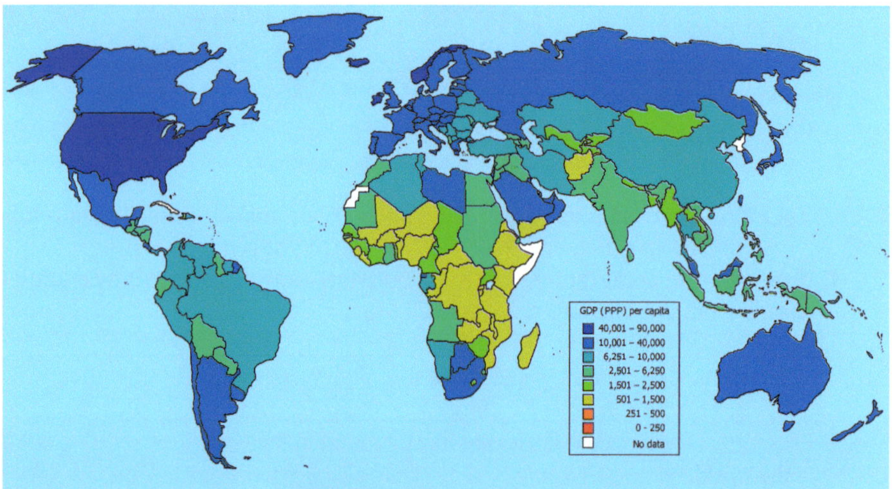

Family house in a country with a high GDP

Family house in a country with a low GDP

Are these images of houses a realistic way to view developed and developing countries?

Use the activities on the Bright Red website to be able to contrast differences in lifestyle and standards of living between rich and poor countries.

However, there are other ways of telling how rich or poor a country is without just looking at money and GDP. We can also look at things such as:

- **literacy** (how many people can read and write)
- **birth rate** (how many babies are born every year in a country)
- **life expectancy** (what age people live to), and
- **infant mortality** (how many babies die in a country in one year)

Table 1 below shows us the differences in indicators of development across four countries.

Country	GDP $ (per capita)	Birth rate per 1000	Infant mortality (death rate) per 1000 live births	Life expectancy (years)	Literacy (% of population)
USA	$59 000	12	6	80	99
Bangladesh	$4200	19	28	73	73
Chad	$634	36	86	51	22
Japan	$42 900	8	2	85	99

Table 1 – Differences in indicators of development between countries

Classroom challenge

1. **Describe** what an indicator of development is.
2. Copy and complete the star diagram to show five ways we can measure if a country is developed or developing.

3. The sentences in the table below have been mixed up. Match up the sentence beginning with the correct ending, and write it out in your workbook.

Beginning	Ending
GDP is......	how many babies are born per 1000 people.
Life expectancy is.........	the earnings of a country divided by the population.
The birth rate is......	the amount of babies who die before age 1.
Literacy is........	how long people are expected to live.
Infant mortality is....	the percentage of adults who can read and write.

4. (a) Use the table below to make up a league table of development for the four countries in Table 1 on page 177. The country that scores the best for each indicator should be given 4 marks. The country with the worst score should be awarded 1. The country with the highest total overall is the most developed. (If there is a draw in any category, give each top country in that category 4 marks, the next country 2 marks, and then 1 mark for the last country.)

DON'T FORGET

Be careful when scoring these, and follow the instructions in the brackets.

Country	GDP (highest figure is best)	Birth rate (lowest figure is best)	Infant mortality (lowest figure is best)	Life expectancy (highest figure is best)	Literacy (highest figure is best)	Overall total
USA						
Bangladesh						
Chad						
Japan						

(b) Which country is the most developed? **Explain** why it has a high score.

(c) Which country is the least developed? **Explain** why it has such a low score.

DON'T FORGET

When answering these questions, try to 'speak like a geographer'. Use the phrases and rules in the table below to score maximum marks in your answer. You should be comparing the countries.

Substantially higher 3 marks	Much higher 2 marks	Higher 1 mark	1 mark – each time a figure from the table is given.
Noticeably lower 3 marks	A lot lower 2 marks	Lower 1 mark	3 marks for saying what the difference is between numbers in the table, for example, birth rate in the USA is ??? lower than Chad.
Identical 3 marks	Equal score 2 marks	The same 1 mark	

(d) Now, work in pairs to mark each other's answers. You should award the scores in the table above each time you see that phrase or make use of the number rules. The more you use these phrases and numbers, and compare countries, the higher your score will be!

5. In a group, make your own 'Developed/Developing World' Top Trumps game. Use this template and list of rules on the next page to help you.

TEACHING NOTES

Follow the link to the CIA World Factbook on the Bright Red website for more data.

Name of country

Flag

Sketch or phrases of things this country is famous for, such as food, landmarks, people, footballers etc.

Population	
GDP per Capita (PPP)	
Life Expectancy	
Death Rate per 1000	
Birth Rate per 1000	

Top Trumps Rules!

1. Usually there are 30 to 32 cards in this game.
2. Deal out all the cards face down to the players.
3. Person to the left of the dealer starts.
4. First player looks at their first card (keeping it hidden from the other players). They choose the category they think is the best and read it out. For example, Life Expectancy.
5. Everyone else reads out what their first card has for that category.
6. The person with the highest score wins all the cards from the other players.
7. Whoever won the cards starts the next round.
8. The person who wins all the cards is the overall winner.

Go Digital!

6. Follow the link to the Scottish Index of Multiple Deprivation (SIMD) interactive map on the Bright Red website. This map shows us areas in Scotland that are poorer (multiply deprived and shown in red) and areas that are least deprived (shown in blue).
   (a) **Describe** what this map tells you about wealth in Scotland.
   (b) Find your school postcode on this map. What does it tell you about wealth in the area around your school?
   (c) Having studied the SIMD map of Scotland, do you think this is a fair way to judge how wealthy a country is? Give reasons why.

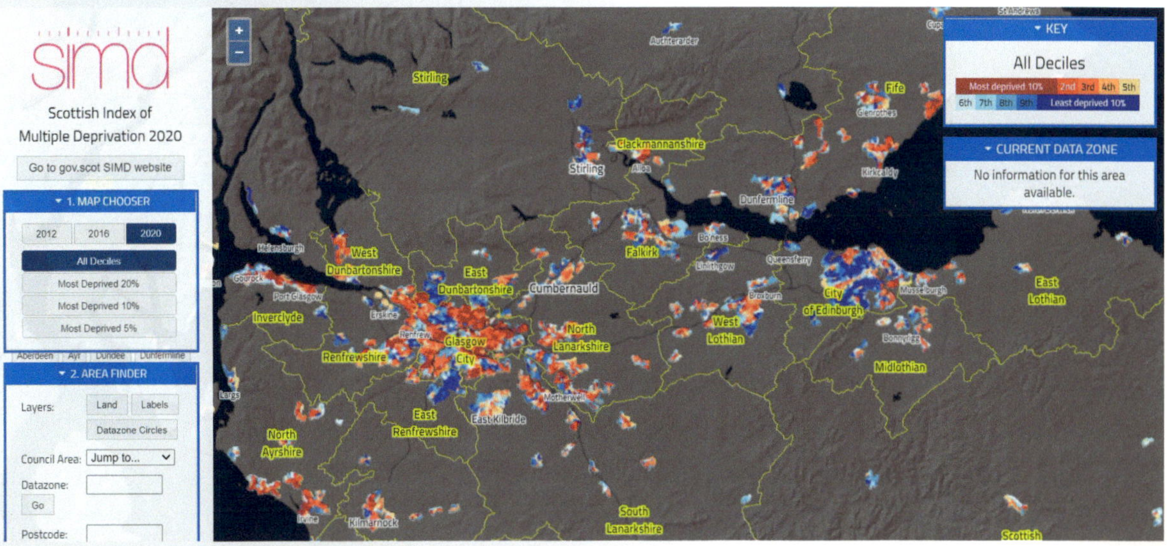

Scottish Index of Multiple Deprivation Map

TEACHING NOTES

Explore developed and developing world themes further with the activities on the Bright Red website.

HOW CAN WE REDUCE DIFFERENCES BETWEEN DEVELOPED AND DEVELOPING COUNTRIES?

The flag of the United Nations

It seems from our learning so far that the world is a very unfair place. There are still many people across our planet who live in extreme poverty and struggle on a day-to-day basis to survive. In an attempt to do something about this, the United Nations (UN) has set a target to end extreme poverty in the world. How can we achieve such an ambitious target?

DON'T FORGET

The UN is an international organisation that brings countries together to talk about and try to agree on world issues.

Sustainable Development Goals

The UN feels that the answer lies with what it calls **Sustainable Development Goals** (SDGs). There are 17 of these. They were launched in 2015 and should all be achieved by the year 2030. The purpose of these goals is not just to end poverty, but also to protect the planet and to allow all people to enjoy peace and prosperity. They are aimed at both developed and developing countries, so we all need to sit up and do something about them. However, the really important thing about these goals is that they are also aimed at young people! This is because it is this generation that holds the key to the future of our planet. That is why it is really important that school students know these SDGs and understand how they are linked. This is sometimes called the 'World's Largest Lesson'. These goals are shown in Diagram 3 below.

Diagram 2 – The five Ps model of sustainable development

The links between these SDGs are shown in Diagram 2 here. This is called the **'5 Ps Model of Sustainable Development'**.

TEACHING NOTES

Go to the Bright Red website to find out more about the 'World's Largest Lesson' and Sustainable Development Goals.

Diagram 3 – The 17 Sustainable Development Goals

Why were the SDGs introduced?

Diagram 4 – Some reasons why the world needs Sustainable Development Goals

Climate-change flooding

Drought in India

n impact on our ocean wildlife and coasts

Classroom challenge

1. How many Sustainable Development Goals are there?
2. **Describe** what these Sustainable Development Goals aim to do.
3. What year should all the SDGs be achieved by?
4. Working in pairs, match up the 17 Sustainable Development Goals with each of the 5 Ps shown below.

People = No Poverty, Zero Hunger etc.

Prosperity =

Peace =

Partnership =

Planet =

5. Redraw the symbols shown on the right, below, in your workbook. Now, match up the goal on the left with the correct symbol.

The SDG icons were modified for the purpose of this exercise.

Goal 1 End poverty
Goal 2 End hunger
Goal 3 Well-being
Goal 4 Quality education
Goal 5 Gender equality
Goal 6 Water and sanitation for all
Goal 7 Affordable and sustainable energy
Goal 8 Decent work for all
Goal 9 Technology to benefit all
Goal 10 Reduce inequality
Goal 11 Safe cities and communities
Goal 12 Responsible consumption by all
Goal 13 Stop climate change
Goal 14 Protect the ocean
Goal 15 Take care of the Earth
Goal 16 Live in peace
Goal 17 Mechanisms and partnerships to reach goals

6. Study Diagram 4 on page 181. Why were the Sustainable Development Goals introduced? Answer the questions below, with the correct figures.

The number of people fleeing war or persecution. ____________

The amount of food wasted each year. ______________

The number of people affected by climate change disasters. ______________

The number of people that go hungry each year. _______________

The amount of people living on less than 1 dollar per day. ___________________

The amount of tonnes of plastic that ends up in our oceans each year. ____________

How many girls in the world are not in school? _____________

7. Do you think the SDGs will be achieved by the year 2030? Give reasons for your answer.
8. Design a T-shirt that could be sold in your school to raise awareness of the Sustainable Development Goals.
   Perhaps you could make up an SDG Mascot? Perhaps the 17 Goals could be listed on the back in the same way tour dates are on a concert t-shirt? Be imaginative and creative! Perhaps your class could even have a competition and a real T-shirt produced of the winner's design.

Front

Back

Go Digital!

9. Look at the 'Lazy person's guide to saving the world' on our website.
   Now, make a plan of what you will do to help the world achieve the SDGs from your couch, from home, from outside your house and from work (school).

SUSTAINABLE DEVELOPMENT GOALS

Case study – Sustainable Development Goals 4 and 5

These are SDGs that you hopefully experience and enjoy!

Sustainable Development Goals 4 and 5

TEACHING NOTES

Discuss with your class what Quality Education and Gender Equality mean.

Many people think we could help the poorer nations of the world out of poverty if we gave them money. However, just giving out money is not going to solve the real causes of why a country is poor in the first place. It is much more complicated than this. Many people believe that the solution to world poverty lies with education and gender equality, and that is why they feature as Sustainable Development Goals.

They can bring down the birth rate, as educated girls want a job and career before marrying. This means less biological time to have a family.

For every extra year a child goes to school, their wages as an adult go up by 10%.

If all children in a developing country went to school, the GDP would increase by 70% by 2050.

How education and gender equality can end world poverty

People's health improves because educated boys and girls are more aware about how to stay healthy.

Lots of highly educated boys and girls means more professionals, such as doctors, lawyers, teachers and business leaders, who can all help the country become richer in the future.

Diagram 5 – How education and gender equality can end world poverty?

Diagram 6 – Girls in Afghanistan getting the chance to learn

School in Burkina Faso

TEACHING NOTES

Find out more about the UN's pledge to end poverty in the teaching notes on the Bright Red website.

Classroom challenge

1. Study Diagram 5 on page 184. Now copy and complete this star diagram in your workbook by answering the questions in the boxes in your own words.

Explain, in your own words, how educating women can bring the birth rate down.

Explain how education can improve health.

If a child attended school for an extra 6 years, how much would their wages as an adult go up by?

How much would the GDP of developing countries rise by if all children were educated?

2. Study Diagram 6 on page 184. Tell your class five ways in which the classrooms shown differ from your classroom.

DON'T FORGET

So, although we all complain about going to school, you must remember it is improving your health and your future wages, raising the GDP of your country, improving the lives of women and reducing our birth rate!

POPULATION

WHAT IS POPULATION DENSITY?

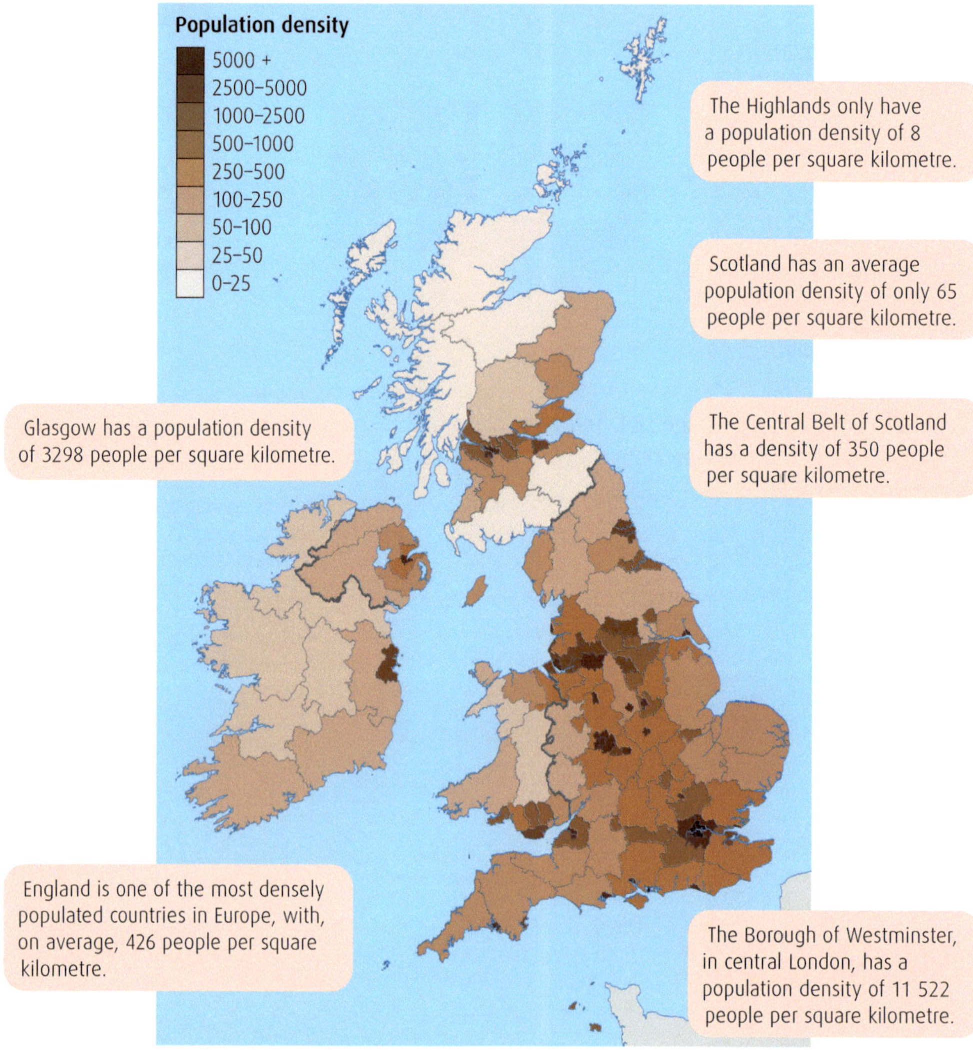

Diagram 7 – Population density of the British Isles

The map above is very interesting to geographers because it tells us where people live in the British Isles. This is usually measured by how many people there are living in each square kilometre of land. We call this **population density.** If lots of people are squashed into a square kilometre, we say the area is **densely populated.** If hardly anyone lives in that square kilometre, we say that it is **sparsely populated.** There is even a formula used to calculate population density for countries. It is:

population density = total population ÷ total land area in km^2

Diagram 7 on page 186 shows us that population density is very uneven across the British Isles. It also shows us that the most crowded places are towns and cities, with London being the most crowded of all.

Glasgow – a densely populated area

The Highlands of Scotland – a sparsely populated area

Classroom challenge

1. **Describe** what population density means.
2. **Explain** how we can calculate the population density of an area.
3. Study Diagram 7 on page 186. Copy out the sentences below but choose the correct word from those highlighted to complete them accurately.

An area which has many people per square kilometre living in it is said to be **sparsely/densely** populated.

An area that has few people per square kilometre living in it is said to be **sparsely/densely** populated.

One of the most densely populated countries in Europe is **Scotland/England.**

Scotland has a population density of **426/65** people per square kilometre.

The most densely populated part of Scotland is **the Central Belt/ the Highlands**.

The Highlands have a population density of **350/8** people per square kilometre.

Glasgow has a population density of **11 522/3298** people per square kilometre.

WHERE DOES THE WORLD'S POPULATION LIVE AND WHY DO THEY LIVE THERE?

On 31 October 2011, a milestone was recorded in the human population of the Earth. It had reached 7 billion people.

However, just like the population of the British Isles, these 7 billion people are not spread evenly across the planet. Some parts are very sparsely populated, whilst others are densely populated.

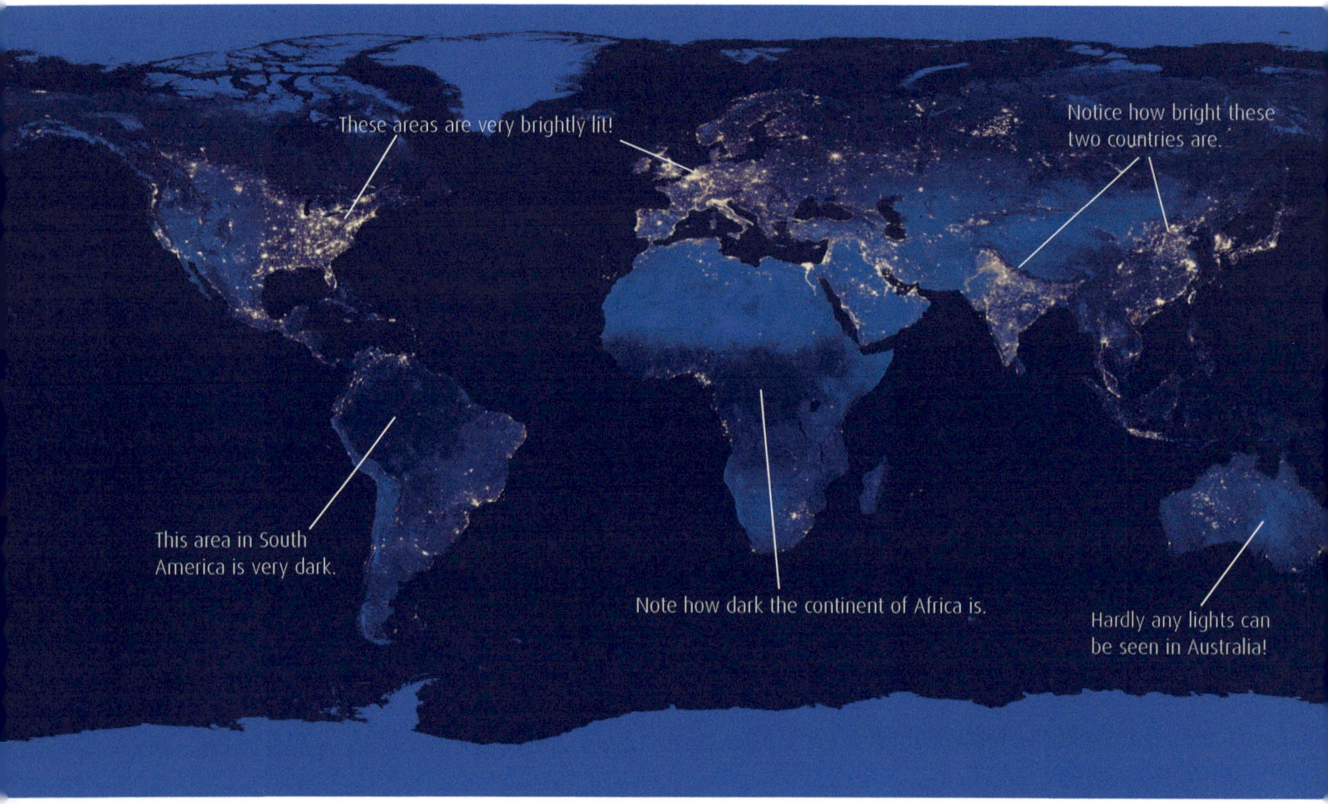

The Earth's street lights from space

The map above is fascinating and useful because it shows the Earth's streetlights from space at night. These light areas indicate where humans are living. Some areas are very bright and well lit, whilst others appear to be in total darkness. Why isn't the human population on our planet spread evenly across the land?

Check out some great activities on the Bright Red website for investigating population growth and density.

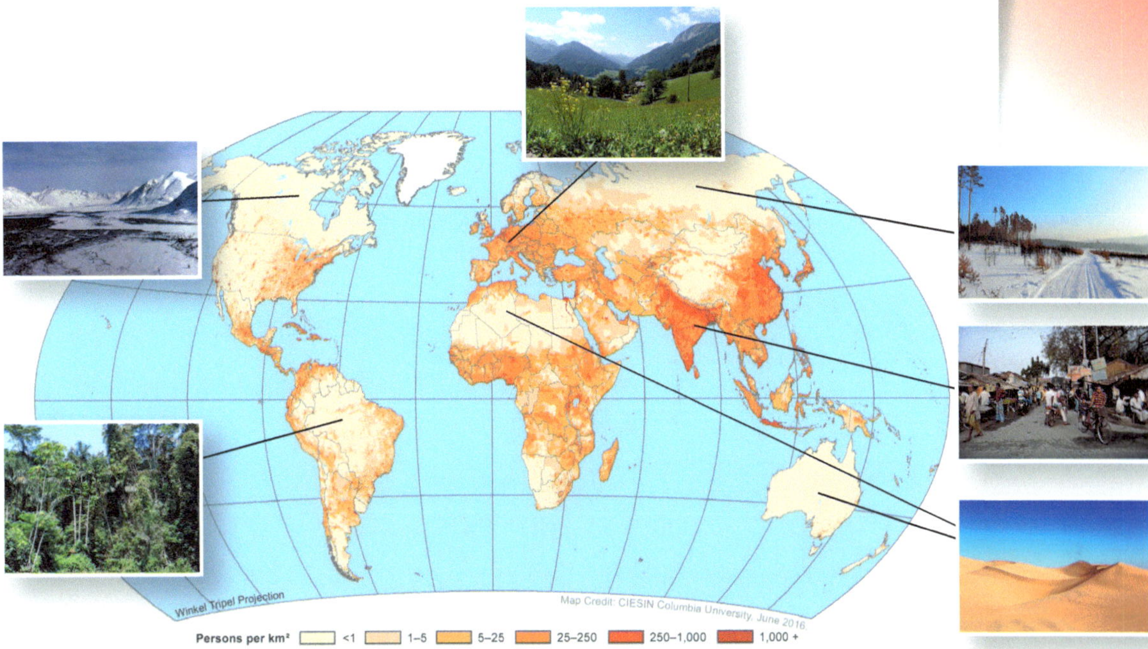

Diagram 8 – World population density per square kilometre

Diagram 8 gives us more detail on global population density. The reason for this uneven spread of people across the planet is because human beings will only live where conditions are suitable for life.

We can see that many of the sparsely populated areas are:

- polar regions (where it is too cold for human survival)
- deserts (where it is too dry for human survival)
- mountains (where it is too steep to build)
- rainforests (where it is hot and humid and soil is too poor to grow food).

Densely populated areas, however, are in places where there is:

- flat land to build on
- a mild climate (not too hot or cold)
- good soil to grow food
- raw materials such as oil to make money and create jobs.

Mild climate, good soil and flat land. Humans like this!

Cold, lack of soil and too steep to build on. Humans don't want to live here.

Too hot, dry and poor soil. Humans don't want to live here.

Classroom challenge

1. World population reached 7 billion on 31 October 2011. How much bigger is it today?
2. Population distribution across our planet is very uneven. However, there are very good reasons for this.
   (a) Imagine the box below is planet Earth. Each square in it represents 1% of the land. Draw these boxes into your workbook. Now use the data below to colour in the squares to show just how little of the Earth's surface is habitable for humans.

This could be set as a homework task.

There is a grid available on the Bright Red website to help with this.

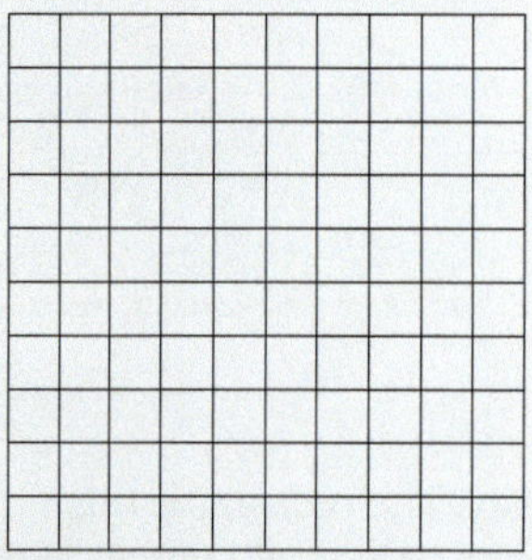

- Water 70%
- Desert 6%
- Too cold 6%
- Can't grow food 5%
- Mountains 5%
- Forest 5%
- Perfect for humans! 3%

   (b) **Explain** what this grid tells you about the land on planet Earth.
3. Look at Diagram 8 on page 188. Now, make your own world population density map. Complete it by studying an atlas and adding the following labels to it. After each label, add the phrase 'sparsely populated' or 'densely populated', using Diagram 8 on page 188 to help you. Colour your map in.

SAHARA	HIMALAYAS	INDIA	AMAZON	GERMANY
SIBERIA	GREENLAND	AUSTRALIAN DESERT		CHINA

TEACHING NOTES

There are world population density maps on the Bright Red website to help with this.

Go Digital!

4. (a) Copy the table on the next page into your workbook. Use the link on the Bright Red website to complete it with the most up-to-date figures. Complete the final column by **analysing** the figures and deciding if it is a sparsely or densely populated country.

   Remember,

   Population density = total population ÷ total land area in km^2

Country	Population	Area (km²)	Population density	Sparsely or densely populated?
United Kingdom		241 930		
China		9 388 211		
Russia		16 376 870		
Bangladesh		130 170		
Netherlands		33 720		
Canada		9 093 510		
India		2 973 190		
Australia		7 692 300		
Japan		364 555		

(b) Copy the phrases below into your workbook. If it is a phrase that would make it easy for humans to survive, colour it red. If it is a phrase that would make it difficult for humans to survive, colour it blue.

Poor soils for growing food

Very dry

Good water supply

Steep slopes

Raw materials for industry and jobs

Very cold

Mild climate

Good soils

No water

Flat land – easy to build on

Very hot

No raw materials

(c) Now, try to **explain** the reasons why some countries are sparsely or densely populated. First, name the two countries from your table that were the most densely populated. Using the phrases above, try to give reasons why they are so crowded.

(d) Name the two most sparsely populated countries from your table, and use the phrases above to **explain** why.

WHAT POPULATION DIFFERENCES ARE THERE BETWEEN DEVELOPED AND DEVELOPING COUNTRIES?

How we count our population

Every ten years, most countries count their populations using a **census**. This is carried out by the government, and it seems they are asking a lot of very detailed, nosey questions. However, the census is essential, as it collects information about who is living in a country so that governments can make plans and policies for the future: for example, how many more schools, houses, hospitals and jobs may be needed.

It is against the law not to fill out a census form!

Population pyramids

Information from sources such as a census helps us to create special population graphs for a country. These are known as **population pyramids**. From these, we can tell:

- the **birth rate** of a country
- the **death rate** of a country – sometimes called the **mortality rate**
- the **life expectancy** of the population (the age people are expected to live to, on average).

However, when we study population pyramids, it becomes very clear that developed and developing countries have very different population structures. In fact, by simply looking at a population pyramid, we can instantly tell if a country is developed or developing. For geographers, this is a very interesting area of study, and it is called **demography**.

TEACHING NOTES

There is some great material to enhance knowledge of population pyramids on the Bright Red website.

Population pyramid – developing country

A geographer can tell at a glance that Diagram 9 on page 193 is the population pyramid for a developing country. To begin with, it has a true pyramid shape, with a wide base and narrow top. We must now try to understand why it is this shape.

This pyramid is very narrow at the top. This means Chad has low life expectancy, and people do not live to a very old age.

Broad base – this means Chad has a high birth rate.

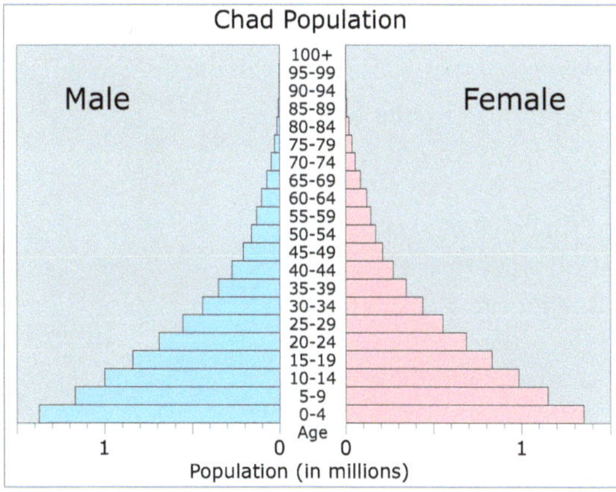

Diagram 9 – Population pyramid for Chad

As we go up the age categories, this pyramid narrows. This means Chad has high infant mortality and high adult mortality (deaths).

Wide base means high birth rate. Why?

One of our children has already died. We need to make sure that some survive.

We don't have pensions. It is our children who look after us when we are old.

Using contraception goes against my religion.

Our birth rate is high because we are subsistence farmers (we grow our own food). We need our children to help us in the fields.

Women like me do not go to school. We have no career. We just work on our farm and marry at a young age. This gives us many years to have children.

Diagram 10 – Reasons why birth rates are high in developing countries

Narrow top means high mortality rates and low life expectancy. Why?

We are **subsistence farmers** and grow our own food, but sometimes our crops fail. We can't get enough to eat, and we suffer from malnutrition and hunger.

Many of us have no access to proper clean water and sanitation (toilets). This is to blame for 80% of all disease in our country. This makes it easy for diseases such as cholera to break out.

It is difficult for us to get medical treatment, as there are few hospitals and doctors in the countryside.

Diagram 11 – Reasons why mortality (death rates) are high in a developing country

Classroom challenge

1. What do we use to count our population?
2. **Describe** why it is important for governments to count their populations.
3. What is the name of the special graph we use to show the population structure of a country?
4. Study Diagram 9 on page 193, showing the population pyramid for Chad.
   (a) This pyramid has a very broad base. What does this tell us?
   (b) Now, study Diagram 10 on page 193. In your workbook, copy the sentences below that are correct.

   - People in developing countries need children to work in the fields.
   - People in developing countries want children to read stories to.
   - People in developing countries need children to look after them when they are old.
   - People in developing countries are subsistence farmers.
   - People in developing countries earn lots of money.
   - People in developing countries have lots of children because many of them die of disease.
   - People in developing countries marry when they are older.
   - People in developing countries perhaps have lots of children because women are not educated.

   (c) Study Diagram 9 on page 193 again. This pyramid gets very narrow towards the top. What does this mean?
   (d) **Explain** three reasons why this is happening (use Diagram 11 on page 193 to help you with this).
5. Copy out into your workbook the speech bubbles from below that contain only the correct phrases about a developing country's population. Colour them in.

Low birth rate

High adult mortality

Low adult mortality

High infant mortality

High life expectancy

High birth rate

Low life expectancy

Low infant mortality

Population pyramid – developed country

This pyramid is much wider at the top than Chad's. This means Austria has **high life expectancy** and people are living to an old age.

Narrow base – this means Austria has a low birth rate.

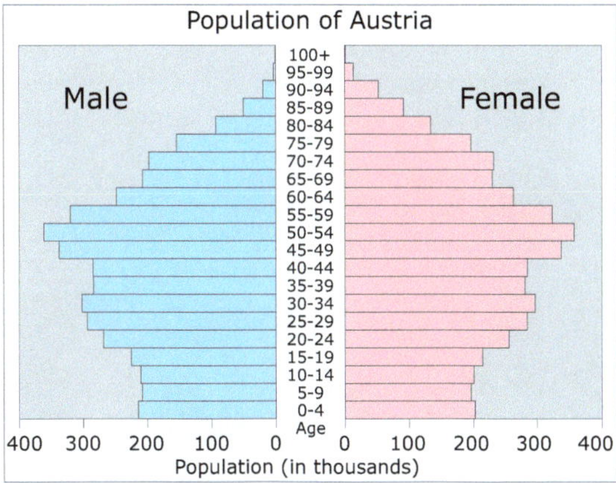

This pyramid does not get narrow as you go up the age categories. This means Austria has low infant and adult mortality rates (deaths).

Diagram 12 – Population pyramid for Austria

This population pyramid for Austria instantly tells a geographer that it is a developed country. It does not have a true pyramid shape. This is a result of the following things.

Reasons for low birth rates

Diagram 13 – Reasons for low birth rate in a developed country

Reasons for low mortality rates and high life expectancy

Diagram 14 – Reasons for low mortality (deaths) and high life expectancy

Classroom challenge

1. Study Diagram 12 on page 195, the population pyramid for Austria.
   (a) This pyramid has a very narrow base. What does this tell us?
   (b) Study Diagram 13 on page 195. Complete the 'Pointless' sentences below by adding in the missing word at the end, using the letter in brackets to help you. Copy them into your workbook.

- People in developed countries don't want too many children because they are **(E)**.
- In developed countries, people can plan their families as they have access to **(C)**.
- People in developed countries don't need children when they are older, as they have **(P)**
- People in developed countries tend to get married when they are older. This means they have less **(B)** time to have children.

3. Look again at Diagram 12 on page 195. What three-word phrase do we use to describe people living to a very old age?
4. Study Diagram 14 above showing the reasons for low mortality (deaths) and high life expectancy.

The numbers below spell out reasons why death rates (mortality rates) are low in developed countries and why people live longer. Use the code-buster to help you find the words by exchanging the number for the correct letter. However, there is a catch. The key words have been jumbled up. Once you have broken the code, unscramble them!

- 14 1 3 5 12   1 5 18 20 23   and   15 14 9 1 20 19 9 14 1 20
- 12 5 9 4 1 3 13   18 3 5 1
- 8 5 8 1 12 25 20   5 20 9 4
- 15 3 8 8 12 4 9 4 15   14 1 3 9 22 14 1 9 15 3 19 20

Code-Buster!

A	B	C	D	E	F	G	H	I	J	K	L	M
1	2	3	4	5	6	7	8	9	10	11	12	13
N	O	P	Q	R	S	T	U	V	W	X	Y	Z
14	15	16	17	18	19	20	21	22	23	24	25	26

5. Look again at Diagrams 10 and 13 on pages 193 and 195. Imagine you were the leader of a developing country. You have decided that the best way to help your country develop is to try to bring down the birth rate. **Explain** three things that you would do to achieve this, and say why you think these would work.

RURAL LIFE

WHAT DIFFERENCES ARE THERE IN RURAL LIFE BETWEEN DEVELOPED AND DEVELOPING COUNTRIES?

The word **rural** describes country life. Life in the countryside in developed and developing countries is very different. When describing life in rural areas, in geography, this often means studying such things as farming. This sounds a bit boring – but there are issues connected with farming in the developed and developing world that should interest us all! At the end of the day, it is where the food we eat comes from.

Rural life in developing countries

In developing countries, 70% of farmers are **subsistence** farmers. This means that they grow their own food to feed themselves and their families, but often have nothing left over to sell. This results in many of these subsistence farmers being poor and stuck in a **vicious circle** of poverty. This means they are unable to escape it.

Diagram 15 – The vicious circle of poverty

In addition to being caught in a **vicious circle** of poverty, subsistence farmers in developing countries face many other problems. These problems are shown in Diagram 16 below.

Diagram 16 – Problems facing farmers in developing countries

Village life in Bangladesh

How can the lives of people in rural areas be improved?

The lives of people in rural areas could be greatly improved if they could break out of the vicious circle of poverty. One of the ways this could happen is if they could produce more crops, then they would have more food to eat but also some extra to sell.

An effort to do this has been made, and started in 1944 in Mexico. It was aimed at improving crop production as well as modernising farming techniques. It was called the **Green Revolution**. One of the most important things introduced was something called HYV seeds. This stands for High Yield Variety. These seeds produce much more harvest than regular seeds, with the most famous ones being Mexipak wheat and IR8 rice. The use of these crops was seen as a big success to begin with.

DON'T FORGET

In countries such as India, the green revolution meant not having to buy these crops from other countries and even being able to sell their own crops abroad because they were producing so much. This made them richer.

However, the Green Revolution was not just all about HYV crops. Other changes were brought in which are shown below.

Diagram 17 – The Green Revolution

Use of machines in rice fields in Bangladesh

Irrigation systems introduced

Classroom challenge

1. Imagine you are in charge of trying to get farmers in a developing country to modernise their farm using 'Green Revolution' techniques. Produce a leaflet, short film or poster to advertise these techniques to them. Use Diagram 17 on page 200 to help you.
2. **Describe** what a subsistence farmer is.
3. (a) **Explain** what a vicious circle is.
   (b) Can you think of a time when you or your friends have been caught in a vicious circle at school or at home?
4. Study Diagram 16 on page 199. Make a larger copy of the diagram below in your workbook. Complete it by adding the answers to the questions in the boxes. Colour your diagram in.

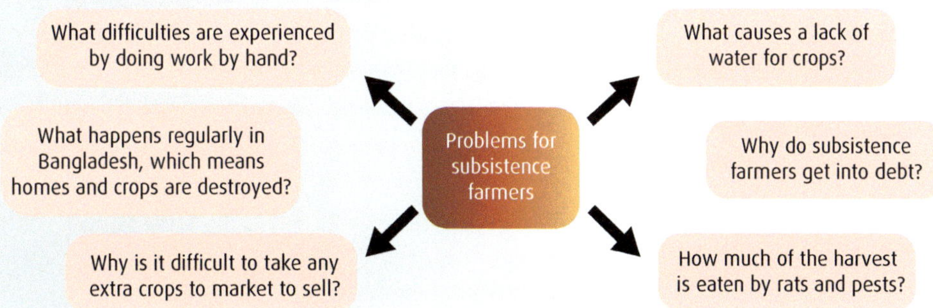

5. **Explain** why the Green Revolution was seen as a big success to begin with.
6. Study Diagrams 16 and 17 on pages 199 and 200. The list below shows phrases summing up the successes and failures of the Green Revolution. Copy and complete the table below by adding them to the correct column. One has been completed for you.

Green Revolution	Successes	Failures
Cheap loans		Poor, landless farmers are unemployed, as machines are doing their work
High Yield Variety crops introduced		
New roads built to market		
Land taken from rich landlords and given to poor, landless farmers		
Irrigation schemes introduced		

- Farmers can take their extra crops to market to sell, make money and break out of the circle of poverty.
- HYV seeds need lots of chemicals, such as fertilisers, which get into drinking water and poison it.
- Crops can now get water, even during drought.
- Richer farmers buy machines so they don't need to pay for workers.
- Farmers get bigger harvests, more food and extra crops to sell at market.
- Lots of other farmers can now travel to market to sell their extra crops. Prices go down, and less money can be made.
- The cost of irrigation water is high.
- Farmers with no land can start growing their own food and crops.
- Rich farmers have less land, and so there is less work for landless farmers.

STRETCH YOURSELF

7. Now, study the table you have just completed. **Evaluate** whether you think the Green Revolution was an overall success. This means you must think about the good things the Green Revolution brought, as well as the bad things. You will need to come to a conclusion at the end in which you state whether you think it was a success or failure.
8. Make up your own word-search using key words to do with the Green Revolution.

There are links to great activities, quizzes and much more on the Green Revolution on the Bright Red website.

TEACHING NOTES

Explaining the impact of an economic activity in a chosen area and beyond is CfE Level 4 work.

Question 7 could be set as a homework task.

Organic farming in Sikkim, India

It is important to remember that the Green Revolution started a long time ago. We must be careful not to think that all farms in developing countries experience the successes and failures we have just studied. There are some areas that have introduced their own farming revolution that could be an example to the rest of the world! Sikkim in India is a good example of this.

Location of Sikkim

Sikkim landscape

In the tiny state of Sikkim in India, farming is most certainly not all about HYV seeds, fertilisers and pesticides. In fact, it has rejected all of this and opted to go completely **organic** with its farm production.

Organic farming means crops and animals are kept without any use of damaging chemicals, fertilisers and pesticides. It makes farming more **sustainable** because it does not damage or destroy the land it is using.

Why did Sikkim go completely organic?

Diagram 18 – Why Sikkim turned organic

Has organic farming been successful in Sikkim?

Turning organic is a very serious business in Sikkim. The state started its efforts to become fully organic in 2003, and it is now a criminal offence to use chemical fertilisers and pesticides. Has this dramatic change to farming in the area worked?

To begin with, many people thought it was a disaster. When chemical fertiliser is suddenly stopped on farms, it takes a long time for natural goodness to build up again in the soil. As a result, in the first few years of organic farming in Sikkim, the harvests failed.

Diagram 19 below shows the successes and problems the area has experienced on its journey to become fully organic.

Learn more about organic farming is Sikkim with the film link on the Bright Red website.

Diagram 19 – Successes and problems of organic farming in Sikkim

Sikkim's chief minister is proud of what is happening in the state. He sees the problems that have been experienced as 'teething' problems. In fact, he hopes that Sikkim can be a model for anywhere else in the world that wants to go fully organic. It is certainly true that the demand for organic food in India has grown rapidly, and Sikkim is starting to feel the benefits of this as demand for its produce increases.

North Sikkim is home to the red panda. Fewer chemicals in the environment help species like this to survive.

Classroom challenge

1. When did Sikkim start to become an organic state?
2. **Explain** why organic farming is said to be sustainable.
3. Make your own field sketch of the Sikkim landscape like the one below. Colour it in and add the following labels to it. One has been completed for you.

Terraced rice fields	**Mountains**	**Organic farm**	**Natural woodland**
Village houses	**Road**	**No pesticides or fertilisers**	

STRETCH YOURSELF

4. Try to **evaluate** if organic farming has been a success in Sikkim.
   Study Diagrams 18 and 19 on pages 203 and 204.
   Now, make up a newspaper article on organic farming in Sikkim. Use the template on the next page help you with this.

TEACHING NOTES

Evaluating the role of agriculture in food production and drawing at least three reasoned conclusions about the environmental impacts and therefore the sustainability of these methods are CfE Level 4 work.

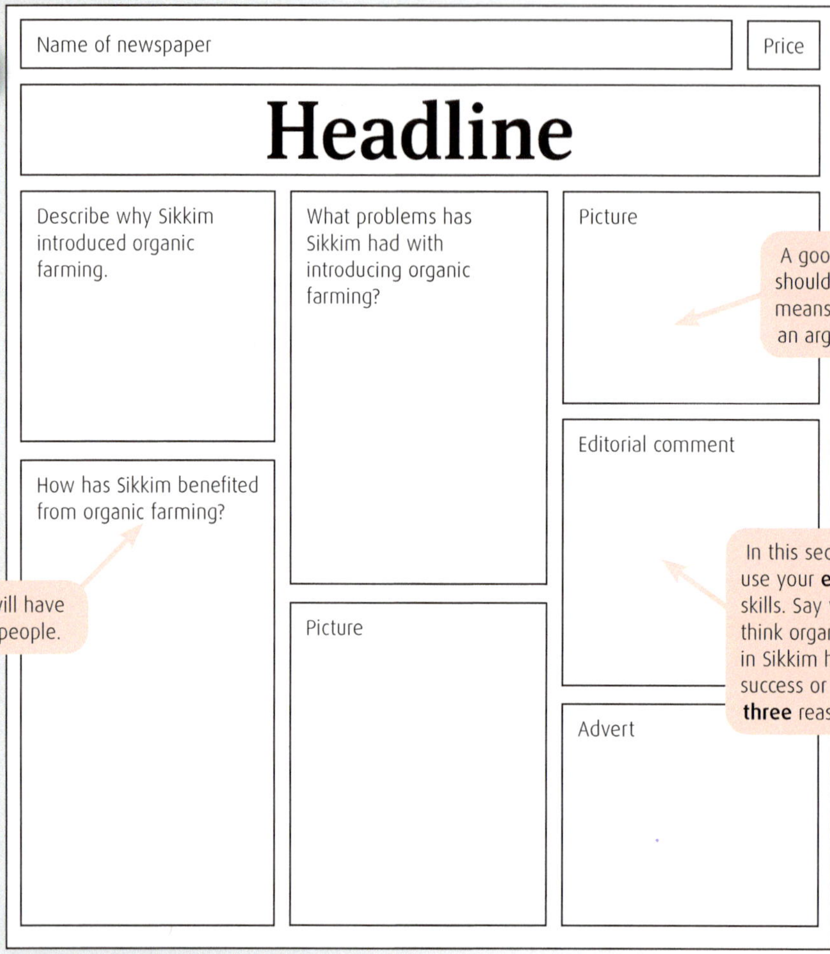

A good newspaper article should be balanced. This means giving both sides of an argument or story.

A good article will have interviews with people.

In this section, you can use your **evaluation** skills. Say whether you think organic farming in Sikkim has been a success or a failure. Give **three** reasons why.

5. In your opinion, do you think it is possible for a whole country such as Scotland to go fully organic, like Sikkim?
Give reasons for your answer.

There are great activities on the Bright Red website to find out more about organic farming in Sikkim.

Rural life in developed countries

Farming in developed countries is very different from that in the developing world. It is mainly **commercial farming** (growing crops or keeping animals to sell, and not for the farmer and family to eat).

In recent years, there have been many changes to farming in rich countries. These changes have brought benefits, but also problems.

TEACHING NOTES

Use the activities on the Bright Red website to find out much more on farming in the developed world.

Diagram 20 – Traditional farm in the UK

What are the different types of farming in a developed country?

In general, there are three main farming types in developed countries.

Arable farming – these are farms that just grow crops. There are no animals on these farms.

Pastoral farming – farms that mainly keep animals (livestock). A dairy farm with cows for producing milk is a good example of this. They may grow some crops for the animals to eat. These are called **fodder** crops.

Mixed farming – when crops are grown and animals are reared on the same farm.

Farming in developed countries can be described as '**intensive**'. This means they are able to produce a lot, even using small areas of land. This is often achieved by using lots of **fertilisers**, **pesticides** and other chemicals. It may also involve squashing farm animals into sheds.

Developed countries also have '**extensive**' farms. These farms generally cover big areas, do not make much use of fertilisers and pesticides and don't need many workers. Sheep farming is a good example of this. However, today, many modern farms producing crops, milk and meat have become so big they can also be described as being extensive.

Sheep farming in Scotland – extensive farming

How has farming changed in developed countries?

For many small farms in developed countries, it is now very difficult to make enough money to survive from farming alone. As a result, many of them have **diversified**. This means they carry out other activities on the farm in an effort to make more money and have a better income. Activities that can be found on diversified farms are shown below.

Diagram 21 – Activities on a diversified farm

The rural landscape in other parts of developed countries has completely altered due to changes in farming itself. This has happened because small farms have been bought by big companies, which do the following:

- rip out hedges
- cut down trees
- put streams underground
- drain marshland

to clear lots of land for growing crops. They want to grow as much as possible in order to make as much money as they can. When farms are managed like this, they are often called an '**agribusiness**'.

Marshland before being drained for farmland

How do we benefit from these changes?

We all benefit from these changes, as most of the food that we buy in the supermarket has probably come from one of these farms. Since they produce crops in such big quantities, it makes our food much cheaper to buy.

These farms also help the country in other ways. There are more jobs in factories that make farm machinery. In addition, if a country can produce a lot of food on its own land, it means it does not have to buy food from abroad, and this is good for the **economy**. In fact, extra food produced by these farms can be sold abroad, once again making money for the economy.

DON'T FORGET

Economy means how money is made and spent in a country.

Typical modern farm in the UK

Classroom challenge

1. What does commercial farming mean?
2. Study Diagram 20 on page 207, showing a traditional farm in the UK. Write out a **description** of what this farm and the area around it looks like. Use the labels to help you.
3. Copy out the passage below and choose the missing words from the word box to complete it.

> In the developed world, there are three main types of farming. __________ farming means only growing crops. Pastoral farming means only keeping l______________. Some crops to feed the animals may be grown on these farms. These are called __________ crops. Many farms produce crops and animals. These are called __________ farms.
>
> If a farm covers a large area but does not need a lot of workers or many fertilisers, we say it is an _____________ farm. If a farm covers a small area and uses lots of fertilisers and pesticides to produce lots of crops, we say it is an _____________ farm.

INTENSIVE   ARABLE   MIXED   EXTENSIVE   LIVESTOCK   FODDER

4. Study the graph below. It shows you the main cereal crops grown in Scotland in 2016.
   (a) **Describe** this graph. Give figures and names of different crops in your answer.

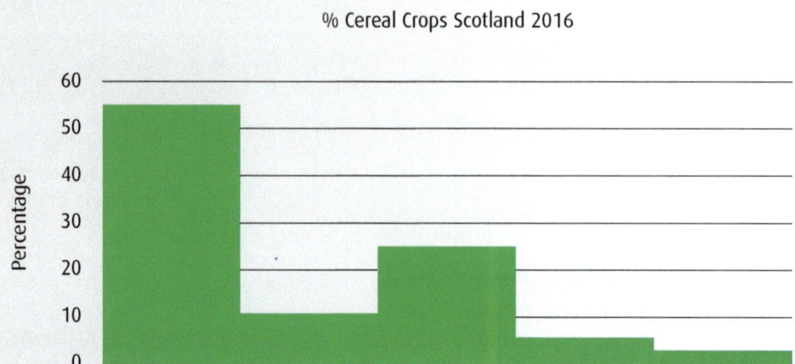

	Spring Barley	Winter Barley	Wheat	Spring Oats	Winter Oats
%	55	11	25	5.4	1.9

Type of cereal crop

Crop production in Scotland 2016

DON'T FORGET

Try to 'speak like a geographer'. It is a good idea to use statements such as 'much higher', 'substantially higher' or 'noticeably lower' when you describe a graph. Look at the table on the next page and try to use these. Compare the crops and give figures for how much is grown, but also for how much one crop is higher or lower than another crop.

(b) Now, swap your graph description with another student in your class. Mark them using the scores for the phrases shown in this table.

Substantially higher 3 marks	Much higher 2 marks	Higher 1 mark	1 mark each time a figure from the graph is given.
Noticeably lower 3 marks	A lot lower 2 marks	Lower 1 mark	3 marks for saying what the difference is between numbers in the graph, i.e. spring barley is ??? (how much) higher than winter barley.
Dominant crop 3 marks	Most common crop 2 marks	Biggest 1 mark	

5. (a) Explain what **diversification** means.
   (b) Study Diagram 21 on page 208. Choose two activities you would want to do on a diversified farm, and **explain** why.
6. Copy the diagram below into your workbook. Complete it by filling in the empty boxes with four ways big companies make more space for growing crops.

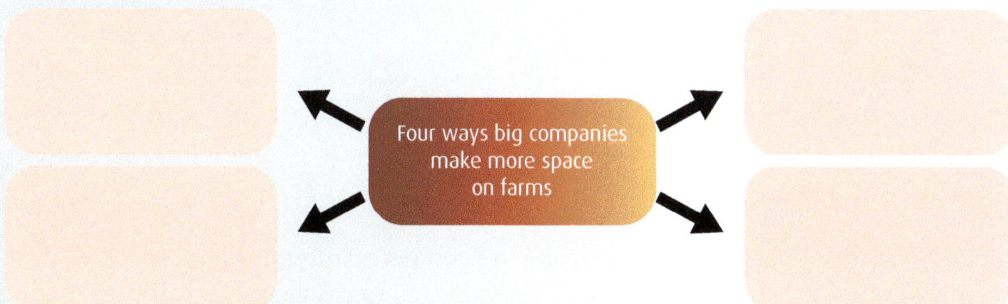

7. **Explain** three good things that these big, modern farms bring for a developed country.

TEACHING NOTES

This can be printed out and played in class. All you need are dice!

Go Digital!

8. Barley seems to be the most popular crop in Scotland. Do some internet research. What things can we make from it?
9. Play the farm simulation game from the Bright Red website with your class. Now answer these questions.
   (a) What natural element does farming totally rely on?
   (b) Which crops did well when it was wet?
   (c) Which crops did badly when it was wet?
   (d) Which crops like warm, dry conditions?
   (e) Which crops did badly when it was warm and dry?
   (f) Would you like to be a farmer? **Explain** the reasons why.

The last part of this activity on the Bright Red website can be completed as a homework task.

10. Follow the links on the Bright Red website to view bigger copies of the maps below showing 'Farm types in Scotland', 'Average rainfall' and 'Relief of the land in Scotland'. Study the maps and their keys. Now use your **analytical** powers to study them.

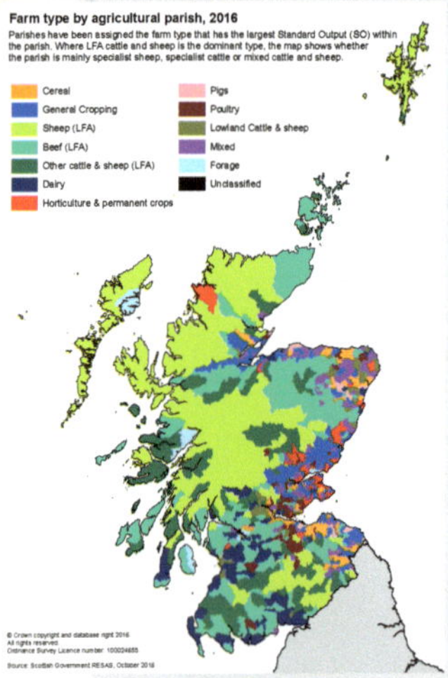

Farming map of Scotland

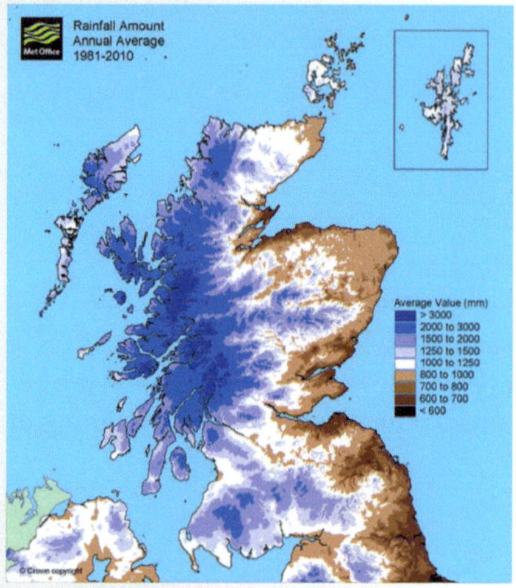

Rainfall in Scotland

Relief map of Scotland. The word 'relief' means the height and shape of the land.

(a) What type of farm is most common in Scotland? (arable, pastoral or mixed)
(b) On what side of Scotland would you find many farms growing crops? (east or west)
(c) **Explain** two reasons why most farms growing crops are on this side of Scotland using the rainfall map and the relief map
(d) In which area of Scotland would you find most dairy farms? (north-east or south-west)
(e) Find out where most sheep farming is in Scotland. What is the relief and rainfall like in these areas?
(f) Use this information to **explain** why you think sheep farming is found in these areas.
(g) What type of farm is most common where you live?

Highland cow calf on a Scottish farm

What problems are caused by modern farming in a developed country?

TEACHING NOTES

Evaluating the role of agriculture in food production and drawing at least three reasoned conclusions about the environmental impacts and therefore the sustainability of these methods is CfE Level 4 work.

STRETCH YOURSELF

Modern arable farming

Study the images below. One shows countryside in the UK with traditional farmland. The other shows the countryside on a modern farm owned by a large company. What big differences do you notice?

Diagram 22 – Traditional farmland versus modern, large-scale crop farming

One of the big problems with large-scale modern farming is the damage it does to the environment, wildlife and the life of people living in the countryside. Some of these are shown in Diagram 23 below.

Diagram 23 – Impact of large-scale modern farming on the countryside

DON'T FORGET

The green slime on this lake is caused by fertilisers getting into the water. This can kill animals.

Poisonous algae

A tractor spraying a field with chemical fertilisers and pesticides

There is no doubt that the countryside in the developed world has been affected by modern farming. Below are some of our much-loved species in the UK that are now endangered.

Would you like to see these species become extinct?

Hedgehog

Water vole

Bee

Tortoiseshell butterfly

Modern, intensive livestock farming

Every year, across the world, 50 billion farm animals are reared on modern livestock farms. Such large amounts of production mean that meat, eggs and milk are all very cheap for us to buy in the supermarket.

However, some people are unhappy about how livestock are reared in these large-scale, intensive farms. Two of every three farm animals are raised in what are known as **factory farms.** They are called this because the farming is carried out almost like being in a factory. Animals are kept in big sheds, and the main focus is on making as much money as possible. People feel this means the welfare of the animals is ignored, and the conditions on these farms upset them.

Egg production on a battery farm

Broiler chickens kept for meat

Is this a fair way to keep animals?

What are the alternatives to these big modern farms?

If we don't want our countryside and its wildlife destroyed by modern farming techniques, what are the alternatives? Also, if we want to eat meat and eggs and drink milk, how can we do this without cruelty to animals?

Perhaps the answer lies with **organic farming** (like in the state of Sikkim in India – see pages 203–206). This means crops are grown without the use of damaging fertilisers and pesticides. This makes farming much more **sustainable** because it does not damage or destroy the environment it is using.

On organic livestock farms, the animals are given space, usually outside (**free range**), and are given food that is natural. This means these animals are much happier and looked after better. It also means that the products from these farms are much better for people's health, as they tend to be free from chemicals. The problem, however, is that organic products are often more expensive to buy.

Why not buy products straight from a farm or from a farmers' market?

TEACHING NOTES

Check out activities on the Bright Red website to investigate modern farming in more detail.

Free-range, organic pigs

Free-range, organic chickens

Classroom challenge

1. Study Diagram 22 on page 213. List the differences you can see between the two different farming landscapes.

STRETCH YOURSELF

2. Look at Diagram 23 on page 213.
   (a) **Explain** why removing hedges and trees can affect wildlife.
   (b) What problem happens when rain washes fertilisers into rivers, ponds and lakes?
   (c) **Explain** why farmers use insecticides and pesticides.
   (d) How can the use of insecticides and pesticides affect food chains?
   (e) What phrase do we use to **describe** when farm workers and their families leave the countryside?
   (f) What are GM crops, and why do some people think we should not use them?
   (g) Name four animal species that are now endangered in the UK as a result of modern farming.

TEACHING NOTES

Evaluating the role of agriculture in food production and drawing at least three reasoned conclusions about the environmental impacts and therefore the sustainability of these methods is CfE Level 4 work.

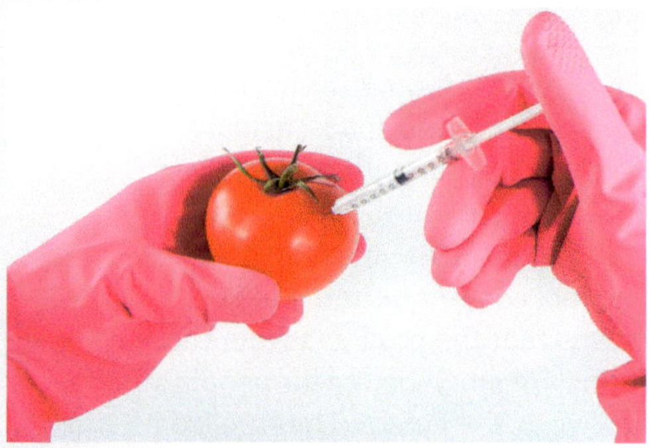

TEACHING NOTES

Describing and making at least three valid conclusions about the impact of human activity on a chosen area is CfE Level 4 work.

3. Unscramble the words below. Use them to complete the sentences and write them in your workbook.

NICROAG	TOCARYF SMARF	EREF GREAN	FREELAW

Intensive farms raising lots of animals in cramped conditions are called __________ _______.

Many people don't like this type of farm, as they feel the _____________ of the animals is ignored.

An alternative is to buy produce from an _____________ farm.

When animals are allowed space to be outside and run around, we call it _______ _________.

Go Digital!

4. Explore the issues with large-scale modern farming further by completing the investigation on the Bright Red website.

The task in question 4 can be completed as a homework activity.

STRETCH YOURSELF

5. Can we farm the countryside in a way that will protect endangered species such as bees, hedgehogs and butterflies? Find out more by visiting the link for Hope Farm on the Bright Red website. From investigating this link, write out what the '6-Point Plan' is to help farm wildlife on Hope Farm.
6. Now, make up a plan for your own farm, similar to that for Hope Farm. Decide what you want to grow on it and what animals you will keep. Make up a key for your fields. Will you be an organic farm? Most importantly, you need to mark on your plan how you are going to protect and encourage wildlife.

Skylark – an endangered species

TEACHING NOTES

Contributing to a discussion on the development of sustainable systems is CfE Level 4 work.

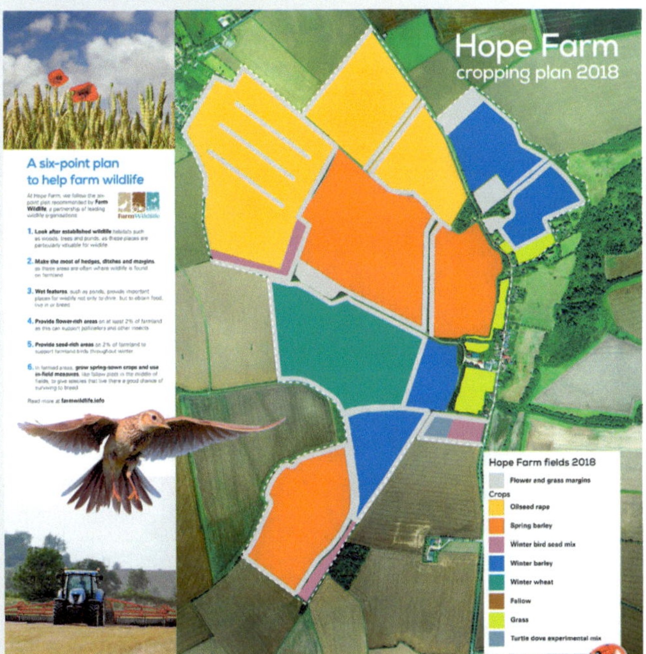

RSPB Hope Farm field plan

Have you enjoyed learning about rural areas in developed and developing countries? Would you like a career that uses the knowledge and skills you have gained from this topic? Why not visit the 'My World of Work/STEM/Developing the Young Workforce' section of the Homework Helpers to find out more?

URBAN LIFE

WHAT DIFFERENCES ARE THERE IN URBAN LIFE BETWEEN DEVELOPED AND DEVELOPING COUNTRIES?

The word **urban** means towns and cities. Life in cities in developed and developing countries is very different.

TEACHING NOTES

Explaining in some detail how any chosen urban area has developed, and evaluating the impact on the society, is CfE Level 4 work.

Urban life in developing countries

STRETCH YOURSELF

Urban areas in the developing world are growing very quickly. This is known as **urbanisation** and is usually a result of people leaving the countryside (rural areas) and **migrating** (moving) to cities.

As we have already found out, life in the countryside in developing countries is tough, and people are often stuck in a vicious circle of poverty. They may also have become unemployed, as the Green Revolution meant machines were introduced onto farms, taking jobs from workers. The reasons people are forced to leave an area are called **push factors**.

Reasons for migrating to cities in the developing world are shown in Diagram 24 below.

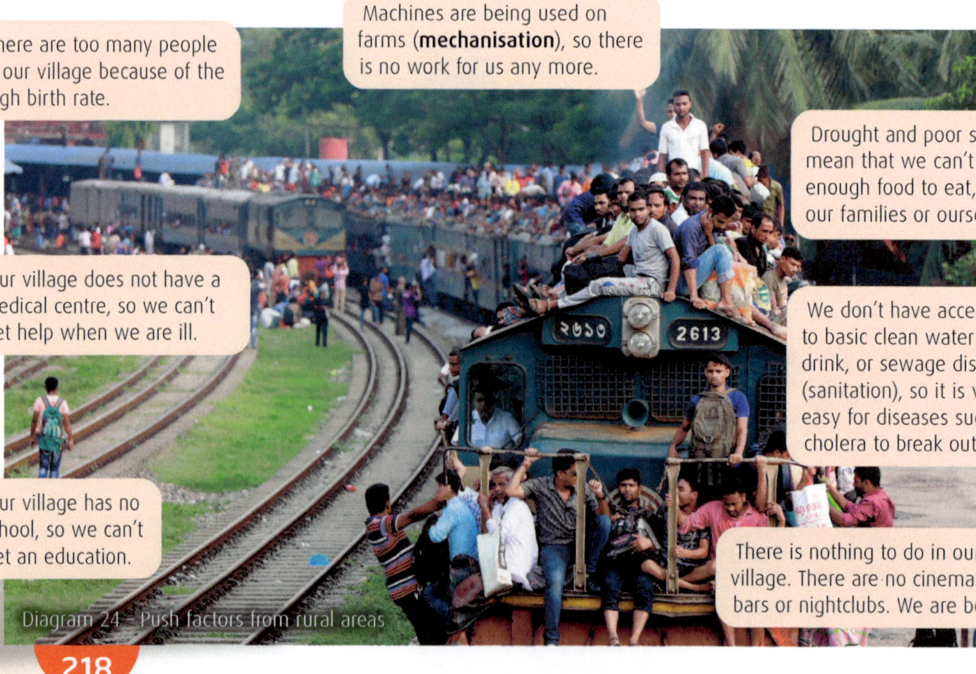

Diagram 24 – Push factors from rural areas

The growth of megacities

As a result of this migration from rural to urban areas, some of the biggest cities in the world are now found in developing countries, and they are growing by the day! Many of them have populations of over 10 million people. We call these **megacities**. To put this in perspective, the population of the whole of Scotland is around 5.5 million!

> **TEACHING NOTES**
>
> Investigate the growth of megacities by following the links on the Bright Red website.

Projected population living in the top megacities in 2030 (in thousands)

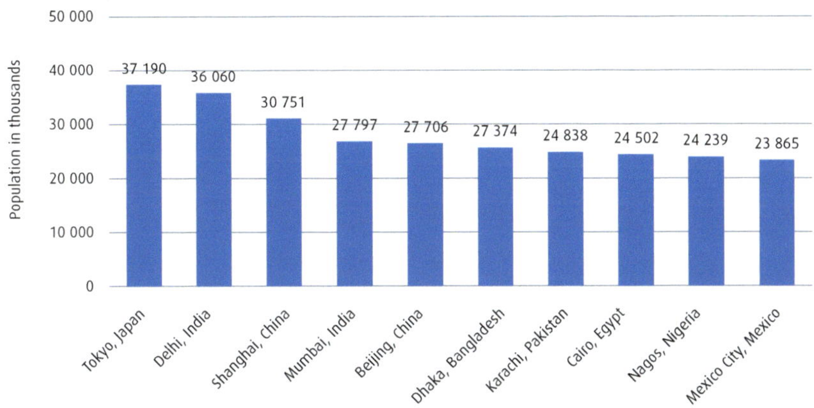

Diagram 25 – Top ten megacities by the year 2030

Diagram 25 above shows us the top ten projected megacities by the year 2030. Nine of them are in developing countries.

We must therefore ask: what is attracting so many people to these cities? These are often called **pull factors.** Diagram 26 below shows Mumbai in India. From the photo, it looks like a very big, attractive city, but it is growing rapidly. In fact, on average, the city is growing by around 3500 people per week.

> **TEACHING NOTES**
>
> Follow the links on the Bright Red website to learn more about Mumbai megacity.

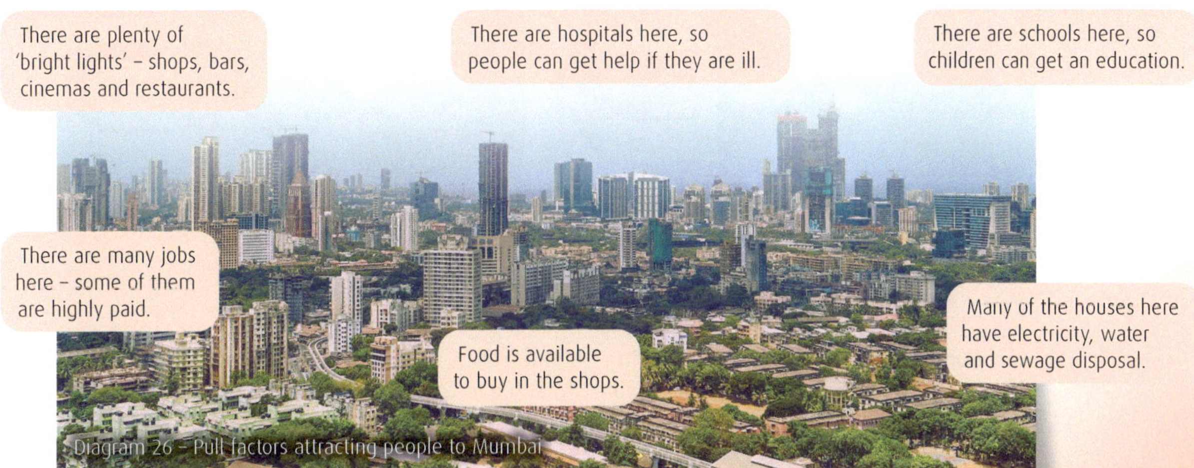

Diagram 26 – Pull factors attracting people to Mumbai

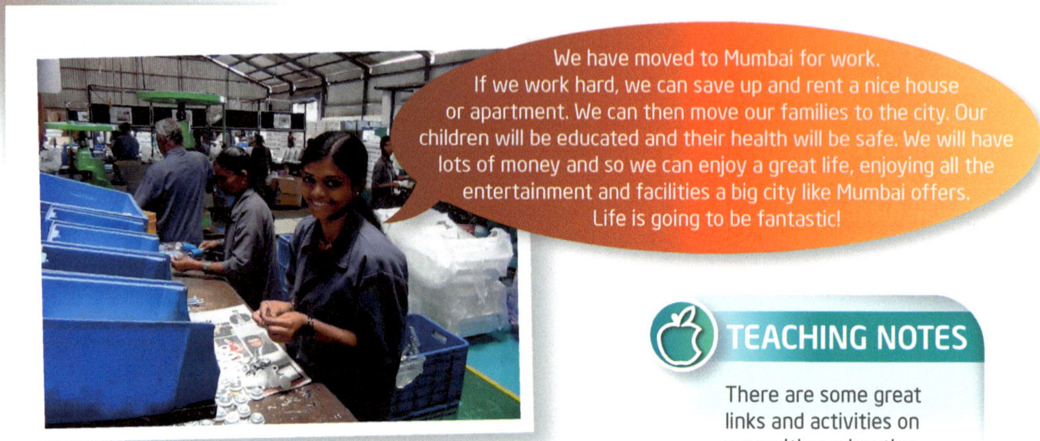

Diagram 27 – The migrant's dream!

TEACHING NOTES

There are some great links and activities on megacities, migration and Mumbai on the Bright Red website.

Classroom challenge

1. What does the word **urban** mean?
2. **Explain** what the term 'push factors' means.
3. **Explain** what the term 'pull factors' means.
4. What size of population do megacities have?
5. Copy out the diagram below into your workbook. Complete it by studying Diagram 24 and Diagram 26 on pages 218 and 219, then give:
   - four reasons, in your own words, why people leave their villages in rural areas (push factors), and
   - four reasons, in your own words, why people may wish to move to a big urban area, such as Mumbai (pull factors).

6. Look at Diagram 27 above, showing 'the migrant's dream'. Do you think these migrants to the city will be able to achieve their dream? Try to think of two reasons why.

7. Think of eight key words to do with urban life in developing countries, and write them down. Now scramble the letters in these words and give them to a partner to see if they can work them out.

Go Digital!

8. (a) Study Diagram 25 on page 219 showing the populations of the world's megacities by 2030. Now, copy out the table below. Use the diagram and the link on the Bright Red website to look up the populations of these cities today to help you complete the table. Tokyo has already been completed for you.

Name of city	Population today	Projected population 2030 (add 000 at the end)	Population increase (subtract population today from projected population in 2030)
Tokyo, Japan	13 617 000	37 190 000	23 573 000
Delhi, India			
Shanghai, China			
Mumbai, India			
Beijing, China			
Dhaka, Bangladesh			
Karachi, Pakistan			
Cairo, Egypt			
Lagos, Nigeria			
Mexico City, Mexico			

(b) **Describe** the table you have just completed in your workbook. Try to point out which cities have the biggest population increase. Use words such as 'much bigger', 'substantial increase', 'large growth'. Try to compare the cities against each other.

(c) Use a blank world map to make your own colourful map showing the location of these ten cities.

DON'T FORGET

In geography, an important skill is to be able to describe tables and graphs. Remember to 'speak like a geographer' as shown on pages 210–211.

TEACHING NOTES

There is a blank world map template on the Bright Red website to help with this.

Problems caused by rural/urban migration

Developing world cities, such as Mumbai in India, are expanding very rapidly due to rural/urban migration. As a city, Mumbai is very successful and is the centre of the film industry in India (Bollywood). The people are very friendly, and it has the nickname of being the 'city of dreams'. It is also the financial capital of India, so there are many very wealthy people living there.

Location of Mumbai

Location of Mumbai in India

Bollywood dancing

In developing world cities, the rich often live in expensive apartment blocks near the city centre. In Mumbai, perhaps the most famous building is Antilia House. It is owned by the billionaire Mukesh Ambani, and the entire high-rise block is home for his family and 600 servants. It is said to be the most expensive family home in the world, as it is valued at over $2 billion!

Downtown Mumbai in the evening

Antilia House

However, there are many problems that have arisen in Mumbai due to all the migrants arriving from the countryside and looking for a better life. One of the main issues is that the 'migrant's dream' does not come true for most people because they can only get poorly paid jobs, which means they don't earn enough money to afford the life they dreamed of. As a result, the biggest problem facing Mumbai is the fact that a huge slum area, where many thousands of migrants have set up home, is found right in the centre of the city. It is called Dharavi (Diagram 28 on page 223). It covers an area of one square mile and has one million people squashed into it in very overcrowded conditions. Slum areas such as this, where migrants build their own shelters to live in, are often referred to as **shanty towns**.

TEACHING NOTES

Explaining in some detail how any chosen urban area has developed, and evaluating the impact on the society, is CfE Level 4 work.

Diagram 28 – Dharavi slum area in the centre of Mumbai

Location of Dharavi in Mumbai

Classroom challenge

1. What is the nickname given to Mumbai?
2. Which part of developing-world cities do rich people tend to live in – the city centre or on the edge of the city?
3. What is the name of the most expensive house in the world, and how much money is it worth?
4. Where do many of the migrants who arrive in Mumbai from the countryside end up living?
5. **Explain** why the 'migrant's dream' life does not often happen.
6. Study Diagram 28 of Dharavi on page 223, and the quote from Prince Charles below. Prince Charles is basically saying that we could learn a lot from life in Dharavi! Give four reasons why he said this.

'I strongly believe that the west has much to learn from societies and places which, while sometimes poorer in material terms, are infinitely richer in the ways in which they live and organise themselves as communities.'

7. Look at the Dharavi street scene.
   (a) Imagine you are a town planner and work for the Mumbai Municipal Corporation (council). You and a colleague have been asked to visit Dharavi and provide a report on the conditions. To get the information, you must carry out an Environmental Quality Survey. Copy the table on the next page into your workbook. Use what you can see in the picture below and the information in Diagram 28 on page 223 to complete the table, by giving each element a score. You should work with a partner. (+ 3 is the best score, and –3 is the worst.)

TEACHING NOTES

There are some film clip links on the Bright Red website that can help with this.

DON'T FORGET

There are no right or wrong answers for completing this table. The scores are totally based on your opinions.

A street in Dharavi

Environmental Quality Survey

	-3	-2	-1	0	+1	+2	+3	
Access to clean water								
Access to sanitation (toilets)								
Density of people								
Quality of buildings								
Litter								
Noise levels								
Air quality								
Amenities (shops, restaurants etc.)								
Condition of roads/pavements								
Parks/open space								
Health of population								
Employment								
Overall total								

STRETCH YOURSELF

(b) You must now report your findings back to the Mumbai Municipal Corporation. This will involve explaining why you awarded certain scores. Present this, with your partner, to your class. It could be in the form of a slide show, poster, speech, film or any other way you want to present your findings.

DON'T FORGET

Carrying out research like this and presenting your findings are really important skills needed for many careers!

TEACHING NOTES

Explaining in some detail how any chosen urban area has developed, and evaluating the impact on the society, is CfE Level 4 work.

How can life in Dharavi be improved?

Over the years, there have been many proposals put forward to try to improve the living conditions in Dharavi. The main reasons why there is a desire to do this are:

- It is a giant slum, located right in the heart of India's financial capital, and it is an embarrassment to the city authorities.
- The land Dharavi is built on is very valuable!

Dharavi – a slum on valuable city-centre land

Proposal 1

Skyscrapers and slums in central Mumbai

The Mumbai Municipal Corporation has come up with a plan to redevelop Dharavi. It is called the **Dharavi Redevelopment Project**. This will involve bulldozing Dharavi completely. The land will be divided into five sectors and then sold to developers. They will then rebuild flats and offices in each sector. The people of Dharavi will be rehoused in high-rise flats (this is similar to what happened in Glasgow and other parts of the UK in the 1960s and 1970s). These new flats will be an improvement because they will have water, electricity and proper sanitation and toilets.

However, there is a catch. Only people who have lived in the area since the year 2000 will be rehoused. Everyone else will be made homeless. Also, they will only be given flats on the ground floor. All other flats and offices will be sold or rented so that the developers can make lots of money. As a result, there is a lot of opposition to this plan.

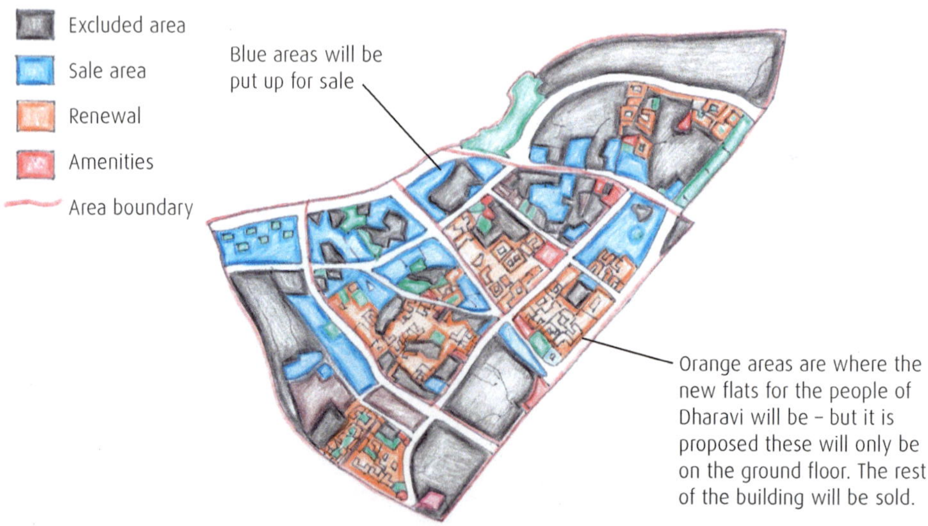

Plans taken from the Dharavi Redevelopment Project

Some people in Dharavi have already been rehoused in high-rise flats. These have very quickly become vertical slums.

Bulldozing Dharavi would destroy the small factories and workshops. 85% of the people of Dharavi would become unemployed.

Many families in Dharavi use their homes as workshops for making things such as pottery. The new flats will have no space for this.

The flats people will be rehoused in are smaller than the houses they have now. It will not help the problem of overcrowding.

If Dharavi is bulldozed, then all the recycling workshops would be destroyed.

Diagram 29 – Problems with the Dharavi Redevelopment Project

Pottery work in Dharavi streets at present

This image shows previous attempts to rehouse the people of Dharavi

Proposal 2

As a result of the problems highlighted with Proposal 1, another proposal has been suggested, by the people of Dharavi themselves. They want the existing area and buildings kept and not bulldozed. This means they keep the workshops, shops, factories, recycling, low crime rates and sense of community. Diagram 30 on page 228 shows what they have proposed for the area.

Diagram 30 – Dharavi improvement suggestions by the local people

Recent changes in Dharavi

A very recent development in Dharavi has been the growth of 'slum tourism'. There are now many tour operators who will take visitors into Dharavi so that they can witness slum life.

Tourists being shown around Dharavi

These tour operators think that this is good for the people of Dharavi because it means that people get to see what Dharavi is really like. They are walked around and shown inside houses, workshops and the general life on the streets. Many visitors cannot imagine that there are actually good things going on in a slum, such as sense of community, workshops, recycling and low crime rates.

If this is carried out **responsibly**, then it can really help the people of Dharavi. In fact, some of the profits from these tour groups are fed back into the community and are used to help set up youth support and education groups. Some tours are now even giving tourists the chance to stay overnight in a slum house with a family, for £22. This means that people of the slum can earn extra money.

However, some people do not approve of this tourism and say it is **exploiting** the people of Dharavi. They feel it is disrespectful and treating the residents as if they were animals in a zoo for people to come and stare at.

Fancy a tour of Dharavi?

Classroom challenge

1. Think of all the words that come into your mind when you hear the name Dharavi. Copy out the wall cartoon below into your workbook. Complete it by adding the Dharavi words you just thought of as graffiti.

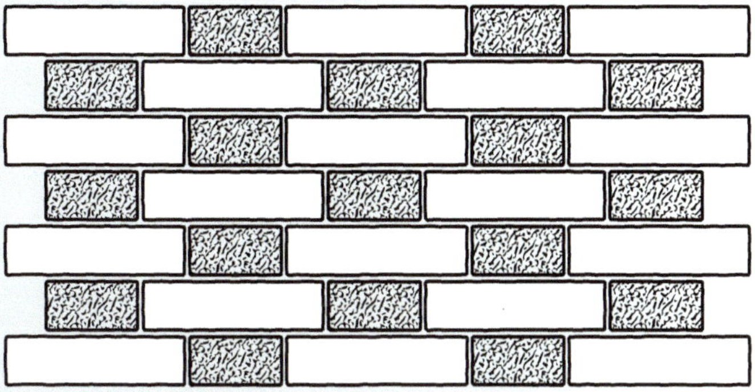

Dharavi Graffiti Wall

2. **Explain** two reasons why the Mumbai Municipal Corporation is keen to redevelop Dharavi.
3. The sentences below have been jumbled up. Match up the beginnings with the correct endings, and write them into your workbook.

Sentence beginning	Sentence ending
The Municipal Corporation of Mumbai want to...	...divided into 5 sectors and sold to developers.
Dharavi will be...	...the year 2000 will be rehoused.
Slum-dwellers will get...	...bulldoze Dharavi and rebuild it.
Only people who have lived there since...	...sold so that the developers can make money.
The rest of the new flats will be...	...a flat on the ground floor.

4. Read Proposal 1. **Explain** why these new flats will be an improvement.
5. Make your own simple sketch of a high-rise flat. Use Diagram 29 on page 227 to write the answers to the questions below as labels around your sketch.

What has already happened to some new high-rise flats in Dharavi?

Why will the redevelopment of Dharavi not solve the problem of overcrowding?

Why will families no longer be able to keep working making pots in Dharavi after redevelopment?

What percentage of people could become unemployed if Dharavi is redeveloped?

6. The people of Dharavi have made their own suggestions on how they feel the slum could be improved.
Imagine you are an architect. You have been given the job of working with the people of Dharavi to redevelop the area. You must listen to their wishes (see Diagram 30 on page 228) and produce an imaginary plan similar to the one below, of what you will do. This plan must be colourful and have a key.

DON'T FORGET

On this plan, mark on the houses and streets. Think of things that would help to make the area better, such as garden space, benches, washing areas, trees and places to meet and chat. Where will taps and toilets be? Also, recycling areas, shops and small workshops will need to be on your plan.

Where will you put workshops?

Where will you put areas for washing clothes?

Where will there be housing with an extra storey added?

How will people be able to get water 24 hours a day?

Where will rubbish be collected?

How will people have access to proper clean toilets?

Where will recycling workshops be?

People like shared areas to meet, chat and celebrate festivals. Where will they be and how should they be designed?

Where will people go to worship?

Where will the shops and market be?

STRETCH YOURSELF

7. Many tour groups are now being taken into Dharavi. **Evaluate** whether you think this is a good thing for the people living there. To do this, state at least two benefits the people of Dharavi get from these tours and at least two problems these tours may cause, then add if you think these tours should happen and why.

Question 7 could be set as a homework task.

Use the links on the Bright Red website to help you.

TEACHING NOTES

Contributing to a discussion on the development of sustainable systems is CfE Level 4 work.

Urban life in developed countries

Urban areas in the developed world are also changing rapidly. However, this change is very different to what is happening in poorer countries. In fact, in the developed world, many people are abandoning city life and going to live in rural areas. Why is this?

STRETCH YOURSELF

Structure of a city in the developed world

Geographers like to use models. This gives us something we can use to compare with the real world. A very popular model used for comparing cities is the **Burgess Concentric Ring Model**. It basically shows that all cities have distinct zones which occur in rings. This is because all cities have grown outwards through time. These zones are important when we are describing change in cities in the developed world.

KEY
A = Central Business District (CBD)
B = Zone of Transition (was old industry in the past)
C = Old Inner City area (these were houses for workers in the old industry)
D = Twentieth century housing areas
E = Modern suburbs/rural–urban fringe

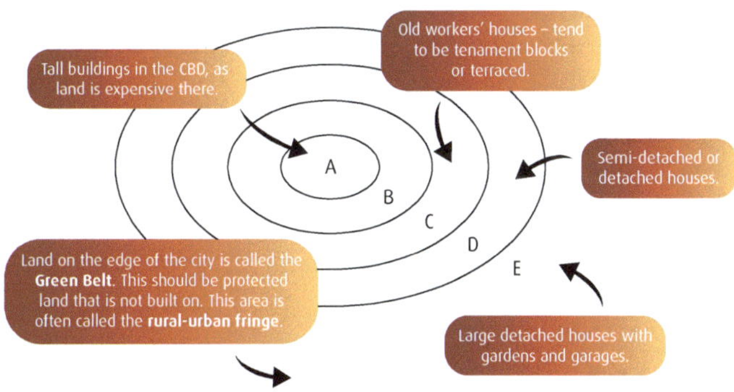

Diagram 31 – Burgess Concentric Ring Model

TEACHING NOTES

Find out much more on developed-world cities with the links and activities on the Bright Red website.

TEACHING NOTES

Explaining in some detail how any chosen urban area has developed, and evaluating the impact on the society, is CfE Level 4 work.

The CBD – Central Business District full of offices, shops, bars, restaurants and transport links

Terraced houses or tenement flats in the inner city

Semi-detached houses built in the 20th century

Detached housing in modern suburbs

Classroom challenge

1. Study Diagram 31 on page 231, Burgess Concentric Ring Model. Copy out the following sentences using the correct word from each pair in the brackets.

- The centre of a town is called the (**EFG/CBD**).
- The buildings are tall here because the land is (**expensive/cheap**).
- Zone B is where there were (**factories/shopping centres**) in the past.
- Zone C is where (**workers/rich people**) lived.
- Houses in the old inner-city area tend to be (**detached/ terraced or tenements**).
- Houses in Zone D were built in the (**twentieth/ nineteenth**) century.
- Large modern houses with gardens and garages are found in the (**inner city/modern suburbs**).
- Land on the edge of a city that should not be built on is called the (**black belt/green belt**).

2. Make your own colourful copy of the diagram below.
   (a) Add the following labels to it:

   CBD   Zone of transition   Inner city   Twentieth-century housing
   Modern suburbs/rural–urban fringe

   (b) As a class, try to add the names of an area in the town or city you live in (or are familiar with) to match each of the zones.

My Concentric Ring Model of .... (name of town or city)

Problems in developed-world cities – the CBD

Edinburgh case-study

Location of Edinburgh

Princes Street in Edinburgh's CBD

TEACHING NOTES

Explaining in some detail how any chosen urban area has developed, and evaluating the impact on the society, is CfE Level 4 work.

Diagram 32 – Problems in Edinburgh's CBD

TEACHING NOTES

View congestion, look at air-pollution levels and check out city-centre property prices with the links on the Bright Red website.

Traffic on Edinburgh's streets

Diagram 32 on page 233 shows us that many of Edinburgh's problems in the CBD come from the fact that it is an old, historic city that is struggling with traffic. It also has other problems that are very common across all cities in the developed world.

Big city centres also lack a sense of community and may even suffer from high rates of crime.

Shops found there tend to be chain stores such as 'Next', 'River Island' and 'Marks & Spencer', which are all selling goods that can be bought in other identical shops across the UK.

Diagram 33 – Problems in developed-world cities

Solutions to problems in Edinburgh's CBD

Congestion – Fast, reliable trams now run into the CBD. These attract passengers who leave cars at home. This helps to reduce congestion and pollution.

Congestion – Cars are not allowed to drive along Princes Street, and new one-way systems keep traffic flowing. This stops congestion and exhaust fumes from cars that are idling.

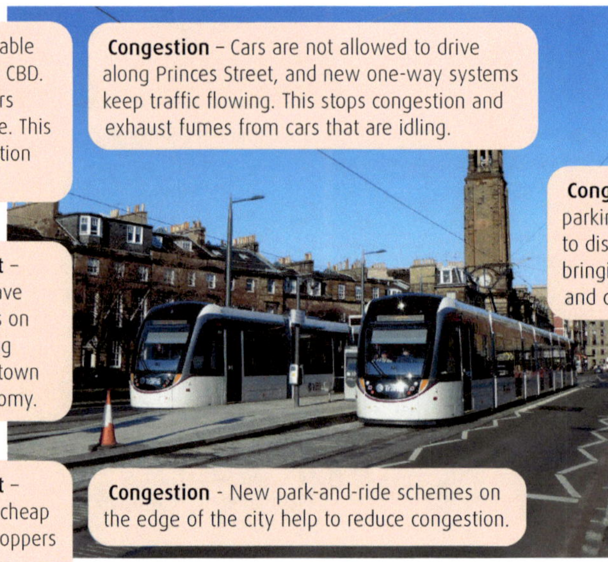

Congestion – Cost of parking is very expensive, to discourage people from bringing cars into town and causing congestion.

Decline of high street – New designer shops have established themselves on George Street, attracting wealthy shoppers into town and boosting the economy.

Decline of high street – Popular shops offering cheap goods are attracting shoppers back to Princes Street.

Congestion - New park-and-ride schemes on the edge of the city help to reduce congestion.

Diagram 34 – Some solutions to the problems of Edinburgh's CBD

People travelling to Edinburgh from outside the city leave their cars at a Park and Ride and take the bus or tram into town. This reduces the amount of cars travelling into the city centre. Do you think a scheme like this works?

Park and Ride scheme at Ingliston, outside Edinburgh

Classroom challenge

1. Study Diagrams 32 and 33 on pages 233 and 234 to help solve these 'Pointless' clues. Write the clues and answers into your workbook.

   (a) The reasons why high streets, such as Princes Street, have gone into decline and shops have closed. (OOTS and OS)
   (b) The two reasons why congestion is bad in Edinburgh's city centre. (NS and LOP)
   (c) The reason why we should be bothered about traffic congestion. (BFH)
   (d) Why the problem of congestion in Edinburgh is set to get worse. (GP and CTD)
   (e) One reason why people no longer want to live in the city centre. (EP)
   (f) Many of the shops on high streets in developed-world cities are this. (CS)
   (g) People do not want to live in developed-world cities because of these. (NSoC and HRoC)

2. Now, copy the flow diagram below into your workbook, completing the missing boxes using the information on Diagram 34 on page 234.

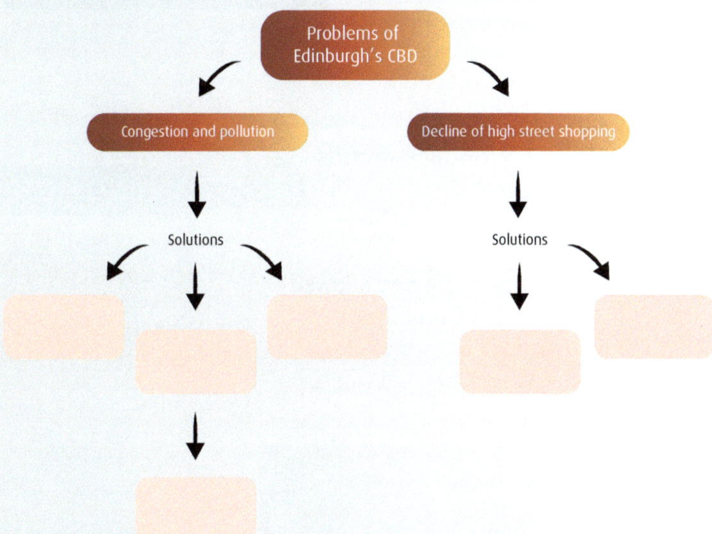

3. (a) Study Diagram 32 on page 233 once more. There is one CBD problem for which no solution is given. Which one is it? (**Hint** – it is not to do with shopping or congestion.)
   (b) Can you think of a solution to this problem?

TEACHING NOTES

Find some interesting points for in-class discussion by downloading the Teaching Notes from www.brightredpublishing.co.uk

TEACHING NOTES

Assessing the impact of developments in transport infrastructure in a chosen area is CfE Level 4 work.

Why not try to carry out a shopping survey of your own? Open the link on the Bright Red website for an example of how to set this out.

Problems in developed-world cities – rural-urban fringe

One of the problems of the CBD that we have identified and is difficult to solve is the fact that people cannot afford to live in city centres because the cost of property is too high. As a result, there has been a movement of people to the suburbs of cities, or to towns and villages outside the city. Many new homes have been built on countryside that has never been built on before. We call these **greenfield sites**.

TEACHING NOTES

Check out the links on the Bright Red website to find out the prices of property in Glasgow and Edinburgh.

New housing on a greenfield site

Protests over building on the Green Belt

STRETCH YOURSELF

Developed-world cities have been growing outwards for many decades now, spreading into the surrounding countryside. This is known as **urban sprawl**. In fact, back in 1947, the Town and Country Planning Act recognised this as a problem and allowed towns and cities the ability to set up a **Green Belt**. This is protected land that surrounds a town or city, which should be preserved as countryside and where any building is strictly regulated.

TEACHING NOTES

Explaining in some detail how any chosen urban area has developed, and evaluating the impact on the society, is CfE Level 4 work.

Cities build upwards when there is a lack of land, or the land becomes expensive

However, recently there has been a lot of building on Green Belt land. Some councils and even members of the UK Government are now arguing that Green Belt land should be developed. The reasons they give for this are:

Edge of Edinburgh in the real world – city ends, countryside begins

Diagram 35 – Reasons for building on the Green Belt

There are many advantages and disadvantages with building on Green Belt land (rural/urban fringe). These are summarised in Diagram 36 below.

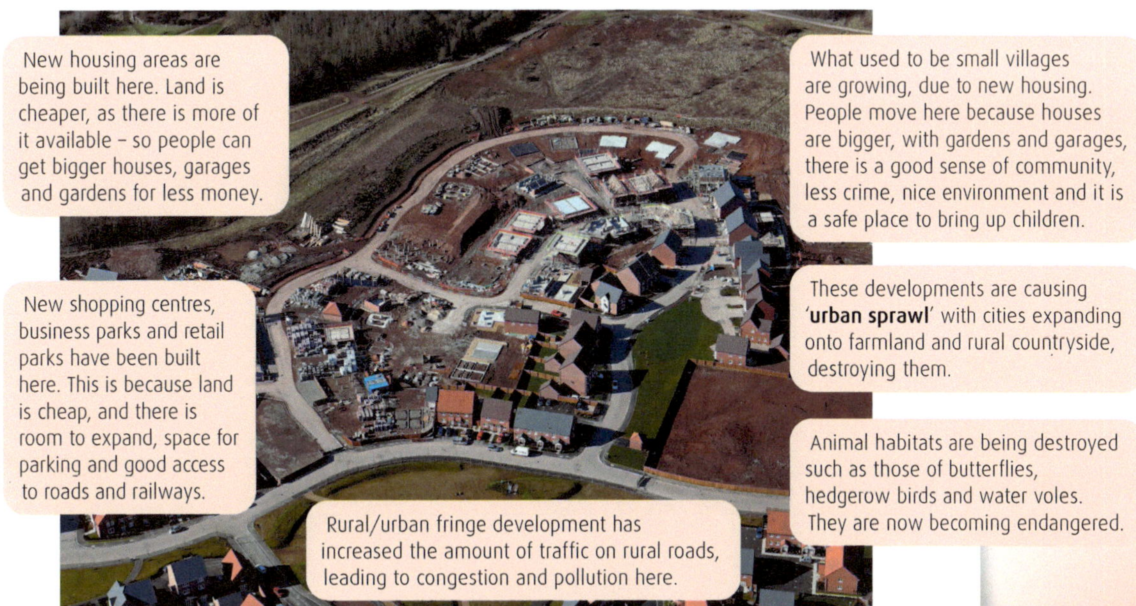

Diagram 36 – Pros and cons of building on the Green Belt (rural/urban fringe)

Classroom challenge

1. Unscramble the words below and then use them to help you answer the questions.

NERGE BTEL FEGRILEDEN TISE BARNU WRALPS

(a) What do we call land in the countryside that has never been built on before?
(b) What do we call it when cities spread out into the surrounding countryside?
(c) What did the 1947 Town and Country Planning Act allow towns and cities to set up?

2. Study Diagram 35 on page 237. **Explain**, in your own words, four reasons why some councils and some people in the UK Government think we should build on the Green Belt.
3. The Brown family are moving. They have chosen this house, which is built on the Green Belt. Study Diagram 36 on page 237, and give three reasons why they should move to this house and three reasons why they should not move there.

The Brown family's new home

We should move to this house because ...	We should not move to this house because ...

4. (a) Imagine you are a town planner. You have been asked by a large national supermarket chain to look for a site for them to build a new supermarket. There are two sites available. One is in the inner city, on land where an old factory will be demolished (**brownfield site**). The other is on the Green Belt (**greenfield site**). Copy out the table and list the advantages and disadvantages of each site. Use the phrases from the word box on the next page to help you.

Brownfield site

Greenfield site

Brownfield site advantages	Brownfield site disadvantages	Greenfield site advantages	Greenfield site disadvantages
Cheap land		Cheap land	

ROOM TO EXPAND	**ROADS TOO NARROW FOR DELIVERY LORRIES**	**LOTS OF CUSTOMERS NEARBY**
LOTS OF ROOM FOR PARKING	**WILL CAUSE URBAN SPRAWL**	
GOOD ACCESS	**NO ROOM TO EXPAND**	**NOT MUCH SPACE FOR PARKING**
WILL DESTROY THE HOMES OF WILDLIFE	**LAND WAS AN EYESORE (ugly)**	**NICE SURROUNDINGS**
LAND IS TOO CROWDED	**WILL CAUSE MORE CONGESTION ON NARROW CITY ROADS**	
VIBRATIONS FROM LORRIES DAMAGE NEARBY BUILDINGS		
VALUABLE FARMLAND IS LOST		

TEACHING NOTES

Explaining in some detail how any chosen urban area has developed, and evaluating the impact on the society, is CfE Level 4 work.

(b) Now that you have completed the table, where will you locate the new supermarket? **Evaluate** both sites and make your decision. (Remember, to evaluate you will need to describe the good and bad things about each site, and decide which one you are going to build on, giving reasons for your choice.)

TEACHING NOTES

Try the games or follow the links on the Bright Red website to learn more about building on greenfield and brownfield sites.

Have you enjoyed learning about urban areas in developed and developing world? Would you like a career that uses the knowledge and skills you have gained from this topic? Why not visit the 'My World of Work/STEM/Developing the Young Workforce' section of the Homework Helpers to find out more?

HEALTH

WHAT DIFFERENCES ARE THERE IN HEALTH BETWEEN DEVELOPED AND DEVELOPING COUNTRIES?

Health in developing countries

Malnourished child

We have already discovered that there are big differences in **mortality** (death) rates between developed and developing countries. We have also discovered that these tend to be higher in developing countries. Why is this?

Our health very much depends on our standard of living as well as the surrounding environment where we live.

In developing countries, a huge cause of disease is the lack of clean water and proper sanitation (toilets). In fact, 80% of all disease in these areas is because of this. Other causes of ill health are shown in Diagram 37 below.

Diagram 37 – Causes of disease in the developing world

Cholera

What happens if you catch cholera?

Cholera is a very serious disease found in the developing world, which kills up to 120 000 people and affects a further 5 million every year. It is caused by comma-shaped bacteria, which, if swallowed, will cause the symptoms shown opposite.

The kind of conditions that cholera thrives in

Cholera thrives in dirty conditions, especially if there is a lack of proper access to clean, safe water or sanitation. Dharavi in Mumbai is an example of the kind of environment cholera would thrive in.

TEACHING NOTES

There are many links, film clips and activities on the Bright Red website that provide lots more detail on cholera.

DON'T FORGET

Symptoms of cholera include severe sickness and diarrhoea, dehydration, coma and death within 48 hours. **Cholera can spread very easily!**

Where does cholera occur?

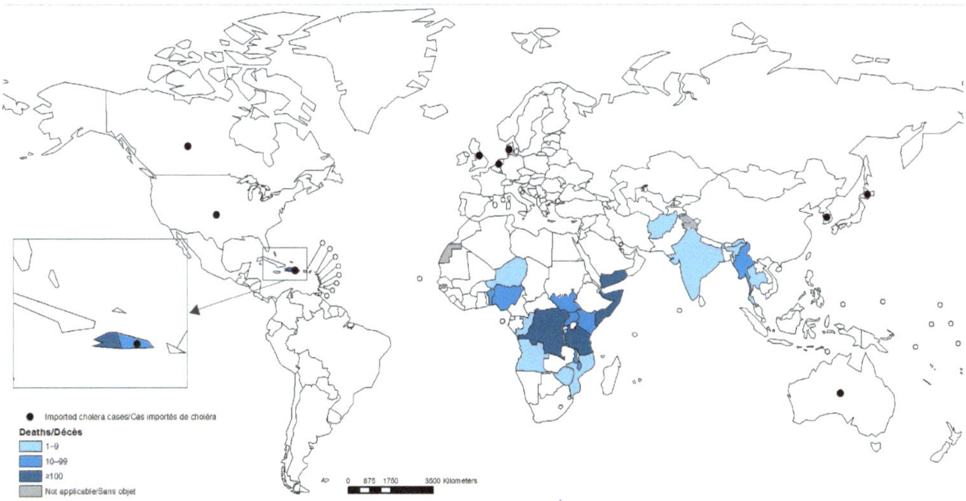

Diagram 38 – Countries reporting cases of cholera in 2016

The map above shows clearly that it is mainly developing-world countries that are affected by outbreaks of cholera.

Classroom challenge

1. What percentage of disease in developing countries is caused by a lack of clean water and sanitation?
2. Study Diagram 37 on page 240. Copy out the sentences below and complete them by filling in the missing words.

- Developing countries have many natural ___________, which help to spread disease.
- Lack of food and a balanced diet can lead to hunger, famine and m______________.
- In developing countries, there is a lack of ____________ staff.
- Disease can spread because people have a lack of education about h_____________.
- Climate makes the spread of disease worse, especially if it is w_______ and w___.

3. **Describe** what would happen to you if you caught cholera.
4. How many people are:
   - killed by cholera every year?
   - affected by cholera every year?

Go Digital!

5. (a) Study Diagram 38 on page 241. Use the online atlas from the Bright Red website to identify the countries that had more than 100 deaths from cholera in 2016.
   (b) Now, use the World Health Organisation link from the Bright Red website to find the world cholera map for 2015. Again, use the online atlas to help you name countries that had cholera in 2015 but not in 2016.
   (c) Now, use the link to the ArcGIS cholera map from the Bright Red website. From this map, find out the following:

   - How many cases of cholera did Afghanistan have in 2015?
   - How many cases of cholera did the Democratic Republic of Congo have in 2015?
   - How many cases of cholera did Haiti have in 2015?
   - How many cases of cholera did Scotland have in 2015?

   (d) Now, make up a bar graph of these figures in your workbook.
   (e) Use your graph to **describe** the amount of cases of cholera that these countries had in 2015.
   (f) Discuss with your class why these countries might have had such numbers of cholera in 2015.

DON'T FORGET

Reading and comparing maps are important skills in geography. They can lead to interesting careers in GIS (Geographic Information Systems)

DON'T FORGET

Remember, to describe a graph, we need to 'speak like a geographer' and pick out figures. You should compare figures from different countries by saying exactly how much higher or lower they are. Also, make use of phrases such as 'much higher', 'substantially lower' and 'noticeably higher'.

What causes the spread of cholera?

Diagram 39 – Causes of the spread of cholera

All our lives, we have constantly been told to wash our hands after going to the toilet and before we eat. We are also taught basic hygiene at school. We know we should not eat or drink things that are not properly cooked or look dirty, and it seems we do all these things for very good reason!

How can we stop the spread of cholera?

There is a vaccination for cholera, but it makes people unwell because it introduces dead cholera bacteria into the body. These make the person's immune system learn how to fight the disease. However, due to the health risks, people only get this vaccination if they know they are going to an area where there is a cholera outbreak.

There are other simple things people can do instead, to treat and prevent cholera.

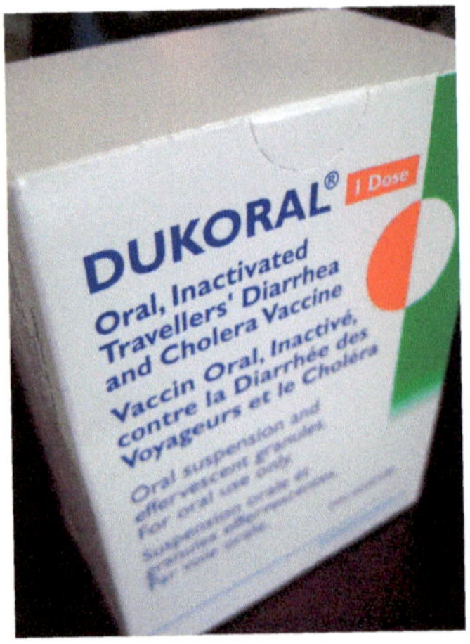

Photo 1 – Cholera vaccine

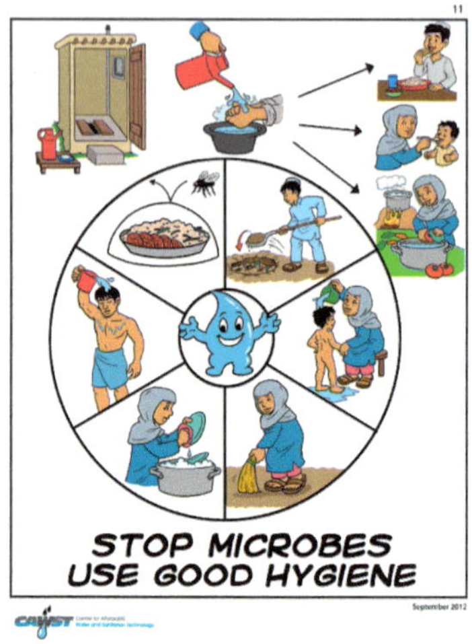

Photo 2 – Hygiene education poster

Classroom challenge

1. Study Diagram 39 on page 243.
   (a) **Explain** the reasons why you think not washing your hands can lead to the spread of cholera.
   (b) **Explain** two reasons why open sewers can cause the spread of cholera.
   (c) **Explain** why people can catch cholera from using the local river for washing and drinking.
   (d) Name two things that people don't do with their food that can cause the spread of cholera.

2. Look at Photo 1.
   (a) What is the name of the vaccination that can be used to prevent cholera?
   (b) **Describe** how this vaccine works.

Go Digital!

3. Copy the diagram on the next page into your workbook or on poster paper. Now, watch the three film clips on cholera from the Bright Red website. As you watch, make notes on how cholera can be prevented.
   Now, complete the speech bubbles on your diagram by adding a statement and a cartoon or symbol on how cholera can be prevented in each bubble. (One has been completed for you. Add extra bubbles if you need to.)
   Colour your diagram in.

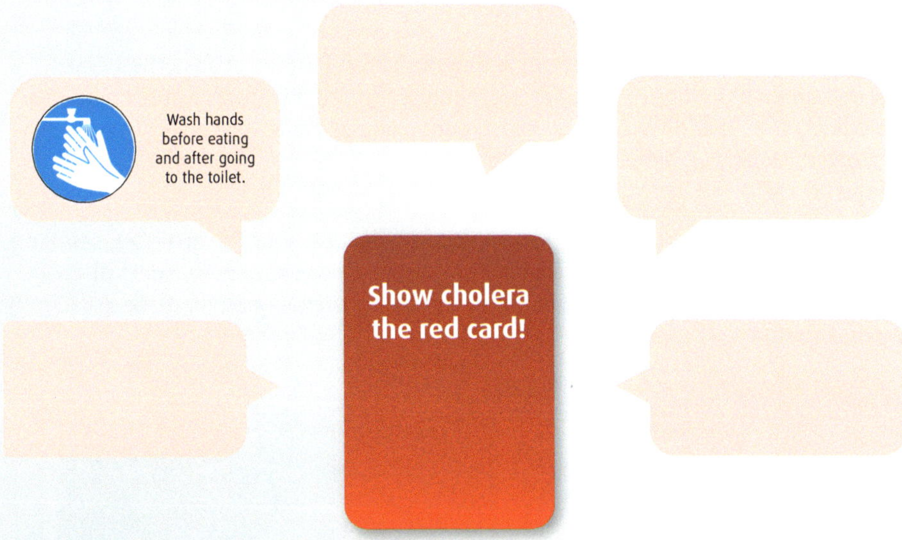

4. Go back to the ArcGIS cholera map from the Bright Red website.
   (a) Look at the cholera map carefully, and select a country that you would really like to go to on holiday but that has a large number of cholera cases.
   (b) Now, imagine you are going on holiday to this country. Watch the film clip and follow the link to the NHS cholera webpage on the Bright Red website. Use them to help you complete the table below on what you should do when you are abroad, to avoid catching cholera.

   Cholera – Dos and Don'ts while on holiday

Dos	Don'ts

Health in developed countries

In developed countries, mortality rates are much lower. This is because they have better standards of living. This means more money to provide clean water, sanitation and medical care. In addition, people earn money and are able to buy food and have a balanced diet. As a result, diseases such as cholera have disappeared in the developed world.

However, longer life expectancy and poor lifestyle choices, such as fatty diet, smoking, alcohol and lack of exercise, mean that other diseases, such as cancer, heart disease and asthma, are common. Rising obesity levels are also causing an increase in cases of diabetes.

Obesity in the developed world

Bad lifestyle choices

Heart disease

Heart disease is an important disease to study because it affects 6.7% of men and 4.2% of women in Scotland. Every year in the UK, 160 000 people die from heart disease, and every 7 minutes, someone will have a heart attack. It has a big impact on the country because it affects people's ability to work, meaning they might have to rely on benefits, as well as putting a lot of pressure on our hospitals. It also causes a lot of emotional stress for families having to deal with relatives with the disease.

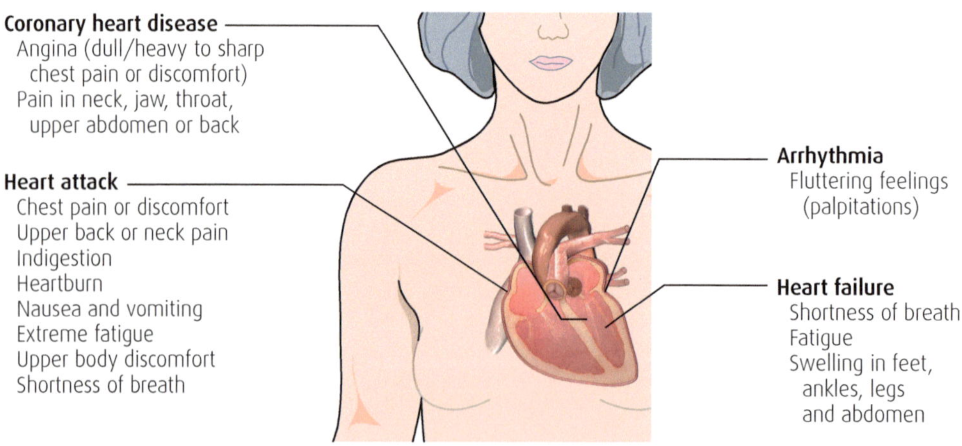

Diagram 40 – Symptoms of heart disease

What is heart disease?

Heart disease is a variety of conditions that affect how well our hearts work. These conditions could be from a build-up of fatty deposits on the walls of **arteries** (the vessels that take blood that is full of oxygen around our body) or problems with how our heart is able to pump blood.

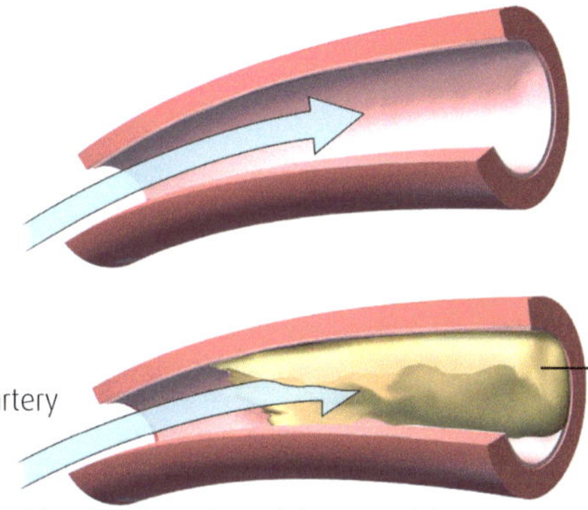

Fatty deposits in arteries (sometimes called plaque)

What are the causes of heart disease?

High blood pressure – puts extra strain on the heart.

Smoking – makes fatty deposits form inside arteries, narrowing them.

Being obese/overweight – this can cause high blood pressure and high **cholesterol**. This clogs up our arteries.

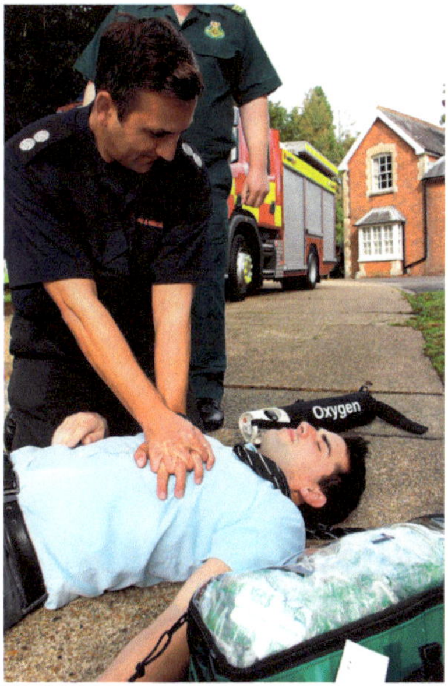

Diagram 41 – The causes of heart disease

Fatty foods – eating too many chips, burgers and cakes can cause a build-up of **cholesterol**. This can then build up as fatty deposits inside our arteries.

Lack of exercise – can lead to higher blood pressure.

History of heart disease in the family – unfortunately, some people are born with a high risk of heart disease and high cholesterol. This clogs up our arteries.

TEACHING NOTES

Follow the links on the Bright Red website to expand knowledge on heart disease, its causes, its symptoms and what we can do to prevent it.

Classroom challenge

1. Copy out the sentences below into your workbook. Write the word 'true' or 'false' after each of them.

- Cholera has disappeared from the developed world because there is money to provide clean water, sanitation and medical care. **True/False**
- Lifestyle choices such as smoking, fatty diet, lack of exercise and drinking alcohol mean that people live longer in the developed world. **True/False**
- Heart disease affects 4.2% of men and 6.7% of women in Scotland. **True/False**
- In the UK, every 7 minutes, a person has a heart attack. **True/False**
- Heart disease is good for a country because people can take lots of time off work. **True/False**
- Every year in the UK, 160 000 people die from heart disease. **True/False**

2. Copy out the diagram below into your workbook. Use Diagram 40 on page 246 to help you complete the missing words.

Symptoms of heart disease

A_________: a dull or sharp pain in the chest

Ind__________n

N______ and V____________.

S_____________ of b_________.

A_____________: fluttering feelings.

S_________ in feet, ankles and legs

F________: tiredness

3. **Describe** what arteries are.
4. What can build up on the walls of arteries?
5. Study Diagram 41 on page 247. Use the code-buster to help you find key words for the causes of heart disease by exchanging the number for the correct letter. However, there is a catch. The key words have been jumbled up. Once you have broken the code, unscramble them!

A	B	C	D	E	F	G	H	I	J	K	L	M
1	2	3	4	5	6	7	8	9	10	11	12	13
N	O	P	Q	R	S	T	U	V	W	X	Y	Z
14	15	16	17	18	19	20	21	22	23	24	25	26

(a) 7 9 8 8   4 12 15 2 15   18 5 19 16 18 21 5 19
(b) 9 8 7 8   20 12 5 18 15 12 8 15 3 19 5
(c) 19 11 9 14 7 15 13
(d) 13 9 12 6 1 25   20 18 9 25 19 8 15
(e) 20 15 2 5 25 9 19
(f) 3 1 11 12   6 15   19 5 18 5 24 9 3 5

What can we do to prevent heart disease?

The main way to treat heart disease is to try to get people to change their lifestyle choices. However, there have also been advances in the medical treatment of heart disease, which now gives people a much better chance of survival.

Eat a better diet!

There are government education campaigns telling us to do the following:

Eat our '5 a day' (eat at least five items of fruit or vegetables every day).

Cut down on high-fat, high-sugar, processed foods.

Look at the labelling on foods, and avoid those with high fat, salt and sugar.

Take more exercise!

This helps to stop people being overweight. It also lowers blood pressure and cholesterol levels.

Stop smoking!

In the UK, smoking in public places has now been banned.

Cigarettes are also now very expensive to buy, to try to put people off smoking.

Cigarettes cannot be displayed in shops.

Very graphic health warnings are found on cigarette packets to shock people into stopping smoking.

Regular cholesterol tests!

People can have regular cholesterol and blood-pressure tests, which mean that action can be taken if any bad signs are found.

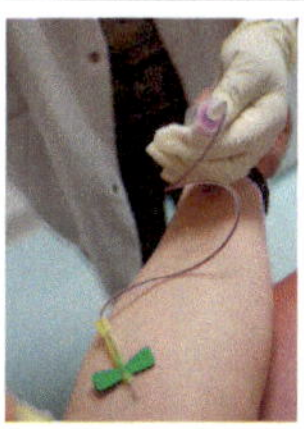

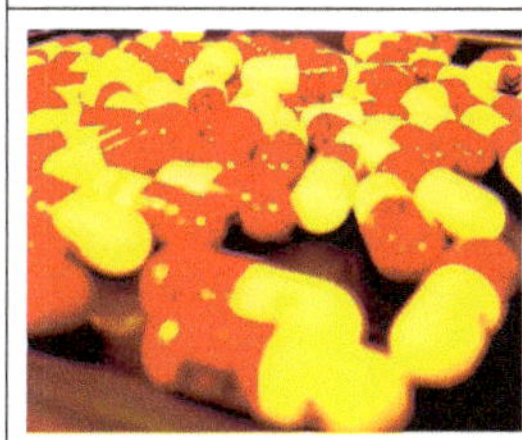

Medical advances!

People with heart disease can now take pills that will thin their blood or lower their cholesterol.

If arteries are clogged up because of fatty deposits, a stent can be put in place (a cage that is inflated by a small balloon that will widen the artery).

Diagram 42 – Ways to prevent heart disease

Classroom challenge

1. Create a 'Heart Disease Awareness' community page poster for Facebook. Use the design below to help you with how to lay this page out.

Cover photos/images/Title of group

Logo

About – say what your group is trying to do

Insert usual Facebook symbols here – Like, Follow, Share, Save

Make at least six separate posts telling your followers how they can avoid heart disease. Diagram 42 on page 249 will help you. Use the Bright Red website for some useful links, but also do some research of your own. You might want to recommend useful websites, film clips and news items that your followers might find useful.
(You can make up how many likes, shares and comments each post has had ☺☺☺☺☺ – nothing rude though!!)

2. Now that you know all about heart disease in the UK, make up a plan of what you think you will do in order to reduce **your** chances of having heart disease. Make at least four pledges in your plan that you want to stick to for the rest of your life!

Question 2 could be set as a homework task.

Have you enjoyed learning about health issues in the developed and developing world? Would you like a career that uses the knowledge and skills you have gained from this topic? Why not visit the 'My World of Work/STEM/Developing the Young Workforce' section of the Homework Helpers to find out more?

MAPPING SKILLS

Marvellous mapping skills!

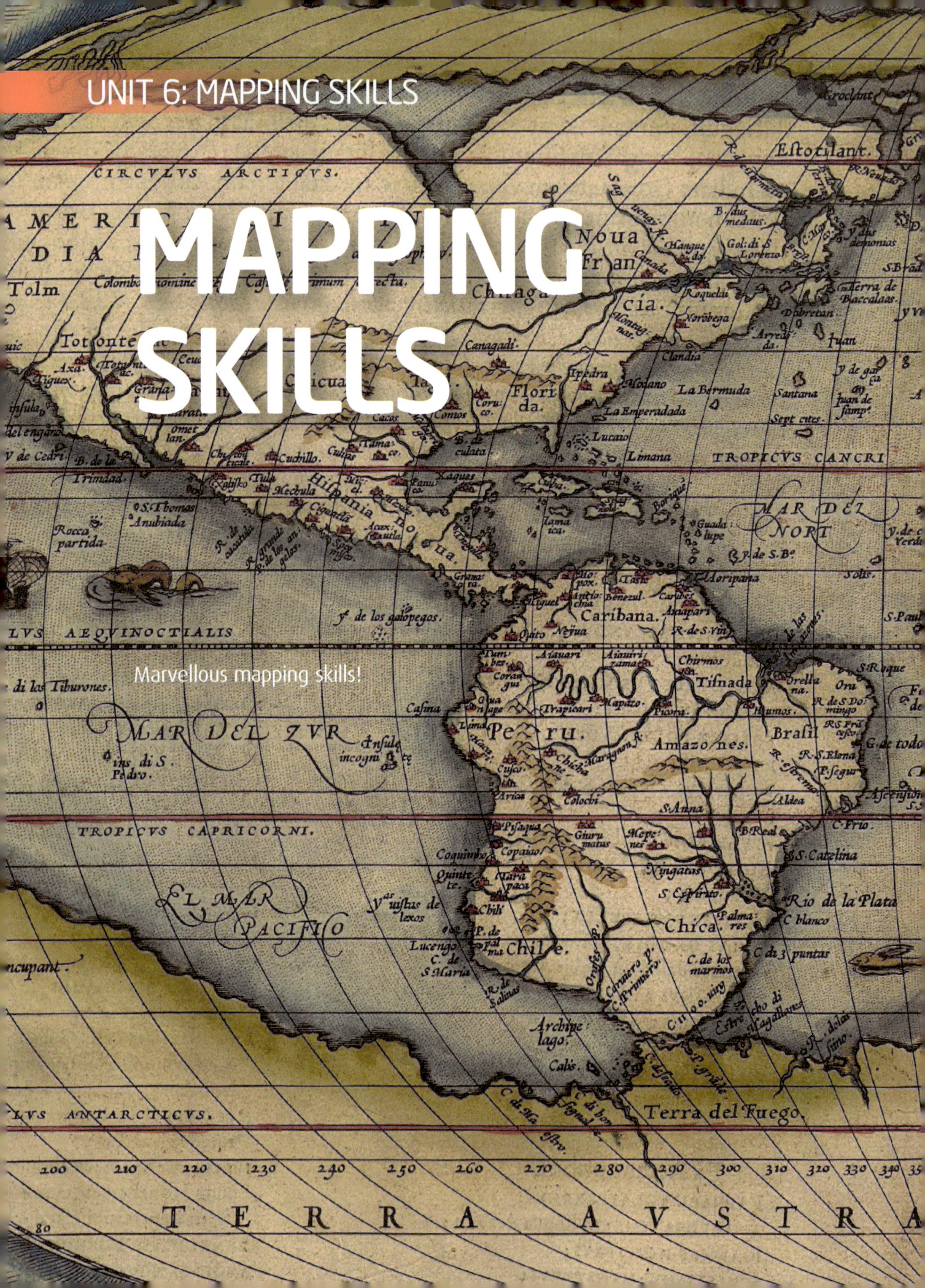

EVROPA
Tartaria
ASIA
China.
India orientalis
Persia
Arabia.
Aegyptus
AFRICA.
Abissini
Manicongo.
Melinde
OCEANVS AETHIOPICVS.
MAR DI INDIA
Psitacorum regio, sic à Lusitanis appellata ob incredibilem earum auium ibidem magnitudinem.
IS NONDVM COGNITA.

MAPPING SKILLS

I can use a range of maps and geographical information systems to gather, interpret and present conclusions and can locate a range of features within Scotland, the UK, Europe and the wider world. SOC 3-14a

Benchmarks

- Reviews at least two simple graphical sources to interpret information and form a conclusion, for example, a map and a graph.
- Uses relevant numeracy and digital technology skills to interpret at least two sources of data from maps and geographical information systems.
- Locates increasingly complex features such as different physical landscape features and human features on maps of Scotland, the UK, Europe and the wider world, for example, hills, mountains, valleys, population.

What's coming up?

- What are physical and political maps?
- What are latitude and longitude and what use are they to geographers?
- Where are the world's continents and oceans?
- River deep, mountain high – where are the world's highest mountain ranges and longest rivers?
- Islands in the stream – where are the world's largest islands?
- Mapping Scotland – making a physical map.
- Mapping Scotland – making a political map.
- Ordnance Survey (OS) mapping skills – four-figure grid references.
- Ordnance Survey (OS) mapping skills – six-figure grid references.

WHAT ARE PHYSICAL AND POLITICAL MAPS?

Maps and atlas work

Did you know that to the ancient Greeks, Atlas was a Titan who, as a punishment, had to hold the heavens on his shoulders?

Atlases in geography, however, are a book of maps. They are used frequently because they tell us:

- Where places are in the world
- What the landscape is like
- The shape of countries, continents and islands
- Information about population and climate

Atlases also show us information using two very different types of maps.

Physical maps

These show us natural things, such as lakes, mountains, rivers and flat land.

Political maps

These show features decided by humans, such as countries, borders and capital cities.

WHAT ARE LATITUDE AND LONGITUDE AND WHAT USE ARE THEY TO GEOGRAPHERS?

All maps in atlases are criss-crossed with thin lines. These are known as lines of **latitude** and lines of **longitude**. They are useful because they help us to find places on a map. More importantly, they quite literally help us to label every spot of land or sea on planet Earth!

Map of North American Great Lakes with lines of latitude and longitude

Lines of latitude – these are lines that cross the map from side to side.

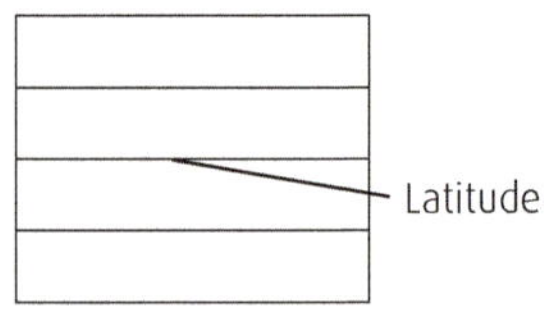

Lines of longitude – these are lines that cross the map from top to bottom.

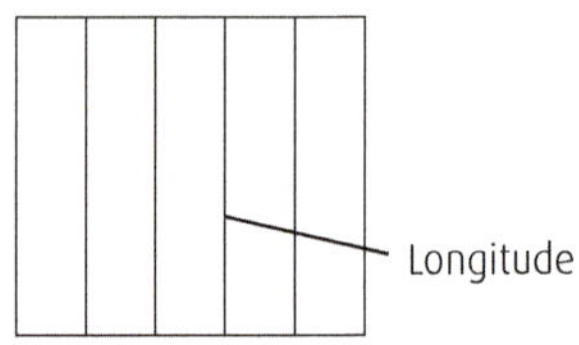

Each line of latitude and longitude has its own number at the end of it.

Important lines of latitude and longitude to remember!

The line of LATITUDE at 0 degrees is called the **EQUATOR**.

The line of LONGITUDE at 0 degrees is called the **PRIME MERIDIAN** (sometimes called the Greenwich Meridian after the part of London it crosses through).

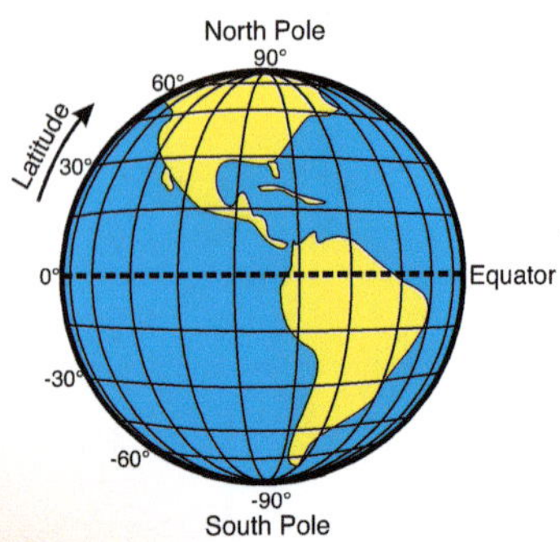

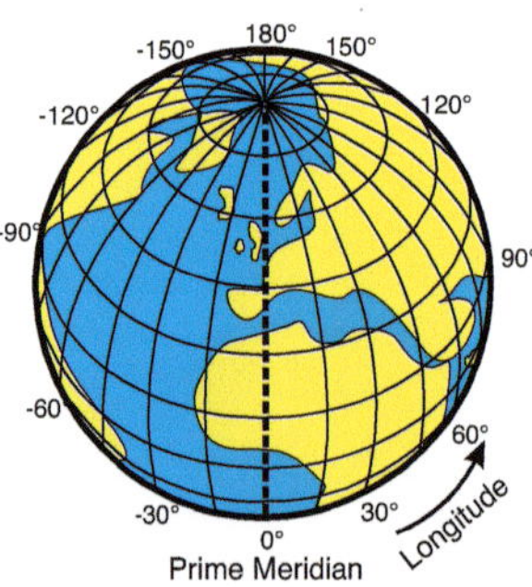

Equator and the Prime Meridian

The Prime Meridian in Greenwich – the left foot is in the west of the world and the right foot is in the east!

A very interesting line of longitude is called the **International Date Line**. It is found in the Pacific Ocean at 180° longitude. It is interesting because lines of longitude are also time lines.

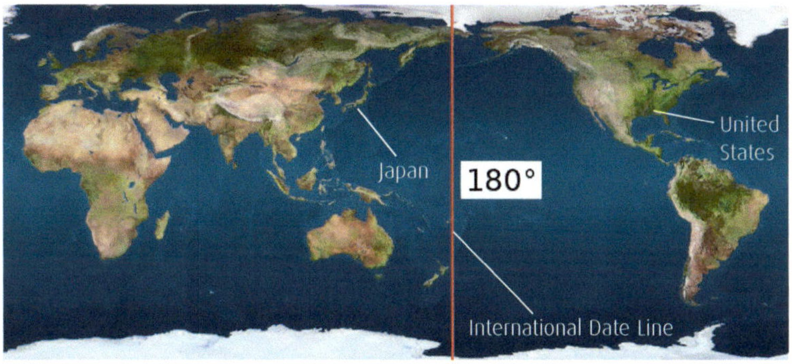

The International Date Line

Try this head-scratcher!

Here's how the International Date Line works. Let's say you fly from the United States to Japan. You leave the United States on Tuesday morning. Since you're travelling west, the time advances slowly thanks to time zones (lines of longitude you are crossing) and the speed at which your aeroplane flies, but once you cross the International Date Line, it's suddenly Wednesday!

On the reverse trip home, you fly from Japan to the United States. You leave Japan on Thursday morning, but, as you cross the Pacific Ocean, the day gets later quickly as you cross time zones. Once you cross the International Date Line, the day changes back to Wednesday!

What do you think would happen if you spent your whole life in a boat crossing the International Date Line every day? Discuss this with your class.

Using lines of latitude and longitude

Diagram 1 – *Titanic* sinking (painting by Willy Stöwer)

When the *Titanic* sank in 1912, a distress message was sent out giving the exact point in the Atlantic Ocean where the ship was sinking. This was done by using latitude and longitude (see Diagram 1 above).

When looking at an atlas and trying to find somewhere, it is best to use the **atlas index**. This is usually found at the back of the atlas, where everywhere is listed alphabetically with numbers and letters after the name. These letters and numbers are the lines of latitude and longitude where you will find these places.

Lines of **LATITUDE** are numbered according to how many degrees north or south of the Equator they are.

Lines of **LONGITUDE** are numbered according to many degrees east or west of the Prime Meridian they are.

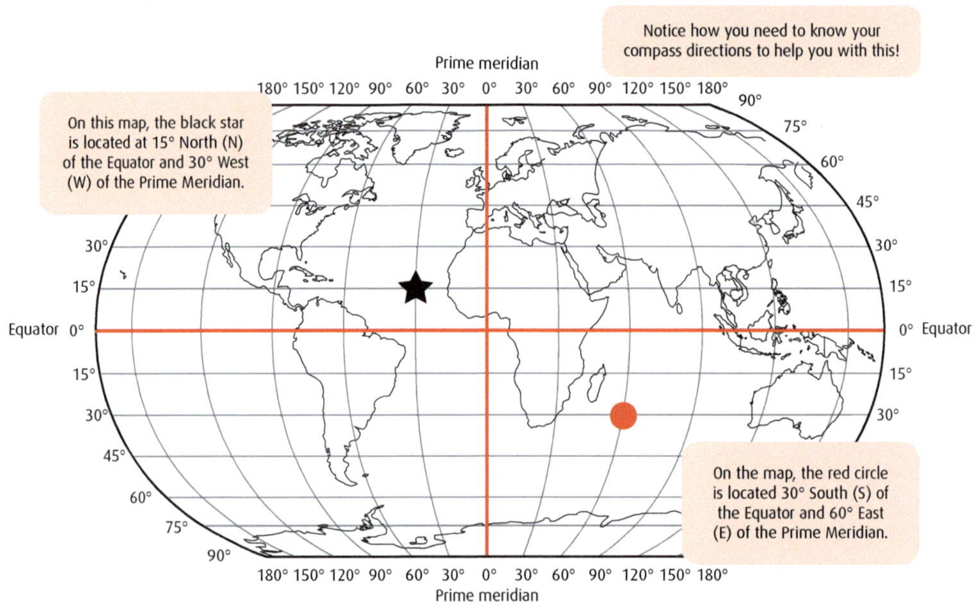

Diagram 2 – How to use latitude and longitude to find things on a map

Classroom challenge

1. Give four ways in which atlases are useful to geographers.
2. **Describe** what a physical map shows us.
3. **Describe** what a political map shows us.
4. Copy and complete the paragraph below into your workbook by adding the missing words from the word box.

> All maps in atlases have thin lines criss-crossing them. These are called lines of ______________ and longitude. Lines crossing a map from top to bottom are called lines of ______________. Lines going from side to side are called latitude. A famous line of latitude is the ______________. A famous line of longitude is the ____________ ______________. They are useful to us because they help us to ___________ where places are on a map. Lines of longitude are also _________ lines. A famous example of this is the ________________ ________ _______.

PRIME MERIDIAN **LATITUDE** **FIND** **LONGITUDE** **TIME** **EQUATOR** **INTERNATIONAL DATE LINE**

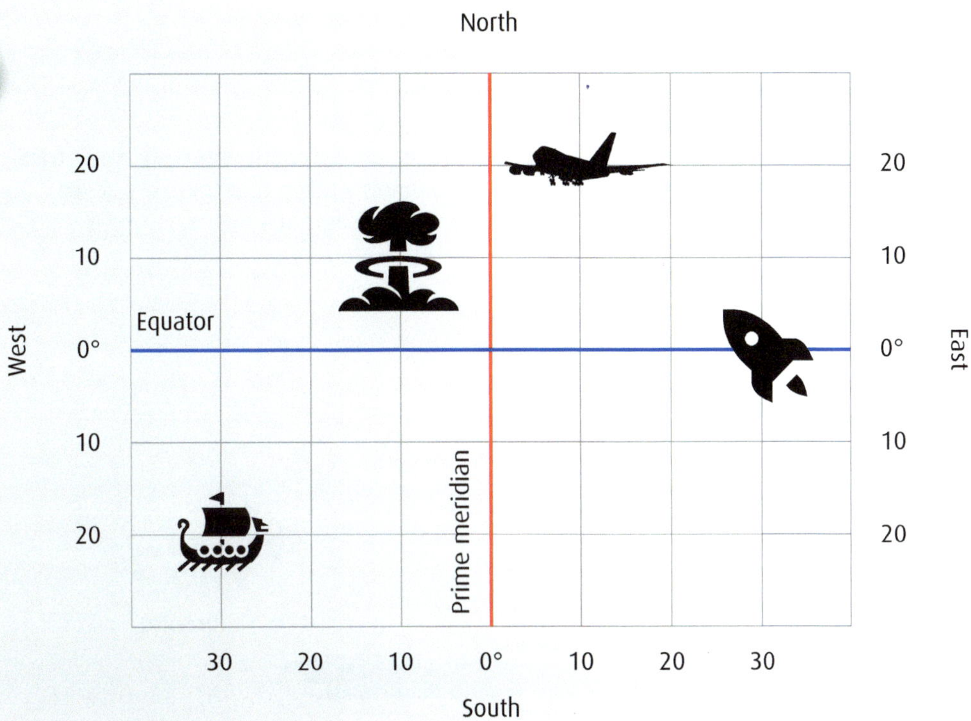

Diagram 3 – Locating things

5. Diagram 2 on page 258 shows us how to use lines of latitude and longitude to find things on a map. Study Diagram 3 on page 259. Now, complete the sentences below giving the correct latitude and longitude.

* An enemy bomber has been detected at 20° North of the Equator and _______ East of the Prime Meridian.

* A pirate ship is sailing 20° ________ of the Equator and ______ West of the Prime Meridian.

* A nuclear bomb has exploded at ________ North of the _________ and 10° ______ of the Prime Meridian.

* An alien rocket has crashed at 0° and _______ East of the Prime Meridian.

6. Now, draw a grid like the Diagram 3 above into your jotter. On it, add your own symbols to represent

- an erupting volcano
- a tornado
- a battleship
- a whale

Once you have added them to your grid, write out a sentence for each – like those in Question 5 – to describe their latitude and longitude.

Question 6 could be set as a homework task.

WHERE ARE THE WORLD'S CONTINENTS AND OCEANS?

A continent is a very large mass of land on our planet. Often, continents – such as Africa – are made up of many different countries. It is commonly taken that there are seven distinct continents on planet Earth. They are shown on Diagram 4 below.

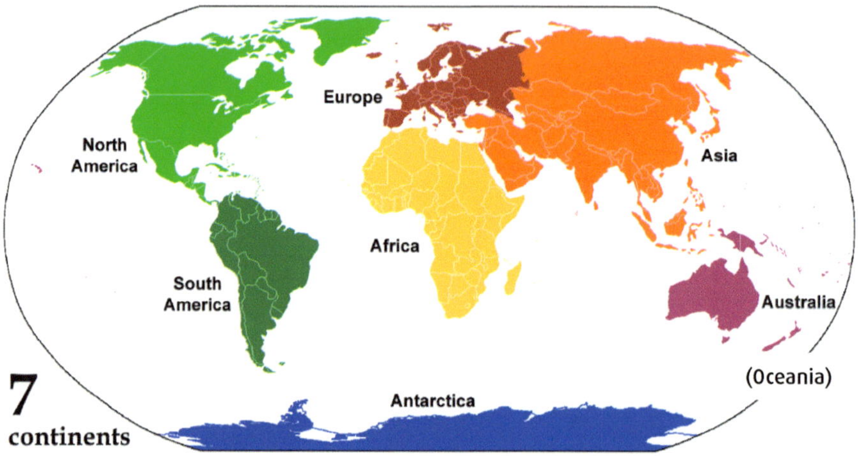

Diagram 4 – Continents of Earth

You are now going to produce some maps for your workbook. You should take your time and present them well.

Classroom challenge

1. Using a blank world map and Diagram 4 above, add the names of the seven different continents onto your map. Mark them out and colour them in a different colour like the example below.

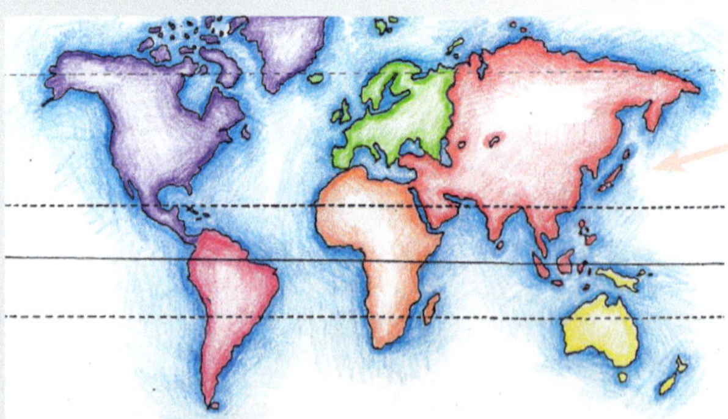

When colouring in maps, try colouring the edges darker and have middle areas lighter. This not only looks better, but also you can read any labels on your map.

There is a blank world map on the Bright Red website and a link to an online atlas to help with this.

2. Use an atlas to complete your map by adding on the names of the world's oceans. There are five oceans in the world, but sometimes on maps their names are split into north and south, such as North Atlantic and South Atlantic.

RIVER DEEP, MOUNTAIN HIGH – WHERE ARE THE WORLD'S HIGHEST MOUNTAIN RANGES AND LONGEST RIVERS?

For this map, you will need to use an atlas from your classroom. All atlases should have a physical map of the world in them. Use this to help you with these tasks.

TEACHING NOTES

Print out the blank World Physical map from the Bright Red website for this activity.

Classroom challenge

1. Eight rivers have been marked on your map with a letter. Copy the table below into your jotter, and use your atlas to match up the name of the river to the correct letter on your map.

Name of river	Letter
NILE	
MEKONG	
MISSISSIPPI	
DANUBE	
YANGTZE	
GANGES	
AMAZON	
RHINE	

The River Nile in Cairo, Egypt

2. Look at your map once again. There are some shaded areas on it. These are the world's highest mountain ranges. Use your atlas to add the correct names of these ranges onto the correct locations on your map. Choose from the options below.

ROCKY MOUNTAINS ANDES ATLAS MOUNTAINS HIMALAYAS ETHIOPIAN HIGHLANDS ALPS

ISLANDS IN THE STREAM - WHERE ARE THE WORLD'S LARGEST ISLANDS?

3. You are now going to use the same map to add the names of the world's biggest or most well-known islands onto the correct locations. Once again, you will need to use your atlas to help you. The islands you need to add are:-

Number	Island
1	Baffin Island
2	Cuba
3	Falkland Islands
4	Greenland
5	Hawaiian Islands
6	Iceland
7	Japan
8	Madagascar
9	New Guinea
10	New Zealand
11	Sri Lanka
12	Sumatra

Don't worry if you can't fit the names onto your map. Just add the number of the island in the correct place and copy out this table into your workbook as a key.

4. Now, complete your World Physical map by colouring it as follows
   Mountains = Brown
   Land = Green
   Sea = Blue
   Add a key to your map.

MAPPING SCOTLAND

Making a physical map of Scotland

1. Now, let's get to know our own country! Use the Scotland Physical map template from the Bright Red website for this. On it, you should mark the following features by looking up their location in an atlas.

The Old Man of Storr on the Isle of Skye

MOUNTAINS/HILLS

- North West Highlands
- Southern Uplands
- Grampian Mountains
- Lammermuir Hills
- Ochil Hills
- Sidlaw Hills
- Pentland Hills

ISLANDS

- Skye
- Shetland
- Jura
- Tiree
- Islay
- Lewis
- Mull
- Orkney
- North Uist
- South Uist
- Rum
- Coll

RIVERS/FIRTHS

- Firth of Forth
- Firth of Lorne
- Firth of Tay
- North Minch
- Firth of Clyde
- Moray Firth
- Pentland Firth
- Solway Firth

2. Now, complete your Scotland physical map by colouring it in.
Mountains = Brown
Lowlands = Green
Sea = Blue

DON'T FORGET

Did you know that we should now only use maps of Scotland that show the true position of Shetland? We should never put Shetland in a box because it does not allow us to understand just how remote these islands are.

Making a political map of Scotland

1. Now, you are going to make a bright, colourful political map of Scotland showing the Local Authority areas. Print out a template map from the Bright Red website and follow the link to the Scottish Government to find out the location of Scotland's local authorities.

DON'T FORGET

Remember to try to colour around the edges darker and shade the middle areas lighter!

OS MAPPING SKILLS

We have already learned how to use latitude and longitude to find places on a map. However, in geography we use Ordnance Survey maps very frequently. They are criss-crossed with thin blue lines that are called **grid lines**. These are important because, once again, they help us to locate things on the map or can be used to give directions. Each grid line has its own special number at the end of it. When we use these numbers to find things on a map, we call these **grid references**.

These grid lines form squares across OS maps which we call **grid squares**.

TEACHING NOTES

Check out the activities and film clips on the Bright Red website for great interactive ways to learn about OS Mapping and grid references.

OS mapping skills – four-figure grid references

The most basic way to locate things on an OS map is to use what we call **four-figure grid references**. To do this, we must first find the two grid lines that cross in the bottom left-hand corner of the square we are interested in (look at the diagram showing the emoji below).

Give the number from the bottom first, which is 12.

Then give the number from the side next, which is 01.

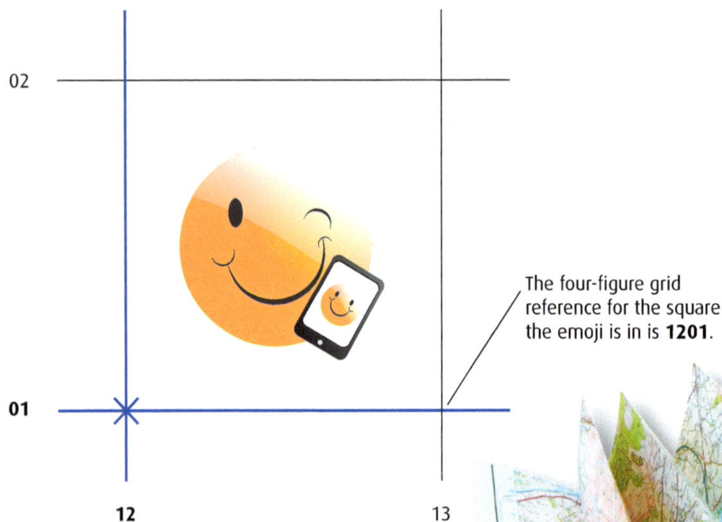

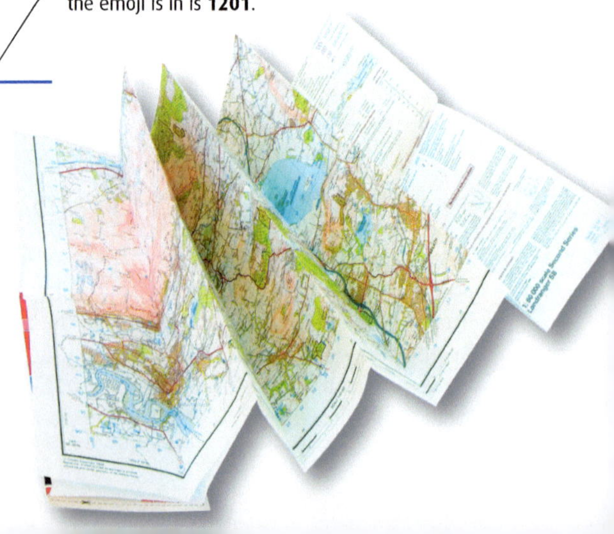

Classroom challenge

Now try this out for yourself!

1. Look at the grid below. Each square has a letter in it. Find each square by following the four-figure grid references listed. Then, for each square, note down the letter in it. These letters spell out two words used frequently in geography when we are carrying out mapping exercises. However, the letters are jumbled up. You will need to unscramble them!

1307, 1812, 1909, 1806, 1509, 1412, 1811, 1410 1512, 1912, 1509, 1712, 1210, 1209

	12	13	14	15	16	17	18	19
12–13	A	B	D	V	O	Y	A	E
11–12	E	N	C	T	C	S	O	A
10–11	S	D	N	E	X	T	N	M
09–10	U	E	Y	R	Z	B	F	N
08–09	V	G	C	E	B	M	P	L
07–08	Q	C	E	F	J	B	S	Y
06–07	R	D	A	C	M	G	E	V
05–06	U	O	C	Y	P	N	L	X

2. Now, let's try out our knowledge of four-figure grid references using a real OS map. Use the OS map of Alton Towers below to complete the following sentences.

- Alton Towers Amusement Park (look for the lakes) is in square __________.
- The hotels are in square _____________.
- Crumpwood Farm is in square_________.
- The castle is in square____________.

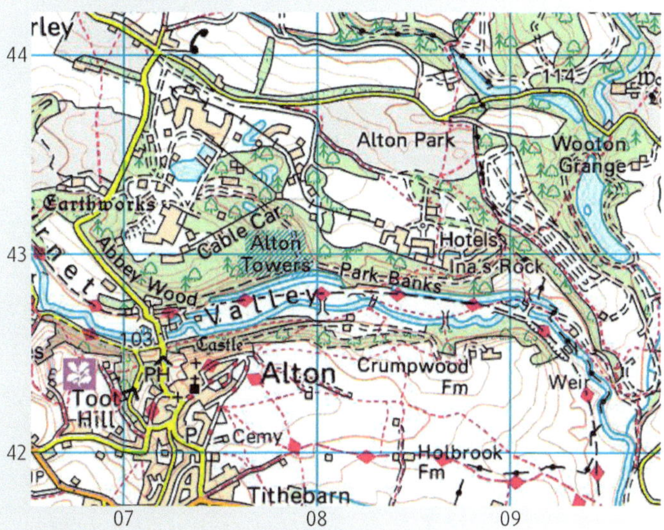

Alton Towers Resort

OS mapping skills – six-figure grid references

Four-figure grid references are good for helping us to locate squares on OS maps. However, if you were out on a Duke of Edinburgh expedition and you needed to phone for help – because someone in your group had broken their leg – using four-figure grid references would not be much use. The reason for this is that a grid square on an OS map is one square kilometre in reality. This would be too big an area for a rescue team to search across.

Did you know that this number can be used in an emergency in the EU, and many other European countries, free of charge on most mobile phones?

As a result, it is much more accurate to use a **six-figure grid reference.** This pinpoints a place to within 100 metres.

To find a six-figure grid reference, we start off exactly the same as we would for a four-figure reference. We find the two lines that cross in the bottom left-hand corner of the square we are interested in. However, we must now also imagine there are 10 further lines dividing up this square.

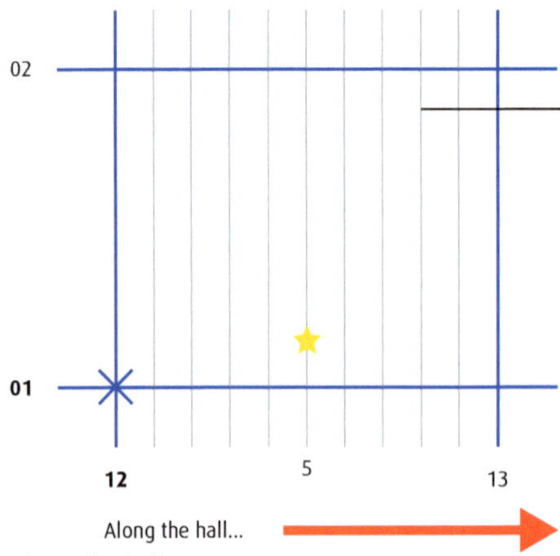

To get us started, we give the first two numbers for the square, which are **12.** We then have to imagine the square is divided up by another ten imaginary lines. If we count across these imaginary lines, we count five across until we are under the yellow star. Therefore, the first three numbers are **125**.

Along the hall ...

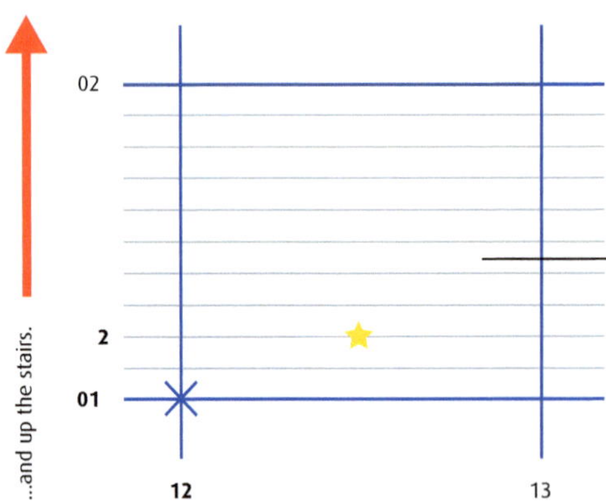

Next, we give the two numbers from the left side for the square that the star is in. These are **01**. We then imagine the square is divided by a further 10 lines running from side to side. We would count two lines upwards until we are level with the star.
Therefore, the second three numbers are **012**. The six-figure grid reference for the star in this square is **125012**.

... and up the stairs

Classroom challenge

Now try this out for yourself!

1. Study the grid square below and use six-figure grid references to complete the sentences.

(a) The whale is at 23_ 14_.
(b) The cat is at _ _ _ 14_.
(c) The ship is at _ _ _ _ _ _.
(d) The quad bike is at _ _ _ _ _ _.

2. Now, let's try out our six-figure grid references using a real OS map.

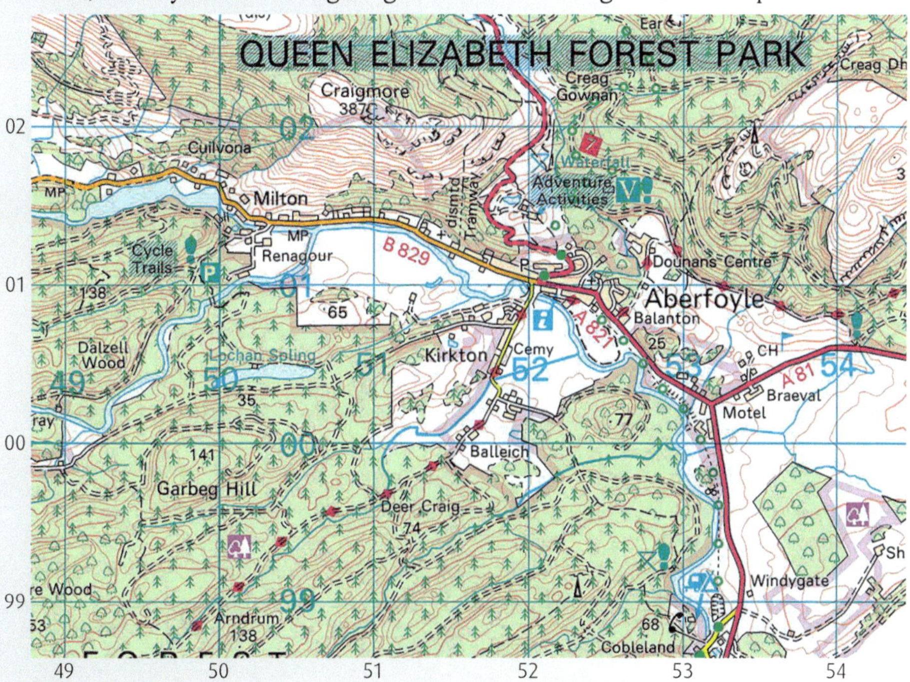

(a) Give the six-figure grid references for the following features on the OS map.

The visitor centre 

The tourist information centre 

The caravan and campsite 

The picnic site 

The parking place 

The clubhouse CH

3. What features/places would you find on the OS map using these six-figure grid references?

496012 = ___________

534003 = ___________

515005 = ___________

493005 = ___________

523016 = ___________

4. Now, make up a six-figure grid references quiz/activity for other students in your class to try.
Draw out your own grid, like the one below, in your workbook. Add your own features on it, similar to those in Question 1. Keep a note of the references for them. Now see if your classmates can give the correct six-figure grid references for them.

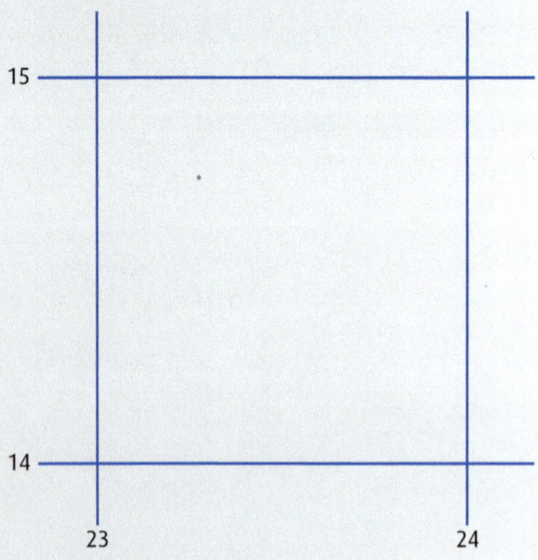

Have you enjoyed learning mapping skills? Would you like a career that uses the knowledge and skills you have gained from this topic? Why not visit the 'My World of Work/STEM/Developing the Young Workforce' section of the Homework Helpers to find out more?

5. In pairs, make up a poster, slide show, film or leaflet which tells school students how to carry out finding four- and six-figure grid references. It should be bright, colourful and easy to understand.

GLOSSARY

Abrasion – When rock fragments embedded in a glacier scrape and scour the land the ice is moving over.

Aeolian erosion – Erosion caused by the action of the wind.

Aftershock – A smaller earthquake that follows a main earthquake.

Agribusiness – When big companies take over farms and run them for maximum profit.

Arable farming – When a farm just grows crops.

Arête – A knife edged ridge found in between two corries.

Biome – Large areas on Earth where the community of plants and animals are shaped by the environment they are in such as the rainforest, hot deserts or the tundra.

Brownfield site – Land that has been built on before.

Burgess Concentric Ring Model – A model that shows how a city should grow outwards and the zones that result from this.

Central Business District – The centre of a city where shops, businesses and offices are found. It is the easiest part of the city to get to.

Climate – The average weather for a place over a long period of time.

Commercial farming – Growing crops or keeping animals to sell, and not for the farmer and family to eat.

Congestion – When roads become blocked because there are too many cars on them. This leads to traffic jams.

Conservationists – People who want to protect the environment.

Convection current – A large circular movement of magma in the Earth's mantle.

Convection rainfall – Rainfall caused by clouds that have formed due to warm humid air moving upwards and condensing.

Core – The zone in the centre of planet Earth.

Corrie – An armchair shaped hollow on the side of mountains that has been glaciated.

Crust – The outer zone of planet Earth.

Densely populated – When there are many people on average per square kilometre of land.

Demography – The study of population.

Describe – To give details about the main characteristics of something.

Developed countries – Countries that are able to provide their citizens with good infrastructure such as clean water, sanitation as well as education and a reliable supply of food. They have a strong economy.

Developing countries – Countries that are not able to provide their citizens with good infrastructure such as clean water, sanitation as well as education and a reliable supply of food. They have a weak economy.

Diversified farm – A farm that has turned to other non-farming activities such as quad biking, running a bed and breakfast or paintball in order to make extra money.

Earthquake – An intense shaking of the Earth's surface caused by seismic waves.

Ecotourism – Tourism that ensures the conservation of the environment and the culture of local people.

Ecosystem – When living things and the non-living environment interact with each other.

Emergents – The tallest trees in the rainforest such as the kapok tree.

Ephemerals – A plant that can grow very quickly and has a short life cycle.

Epicentre – The point on the Earth's surface directly above the focus of an earthquake.

Epiphyte – A plant that grows on another plant.

Equator – The name of the line that is zero degrees latitude.

Erosion – The wearing away of the landscape by wind, water or ice.

Evaluate – To look at the advantages or disadvantages of something and form a conclusion. Often you may have to give evidence for your decision.

Extensive farming – When a farm covers a large area but does not require many workers or input.

Exfoliation – When layers of rock break apart in a similar way to the layers found in an onion.

Explain – To give the meaning of something or to give reasons for something happening.

Firn – Granular snow found in glaciers before it has been squashed to form ice.

Flash flood – Sudden and rapid flooding of an area.

Fold mountains – Mountains that form on the edges of plates where they collide. Examples are the Alps or Himalayas.

Frost Shattering – When water in cracks in rocks freezes and expands to shatter the rock.

Glaciation – A time when the landscape is covered in ice and glaciers.

Glacier – A huge mass of ice that moves slowly.

Green Revolution – When new seeds and technology was introduced to farmers, especially in the developing world, to help increase production.

Green belt – An area of land surrounding a town or city which should be protected from development.

Greenfield site – Countryside that has never been built on before.

Gross Domestic Product (GDP) – This is the value of all the goods and services produced in a country in one year, divided by how many people live in the country (per capita).

Hanging valley – Where a smaller valley meets the sides of a U – shaped valley. They may have a waterfall falling from the end of them.

Indicators of development – Figures used to show how developed or developing a country is.

Indigenous – People with distinct cultures and life styles which have been shaped by the landscapes and environments in which they live.

Infant mortality – The death of babies before the age of one.

Intensive farming – When a farm produces a lot, even on a small area of land.

International date line – The name of the line that is 180° longitude.

Irrigation – To water crops.

Latitude – Lines that cross a map from side to side. They tell us how far north or south of the equator places are.

Leaching – The loss of nutrients in the soil due to rainfall.

Life expectancy – How long people are expected to live for.

Literacy – The ability to read and write.

Longitude – Lines that cross a map from top to bottom. They tell us how far east or west of the prime meridian places are.

Magma – Molten material in the Earth's mantle.

Mantle – The molten zone underneath the Earth's crust. This is the thickest zone.

Mechanisation – When machines take over work that was done by hand before.

Megacities – Cities with a population of over 10 million people.

Mid Atlantic Ridge – A line stretching down the middle of the Atlantic Ocean where the North American plate is moving away from the Eurasian plate.

Migration – When people or animals move from one place to another.

Misfit stream – Often found flowing along the floor of a U-shaped valley. They look too small to form the size of the valley they occupy.

Organic farming – This means crops and animals are kept without any use of damaging chemicals, fertilisers and pesticides. Animals are usually allowed to roam free (free range).

Pangea – The name of mega land mass that existed 250 million years ago.

Pastoral farming – When a farm mostly keeps livestock (sheep, cows etc).

Permafrost – Permanently frozen ground.

Physical map – A map that shows natural things such as mountains, rivers and seas.

Plates – The name given to the large sections that the Earth's crust is broken up into.

Plate tectonics – The study of the Earth's plates and their movement.

Plucking – When rocks are pulled from the ground when a glacier moves over it.

Political map – A map that shows man made features such as countries, capitals and borders.

Population density – How many people on average there are living on a square kilometre of land.

Population pyramid – A special graph that shows the age and sex of the population of an area or country.

Precipitation – Anything that falls from clouds in the sky such as rain, hail, sleet and snow.

Prevailing wind – When winds constantly blow from a certain direction.

Prime meridian – The name of the line that is zero degrees longitude.

Pull factors – Reasons that attract people and make them want to move to a certain area.

Push factors – Reasons why people may decide to leave a place and move to another.

Pyramidal peak – Sharply pointed mountain tops formed due to frost shattering with two or more corries on their sides.

Pyroclastic flow – A fast moving eruption of hot ash, gases and pumice from a volcano.

Ribbon lake – A long, thin lake found in valleys created by a glacier.

Ring of fire – An area that experiences lots of volcanic activity and earthquakes around the edges of the Pacific plate.

Rural – Countryside areas.

Rural depopulation – When people leave countryside areas to go and live elsewhere.

Scottish Outdoor Access Code – Some basic rules, information and guidance on how to behave in the Scottish Countryside.

Seismic waves – Sometimes called shock waves. These are ripple like movements of the ground which come from the epicentre of an earthquake.

Seismometer – An instrument used to measure the direction, strength and length of time of an earthquake.

Shanty town – A deprived area of a city with makeshift buildings made out of plywood, corrugated metal and other temporary materials.

Shifting cultivation – When land is farmed for a short time then abandoned so that the soil can rest and become fertile again.

Shock waves – Sometimes called seismic waves. These are ripple like movements of the ground which come from the epicentre of an earthquake.

Sparsely populated – An area where very few people live.

Striations – Scratches made in rock due to abrasion by glaciers.

Subsistence – A traditional way of life which involves living off the land.

Sustainable – When an activity is carried out in a way that that meets the needs of today's people but does not damage the environment for future generations.

Sustainable Development Goals – 17 targets set by the United Nations to try to achieve a better and more sustainable future for everyone on the planet.

Tsunami – A wave caused by an earthquake or volcanic eruption under the ocean.

U-shaped valley – A glacial valley with very steep sides and a broad, flat valley floor.

Urban – Areas, usually towns and cities, where there is a high population density.

Urban sprawl – When a town or city grows so large that it starts to spread out onto the surrounding countryside.

Urbanisation – When an area becomes more urban.

Volcano – A cone shaped opening in the Earth's crust from which lava, ash and gases may escape from.

Weather – What happens day to day with elements that can be measured such as temperature, wind speed and air pressure.

Weathering – The breaking up of the landscape due to the action of elements of the weather.

Xerophytes – Plants such as a cactus which can withstand droughts and are adapted to living with very little water.